DAVID'S
MIGHTY MEN

DAVID'S MIGHTY MEN

A Tribute to 21st Century Christian Laymen

In Honor of All Christian Laymen
Who Have Been to Their Pastors as
David's Mighty Men of Valor
Were to Their Shepherd King

C. David Jones

Requests for information should be addressed to:
Dr. C. David Jones
1811 Brandywine Trail
Fort Wayne, Indiana 46845-1577

E-mail: Dr.C.DavidJones@PhalanxAssociatesInc.com
or
drcdavidjones@verizon.net

Website: http://www.chapelquartet.org/theminyan.htm

ISBN: Hardcover 978-1-4415-5278-5
Softcover 978-1-4415-2645-8

Library of Congress Control Number: Hardcover 2009932809
Softcover 2009926084

All Scripture quotations, unless otherwise indicated, are taken from the Holy Bible, New International Version®.NIV®. Copyright © 1973, 1978, 1984 by the International Bible Society. Used by permission of Zondervan.

Scripture quotations marked (LBP) are taken from the HOLY BIBLE, THE LIVING BIBLE PARAPHRASED, copyright © 1971. Used by permission of Tyndale House Publishers, Inc., Wheaton, Illinois 60189. All rights reserved.

Printed in the United States of America

This book is printed on acid-free paper.

To order additional copies of this book, contact:

Xlibris Corporation
1-888-795-4274
www.Xlibris.com
Orders@Xlibris.com
43658

Dedicated to

Barbara Ann Hillman Jones

my devoted and faithful wife, my partner in the Christian ministry,
my editor, best critic and loyal fan

Contents

FOREWORD

EVERY MAN who is a success, regardless of how gifted he may be, did not manage to achieve his goals, rank, station or wealth by his own efforts, but he is indebted to a number of key persons in his life without whose mentoring, support, and encouragement he would quite likely have been a miserable failure!

*　　*　　*

KING DAVID of Israel was surrounded by a magnificent corps of extraordinarily strong, courageous, unflinchingly brave and self-sacrificing men who were his confidants, his personal bodyguard, and comrades-at-arms. They were the special elite corps of fearless warriors whose devotion to their king placed his welfare and that of his kingdom above their own personal safety—every one of these champions would gladly have sacrificed his own life to honor, advance and protect the life of their king. The annals of Holy Scripture single them out by the accolade that marks them as **David's Mighty Men**. Their names are recorded in the Hebrew Old Testament book of II Samuel, chapter 23, verses 8-39. They were thirty-seven of the most fierce and dedicated warriors that ever lived. In a parallel list of these men which is recorded in I Chronicles 11:11-47, the number of warriors is expanded by 16 names (I Ch. 11:41-47), probably because additional men were added to replace those who had died, some in battle, giving their lives for their king.

They were truly men of extraordinary valor, physical might and unwavering loyalty. They were a combination of "combat commandos," "stealth rangers," "navy seals," "green beret," "special ops" and "Delta forces" who had acquired the skills of battle demanded to survive and conquer in hand-to-hand warfare. They engaged in clandestine operations and were often outnumbered by staggering odds pitted against them, yet they stood their ground. Time after time on fields of battle they were "the last men standing."

They defended their king and gained victory over their enemies by sheer strength of determination and by the inexplicable physical and mental character with which they were endowed by their God, Yahweh, Who Himself had chosen David as their king.

"These are the names of David's Mighty Men:

"**Josheb-Basshebeth,** a Tahkemonite, was the chief . . . he raised his spear against eight hundred men, whom he killed in one encounter.

"**Eleazar** son of Dodai the Ahohite . . . he was with David when they taunted the Philistines that were gathered at Pas Dammim for battle. The men of Israel retreated, but he stood his ground and struck down the Philistines till his hand grew tired and froze to the sword. The Lord brought about a great victory that day.

"**Shammah** son of Agee the Harrarite. When the Philistines banded together . . . Israel's troops fled from them. But Shamma took his stand in the middle of the field. He defended it and struck the Philistines down, and the Lord brought about a great victory.

"**Abishai** the brother of Joab . . . he raised his spear against three hundred men, whom he killed.

"**Benaiah** son of Jehoida was a valiant fighter from Kabzeel . . . he struck down two of Moab's best men. He also went down into a pit on a snowy day and killed a lion, and he struck down a huge Egyptian. Although the Egyptian had a spear in his hand, Benaiah went against him with a club. He snatched the spear from the Egyptian's hand and killed him with his own spear. And David put him in charge of his bodyguard."

Abishai, Benaiah and another warrior risked their lives to break through the lines of the Philistines and draw water from the well near the gate of Bethlehem to bring back to David a drink from that well. Although he longed to taste that water, David poured it out as an offering unto the Lord rather than to drink water for which his loyal and devoted warriors risked their lives. There were also among David's Mighty Men the following warriors:

> "**Ashel** the brother of Joab, **Elhanan** son of Dodo from Bethlehem, **Shammah** the Harodite, **Elika** the Harodite, **Helez** the Paltite, **Ira** son of Ikkesh from Tekoa, **Abiezer** from Anatoth, **Mebunnai** the Hushathite, **Zalmon** the Ahohite, **Maharai** the Netophathite, **Heled** son of Baanah the Netophathite, **Ithai** son of Ribai from Gibeah in Benjamin, **Benaiah** the Pirathonite, **Hiddai** from the ravines of Gaash, **Abi-Albon** the Arbathite, **Azmaveth** the Barhumite, **Eliahba** the Shaalbonite, **the sons of Jashen, Jonathan** son of Shammah, the Hararite, **Ahiam** son of Sharar the Hararite, **Eliphelet** son of Ahasbai the Maacathite, **Eliam** son of Ahithophel the Gilonite, **Herzo** the Carmelite, **Paarai** the Arbite, **Igal** son of Nathan from Zobah, the son of Hargri, **Zelek** the Ammonite, **Naharai** the Beerothite, the armor-bearer of Joab son of Zerubiah, **Ira** the Irhrite, "**Gareb** the Ithrite, and **Uriah** the Hittite. There were thirty-seven in all."[1]

To the above list of heroes sixteen additional names are added in the list of David's Mighty Men recorded in the Old Testament book of I Chronicles 11:10-47:

> "**Zabad** son of Ahlai, **Adina** son of Shiza athe Reubenite, who was chief of the Rubenites, and the thirty with him, **Hanan** son of Maacah, **Joshaphat** the Mithnite, **Uzzia** the Asterathite, **Shama** and **Jeiel** the sons of Hotham the Aroerite, **Jediael** son of Shimri, his brother **Joah** the Tizite, **Eliel** the Hahavite, **Jeribai** and **Joshaviah** the sons of Elnaam, **Ithmah** the Moabite, **Eliel, Obed** and **Jaasiel** the Mezobaite."

These last sixteen great warriors apparently were added to take the place of those soldiers who fell in battle from among the first thirty-seven warriors, and are evidence that as David's kingdom grew other great men were drawn by his magnetism to follow him as their king.

The following twelfth chapter of I Chronicles records a list of other warriors who volunteered to join David in the ranks of his army. If the numbers in the ranks are totaled, it shows an army of 340,800 men including officers and warriors armed with every type of weapon and ready for battle. That is an impressive army in any day, considering that in the recent war in Iraq the Allied troops were only about half that number.

David was only 30 years old when he became the king. He reigned over the tribe of Judah for 7½ years and over all of Israel for 33 years, making the total length of his reign 40 years. Not long after becoming king over Israel, David made his capital in the city of Jerusalem. Standing high on Mt. Zion and surrounded on three sides by valleys, the capital city was easily fortified into a nearly impregnable fortress guarded by high walls, battlements, parapets and massive gates. Within the walls of this carefully planned city David would set in motion the building of a magnificent Temple, which his son Solomon would complete.

With the assistance of his commanders and seasoned warriors, David was very successful in expanding his kingdom. He completely conquered the Philistines, Moabites, Syrians, Edomites, Ammonites, Amalekites, and all the neighboring nations. "The LORD gave David victory wherever he went" (2 Samuel 8:6).

David took a small, insignificant and beleaguered tribal nation and, with the devoted loyalty and assistance of his corps of Mighty Men, in a few short years he developed it into a mighty kingdom. The dynasty of the Pharaohs of Egypt to the southwest had declined. The nations of Mesopotamia, Assyria and Babylonia to the east had not yet emerged from city states. Israel commanded a strategic position on the international highway between Mesopotamia (Eurasia) and Egypt (Africa). Under the leadership of David, supported by his Mighty Men, this relatively tiny nation became almost overnight not what today would be considered a world empire but perhaps what at that time in history was in fact the single most powerful kingdom on earth.

*   *   *

Over the half-century of my active years in Christian ministry, both as a pastor and as a professor in academia, like my namesake David I have had the good fortune to have been surrounded by a host of men—and women—who have been to me what King David's Mighty Men were to him. Without the loyalty and support of these devout Christian warriors, I would have been vulnerable and defeated by the adverse circumstances that on more than one occasion posed major serious threats to my pastoral career and to the congregations I served. Because of these good and loyal men we experienced the measure of success that we marked as "victories" which The LORD gave to this 20th Century pastor/shepherd. Some of these successes are reported in the following chapters.

This book is written as a tribute to those marvelous warriors of the faith without whose help none of those victories would have been won. The kingdom which we sought to build was not our own, but it is the Kingdom of God and His righteousness. For the lives and comrades-at-arms who helped us fight the good fight and for the favor shown to us by the LORD in our labors for His kingdom, I am enormously and everlastingly grateful. Among the eighteen men about whom I have written in this book are skilled journeymen technicians and craftsmen, master builders and developers and contractors, successful farmers, educators, military personnel, corporate managers and executives, and a physician. They represent a broad cross-section of lay Christians found in churches around the world today. To these friends I owe an inexpressible debt of gratitude and credit, and to God belongs the glory for all that we achieved working together with Him. None of these friends had to engage in hand-to-hand combat to defend me, nor were their exploits as dramatic as those of Josheb-Basshebeth, Eleazar, Shammah and the others among King David's mighty men, but the men whose names appear in this book were loyal partners and co-workers with me in ministry, they were trusted confidants, and true friends. It was not just their spiritual leadership within their respective congregations, but it was their personal friendship, their encouragement, and their camaraderie both within and apart from the congregational settings that meant so much to me then and for which I will always remain grateful.

In order for us to understand the significance and importance of the valiant warriors who surrounded David and supported and protected him, the Bible tells us a great deal more about the young shepherd king David than it does about David's Mighty Men themselves. Yet without the aid and protection of those brave and loyal warriors, it is highly unlikely that David would have survived the assaults made upon him by King Saul and his other adversaries. The Biblical writers were quite correct in paying tribute to those loyal heroes who were so vital to David's survival and success.

Admittedly certain parts of this book are autobiographical in their construct. Perhaps that is partly because the stories in each chapter are told in a first-person narrative genre. The purpose of these vignettes is to provide a background to assist the reader in appreciating the setting in which these men were partners with me in giving leadership for their respective congregations. To provide the reader with a brief background about the writer I have included a Prologue which tells a little bit about my entrée into the ministry. The reader may skip the Prologue and begin with the first chapter, and if your interest is piqued you can go back and read the Prologue to get some idea of how this all began. Please forgive me for having interjected into each of the chapters certain facts and details which may appear to be more personal than they are descriptive of each man and the special role he contributed to provide the support and relationship that made our work together a joy and a success.

I debated about whether or not to relate some of the incidents and circumstances reported in some of the chapters: my inclination was not to mention anything that might reveal the bad or difficult situations and dynamics that developed in certain instances, but I felt that to hide or ignore those factors would be cowardly and unfaithful. My father used to say to us that "a half-truth is no truth at all." It might have given the false impression that everything was always peaches and cream, that everything went just hunky-dory all of the time, and that we never encountered a hitch or a glitch but that all of the churches I served were model congregations. Any veteran pastor and every seasoned churchman would know that such churches simply do not exist, at least not for very long at a time, because as human beings, including both the clergy and laity, we are all flawed creatures in constant need of God's mercy and grace. If I ever had found a "perfect" church, it would have ceased being perfect the moment I arrived on the scene, because I would have brought with me my own human frailties and imperfections. Although I have endeavored not to bore the reader with all of the gory details of every single one of our foibles and sins, there is enough within these chapters to indicate that these men and their pastor were as vulnerable as anyone else, but that by God's goodness we not only survived but in many cases were granted what for us were significant victories and successes in our common mission to live and proclaim the Gospel of Jesus Christ.

Those fellow pastors and lay church leaders who read this book will recognize among its pages men and women whom they know as twins of some of their own colleagues and parishioners—Christian warriors who at considerable cost and sometimes risk to themselves have stood their ground in the thick of the battle and by their faithfulness have helped win the victory and achieve the successes that God has granted. It is my sincere hope that others will be inspired by the biographical sketches of these modern day heroes of the faith, and will volunteer to join the ranks of this grand company of Christian warriors.

NOTES:

1   The number 37 does not compute with the number of names given. Even if the names given in 2 Samuel 23: 8-23 are included there are only 36. It appears that from among David's mighty warriors there were men whose names were not transmitted or were inadvertently omitted or lost, or that have been corrupted (v. 32; cf. I Chr 2:34.) See The Jerome Biblical Commentary. Englewood Cliffs, NJ: Prentice-Hall, Inc., 1968, p. 178."

PROLOGUE

MY BRIDE, Mary Elizabeth Hollis Jones, and I had been married for less than a week when I received a telegram from Mary's father, the Reverend Lewis J. Hollis, Pastor of the Assemblies of God Church in El Dorado, Kansas. The telegram was short and to the point: *Pastorate available in Columbus, KS; will you accept appointment?*

I had just completed my sophomore year and Mary Elizabeth had completed her freshman year at Central Bible College, Springfield, Missouri. On Thursday morning, May 25th, 1951, Mary and I were united in marriage by the Reverend Wilfred Brown, General Treasurer of the Assemblies of God denomination. We were married in the Brown's living-room across the street from the college campus. Katie McVey was Mary's maid of honor and Alexander Llewellyn Hunter was my best man. Later Katie married a minister, and Al Hunter had a good career as a Christian educator and as a pastor. Mary and I planned to find summer jobs at Armstrong flooring company in Lancaster, Pennsylvania. Mary's parents had given us a 1949 Chevrolet as a wedding present, so we packed our few belongings in our car and immediately following our wedding ceremony we headed for my parent's home in Columbia, PA, just seven miles west of Lancaster. My father was serving the First Assemblies of God Church in Columbia, and I had graduated from Columbia High School with the class of 1949.

The Sunday morning following our wedding Mary and I attended Sunday Worship Service at my father's church and decided to drive to Washington, DC for a short honeymoon before seeking employment at Armstrong's the following week. I had graduated from Langley Jr. High

School in Washington, DC in 1946 and wanted to show Mary our nation's capital city.

When we returned to my parent's home following a weekend in the District of Columbia, to our great surprise a telegram from Mary's father was waiting for us. Upon reading its abbreviated message, there seemed no doubt in our minds that God had a different plan for us . . . He had given to us a call to pastor a church in Mary's home conference, to which I was offered an appointment "sight-unseen" by Bishop Victor Greissen of Wichita, Kansas. I went to the local Western Union office and wired Mary's father back, "Yes, I will accept the pastorate."

We had gladly accepted the "call" to my first pastorate. If that was what God wanted us to do, and since He had providentially opened a door of ministry to us, we felt that He was calling us and we were not to question His divine providential leading. Without thinking past that commitment to follow God's unfolding will for our lives, we had packed our few belongings and the following day, amid the tears and best wishes of my parents, we headed back across the Pennsylvania Turnpike toward Kansas.

We were driving along somewhere in Indiana when it hit me like a ton of bricks: what had I done? I had accepted the pastoral appointment, sight-unseen, to a congregation I had never met and who had not had the opportunity to meet me. I was going to have to stand in the pulpit on Sunday morning and preach to a congregation of total strangers . . . and I didn't have the slightest idea what I was going to say!

I had preached a couple of sermons to the youth group in my father's church, and one time he had allowed me to preach a sermon in a Sunday evening "evangelistic" service. I had spoken to the youth group in a neighboring church across the Susquehanna River in Wrightsville, PA, and I had spoken briefly once or twice at one of the "out-station" preaching "churches." These churches allowed ministerial students from the Bible College to conduct Sunday worship services in some of the small rural communities and country school-houses around southern Missouri. But, like most young ministers I certainly had no "barrel" of sermons like a mature and seasoned senior pastor would have. I wasn't even ordained and I didn't even have a preaching credential of any sort. In fact, I was still a college student and a minor only 19 years of age.[1] Why in the world had Bishop Greissen appointed me to this church? What kind of a church would it be? What would the parsonage be like? What would the congregation think of me? What in heaven's name would I say to them? What should I preach about?

With sweat breaking out on my brow, I turned to Mary Elizabeth as we drove along, and I admitted in panic, "I don't have the foggiest notion of what I am going to say or preach about on Sunday morning! Mary, you better find a pencil and paper and write down whatever I tell you." We prayed and asked God for

His guidance and were totally dependant upon Him and the prompting of His Holy Spirit to provide me with the words to speak from my new pulpit.

Both Mary Elizabeth and I had been reared in Pentecostal parsonages, and our fathers were both men of great faith, and our mothers shared that faith with them. We certainly were striking out on a life-long adventure of "faith." Ah ha, that was it, I would preach about faith. The great faith chapter written by St. Paul to the Hebrews came to mind. I had Mary look up Hebrews 11 in the new Thompson Chain Reference Bible that she had given to me as a wedding present on the morning we were married, and she read aloud the words of that New Testament Scripture as I drove westward.

Yes, "*Faith* is the substance of things hoped for, the evidence of things not seen!"

Mary wrote down the thoughts that came to my mind as we drove along. It was a rambling kind of extemporaneous paraphrasing of my simplistic but fervent understanding of the Biblical meaning of faith, interspersed with examples of answered prayers taken from throughout the Scriptures and from my very limited experiences as a fledgling teenage "preacher." I just wish I had kept those notes written in Mary's handwriting, but over the years they were lost in the shuffle.

From St. Louis, Missouri, we drove drown route 66 straight to Columbus, Kansas. On June 6th, 1951 we managed to find the parsonage which was adjacent to the little one-room clapboard church house that had been a former Methodist Church before the Methodist Congregation had built its handsome new brick church along the main highway that ran through the town. The previous minister had not yet vacated the parsonage, so there was no room for our few belongings. However, since we had no furniture of our own, the pastor and his wife offered to sell us their bed, a tattered and worn out sofa and chair in the living room, and an old second-hand dining room table and chairs. We only had a few dollars, but agreed to send them the balance as we were able. The transaction saved my predecessor from having to rent a U-Haul trailer or truck to move what we had purchased, and we were glad to acquire the few essential sticks of old used furniture so that we could "set up housekeeping" in a Spartan kind of fashion.

The pastor was not going to move out of the parsonage until the following week, so he would preach that following Sunday, and I would actually "take over the reins" of the parish and begin my pastoral duties on the following Sunday, June 11th, 1951. That weekend there was a District Fellowship Meeting in Oswego, KS, the next town west of Columbus, just across the Oswego River. It was the town in which Mary Elizabeth was born on March 3, 1932. The fellowship meeting and the worship service were held in the "home" church of her parents, which was the very church in which her father Lewis J. Hollis found Christ as his personal Savior and Lord.

We spent that first weekend in June in El Dorado, Kansas with Mary's family and worshiped with the congregation pastored by her father. Not knowing quite what to expect or what awaited us when we would return to Columbus during that following week, we returned with the mixed emotions of both excitement and apprehension. The days seemed to fly by as we swept out the parsonage, unpacked our few belongings, stocked in a few groceries, and Mary went about the task of trying to make our new "home" look presentable and comfortable. I busied myself going over to the old church house next door, trying to get my bearings, praying and attempting to prepare my heart and mind for my first Sunday as a Christian minister.

That first Sunday morning Mary and I dressed in our wedding outfits: I had a double-breasted navy blue pinstriped suit and Mary wore a pretty pink tailored suit and a little white hat with a puff of feathers, white platform pumps and white gloves. There were thirty-one souls, counting the babies and children and the new preacher and his wife who gathered for worship that morning.

Mary Elizabeth played the piano and I led the service; we sang a selection of favorite beloved hymns, I read the Scriptures and received the offering; and when the time finally came for the sermon, I turned to Hebrews chapter 11 and began a running "expository" paraphrasing of the succession of verses interspersed with as many illustrations as I could think of including both those which were in my sermon notes and whatever else spontaneously popped into my mind as I rambled along. I can't remember how far I managed to get as I moved along from one verse to the next, but as I recall the sermon was at least 40 minutes long, which was the minimum accepted standard for sermons in Pentecostal churches of that era. For me, it was a matter of "monkey see, monkey do." I had listened to sermons preached by my father and by other Assemblies of God ministers and by professors, visiting guest pastors and evangelists and the senior seminary students who spoke in the Chapel services at college. I endeavored to mimic their collective example as closely as I could, and I understood that whatever I said needed to be said with conviction, verve, enthusiasm and of course . . . loudly so everyone could hear, especially the hard of hearing. There were no public address systems in the majority of our churches in those days and preachers were expected to "speak up" in a style not terribly unlike what is still today found in many of the Black churches and the conservative and fundamentalist "hell, fire, and brimstone" rural congregations across the land.

In the back of my mind was the keen awareness that an essential and standard part of every Pentecostal service was the traditional "altar call" invitation to the unconverted to come forward and kneel at the communion rail to confess their sins and acknowledge Jesus Christ as their Savior. Following the standard invitation call to the sinners, there was generally an invitation to anyone who desired prayer for divine healing to come forward to kneel at the altar/communion rail. The traditional ritual for healing consisted of anointing the seeker with symbolic olive oil and the laying on of hands by the minister and the elders of the church who would then offer up prayer and supplication on behalf of the seeker for divine healing. This was all in accordance with the New Testament Epistle of James 5:13-16.

I knew that the congregation was waiting to see if their new young pastor would follow the traditional pattern for the worship services and offer prayer for the sick. Many parishioners fully expected that if the minister were truly a man of God and a man after God's own heart as King David was, then when their minister prayed for their healing, God would be gracious and look down from heaven with favor and grant His miracles of divine healing to the supplicants. I had witnessed my father offer prayer for the sick hundreds of times, and Mary's father had done the same in the churches he pastored, and amazingly enough . . . by God's grace and mercy people were healed and miracles occurred often enough to encourage the faith of these Pentecostal believers and to cause them to rejoice that they knew a Savior who was "the same yesterday, today, and forever." He who wrought miracles throughout the long history of ancient Israel and among the early Apostolic Christian Church to the present time is still able to work miracles of healing, mercy and grace.

In the back of my mind, however, was the frightening awareness that if I were to pray for the sick and nothing happened, I would no doubt be considered by the congregation to be a fraud, just another young up-start kid with a "preacher's itch" that needed scratching at their expense, but I would not be considered a genuine and true "man of God" to whom they could turn as their spiritual leader and pastor. I was honestly afraid to pray for the sick that first Sunday morning for fear that if no one was healed I would be marked as a sham and an imposter, another wolf in sheep's clothing hiding behind a "clerical collar."

So I said to the congregation, "You all come back next Sunday morning, and next Sunday at the close of the service I will pray for the sick." I would hold out the carrot that perhaps God would look down in His infinite mercy and grace and grant to those who may need His healing touch some miracle of health and wholeness to their relief and to his own honor and glory. But I just didn't have the courage and faith to put God to the test that first Sunday. I thought that just in case God did not answer our prayers for healing, I would be all washed up, but at least I would give myself one whole week in the role of a pastor before I would subject myself to the litmus test like Elijah had done on Mt. Carmel.

Sunday evening we held the usual "evangelistic" service, we sang more hymns, I called for "testimonies" from the congregation. Mary Elizabeth and I sang a couple of duets, she played a musical selection on her accordion, and I played a musical number on my "C" Melody saxophone (my "sanctified pipe" as we called it). I preached what I believed was a typical "evangelistic" sermon about the wrath of God against unrepentant sinners and His gracious mercies and loving forgiveness toward those who were truly sorry and genuinely repentant for their sins. We sang a "hymn of invitation" (a favorite was "Pass Me Not O Gentle Savior"). As I gave the altar call, many of the folks came forward to pray, to confess their sins again, and to pray for their unconverted loved ones, friends and neighbors. Once more they would rise from the altar feeling that they had made their peace with God and could begin the coming week with a clean slate.

*   *   *

That next week just seemed to fly by, and before I knew it Sunday morning quickly came around again. There were thirty-two people present that morning—apparently everybody was coming back to see if anything would really happen when I prayed for the sick and infirm. We sang the usual selection of old fashioned gospel hymns, offered our prayers of thanksgiving and supplication, received the morning offering, the Scriptures were read, there was a special duet, and finally it was time for the morning sermon. I cannot recall the exact Bible verses which were my sermon text, but I remember that I began with the verses where I had left off the previous Sunday morning, once again reciting the stories from Hebrews chapter 11 about the great heroes of the faith. The minutes went by and finally after having spoken the required 40 to 45 minutes I stuck a "period" in the sermon discourse, not quite having completed the chapter, but announcing that the following Sunday morning I would continue our sermon series on "Faith."

Now the inevitable time had come for the show-down: I would anoint with oil and offer prayers to God for any persons who desired prayer for divine healing.

Secretly I was hoping against hope that no one would come forward for prayer; but much to my anguish and consternation five people stood and moved out of their pews to the center isle and came forward to the front of the altar for prayer. I began praying first for the person on my left as they faced the chancel platform, and I began by asking each one what it was for which they wanted me to pray. One person had a bad summer cold and a runny nose; I anointed him with oil and prayed a simple prayer, feeling somewhat relieved because I reasoned that by and by their cold would go away whether by divine miracle or by the course of the wonderful recuperative nature of our physical immune systems. So far I was safe.

Another person had an ear ache, and I knew that too would eventually pass. The next person had an upset stomach and indigestion, and I thought that would also go away in time. Another person was suffering from "hay fever" and

I knew that eventually the pollen count would go down and their sinuses would clear up. So far so good: they would get better and I would pass muster.

But at the end of the line was an elderly gentleman in his eighties, a Mr. Matthew Oceanbeam. He looked me in the eye and said loudly enough so that everyone in that little church could hear him, "Preacher, I've got cataracts, and I want you to pray that God will heal my eyes from these cataracts!"

I was stunned. The jig was up, for sure. It was one thing to pray and ask God to heal a runny nose, or a tummy ache, or any of the common ordinary chronic illnesses that come and go with the seasons; but cataracts would not just go away—that would take a real true genuine miracle from Almighty God. I didn't know what else to do but to anoint Matt Oceanbeam with the consecrated olive oil and pray that God somehow would be kind enough to grant Matt, and all the rest of us, an indisputable miracle!

I didn't have the courage to ask anyone of the seekers for healing if they felt any better or if God had done an on-the-spot miracle for them—that was just pushing my luck too far. So after I had prayed and the supplicants had returned to their respective pews, I said to the congregation: "Now let's all trust the Lord this week and we will continue to all pray for each of those for whom prayer had been offered, and let's all come back next Sunday and we will see what God has done for us during this coming week."

I let it go at that. What else could I do? At least I would give myself another week as their pastor. And maybe by some unexpected chance at least one of the five supplicants might feel somewhat better and we would all give to God thanks for hearing our prayers and for small gifts from above.

*   *   *

The following week passed quickly, and once again it was Sunday morning and time for worship. Again we followed the usual unwritten liturgy that was our common practice, and again the sermon time rolled around. Once more I preached from the great faith chapter, Hebrews 11, and again I reiterated the stories of the saints and martyrs listed in that chapter, expounding and expanding upon each saint in chronological order, and again the time passed and the sermon time came to an end.

It was with dread that in order to keep my promise to the congregation, feeling a considerable temerity and a great deal of doubt and angst, I asked the congregation if during the past week God had done anything special for anyone present. There was a long silence and heads turned as parishioners looked around to see if perchance there might be anyone present for whom God had worked a special miracle.

To my utter amazement and complete astonishment and total surprise, old Matt Oceanbeam stood in his pew . . . and then he moved out of his pew into the center isle and came forward to where I was standing in front of the communion rail altar. He said, "Pastor Jones, this past week my cataracts broke loose from my eyes and dropped off just like fish scales and I can see like when I was a young man." The congregation did not seem to be surprised, but there were hands raised in praise and thanks to God and many *"Amen"*s. After all, it was what they were used to expecting when they prayed to God. Sure God didn't always answer their prayers in exactly the way they wanted Him to do, but every now and then, when they really needed Him, He would look down from heaven as a loving Heavenly Father and touch their bodies with a miracle of healing or He would answer their other prayers for His help with other things, like sending rain when their crops needed water, or doing some other thing that was desperately needed for their survival and well being. So why shouldn't God heal Matt Oceanbeam's cataracts!

In my heart I breathed an enormous sigh of great relief—God in heaven had actually heard our prayers and in His great and infinite grace and mercy He had granted to Matt Oceanbeam, and to our little congregation as well . . . and especially to me, a remarkable miracle of divine healing. The same God who had honored the prayers of my godly father and of Mary Elizabeth's righteous father had also heard our humble and faltering prayers and had confirmed our faith and trust in Him by answering our prayers as well. How marvelous! How wonderful is my Redeemer's love for me!

But Matt Oceanbeam didn't stop there. He looked imploringly at me and said loudly enough so that everyone present could hear him: "Pastor Jones, I want you to anoint my ear and pray that God will heal the cancer that is growing on my ear. If God can heal my cataracts He can just as surely heal the cancer that is eating up my ear."

"Oh, no!" I thought to myself. Why couldn't we have just quite while we were ahead? Wasn't it enough to ask and receive from God one marvelous and amazing miracle? Why did we have to push our luck and ask Him for another incredible miracle?

It was with a wave first of almost unbelievable surprise and joy that we had heard Matt Oceanbeam account his miracle of the healing of his cataracts; and then with a roller-coaster drop my faith took a nose-dive and I thought a second miracle was too much to ask of God. Nevertheless, with no sense of faith on my own part to believe God for a second miracle, I once again anointed Matt Oceanbeam and asked God to heal the cancer that was there on his ear, big as life, a black and ugly malignant tumor growing on his ear that everyone could see.

As much as I was grateful for the first miracle from God, I didn't have the faith to believe for a second miracle, and it was obvious that when I finished praying the ugly cancer was still there—there was no instantaneous disappearance of the malignant growth.

So I followed the same tack I had taken the previous Sunday, and I asked the congregation to continue to pray for Matt Oceanbeam and for one another throughout the following week, and I urged them to be sure to come back to church again the next Sunday and tell us if God had done anything special for them during the next seven days. I offered a benediction and hurried to the front door of the church to greet the parishioners as they departed.

* * *

During the following week I relived over and over again the events of the previous Sunday morning, and all week long I had a sense of anticipation but also an overwhelming fear and dread that nothing miraculous would happen and that Matt Oceanbeam would show up for church with that same ugly tumor glaring at us in mockery of our faith.

I can't tell you what I preached about that fourth Sunday morning, but I believe that I continued on with the theme of "faith" and God's miraculous wonderworking power. At the close of the service I again asked the congregation if there was anyone present for whom God had done anything special during the previous week. There was a pall of silence over the congregation and all eyes turned toward Matt Oceanbeam. Then, to everyone's astonishment, once again Matt Oceanbeam stood to his feet and began to speak:

> "Pastor Jones, the same God who healed me of my cataracts has also healed and delivered me from the cancer that was eating away my ear. This past week that old cancer shriveled and dried up like an old prune and it fell off my ear like a big scab, and under that old tumor there is new skin, soft and pink and shinny like a babies. I have truly been healed by the Lord!"

I could hardly believe my ears or my eyes, but sure enough, the cancerous growth was gone. For the second time in a row God had looked down from His heaven and had heard our simple prayers and had honored our faith in Him and in His miracle working power. I invited the congregation to stand and lift their hands toward heaven and to join me in offering unto God our thanksgiving and praise for His goodness to Matt and to all of us. There were some tears of joy and some hugging and back slapping and hand pumping and congratulations and best wishes to Matt, and there was a spirit of hope among some of the members that maybe God had smiled on their congregation and sent them a young pastor who like the shepherd boy David believed and trusted in God. This new young pastor of theirs might not be the most learned Biblical scholar nor the most erudite or profound preacher, but maybe, just maybe this boy pastor might know the same God that King David and the other saints of old knew.

*   *   *

Columbus, Kansas is the center of Cherokee County government and the Cherokee County Court House sits smack-dab in the middle of the town square. Like many Midwestern towns, the county court house is surrounded on all four sides by streets upon whose opposite side, facing the court house, are arrayed a battery of stores and business establishments. There is a bank on one corner and a hardware store on another corner. You could also find a US Post Office, a 5 & 10 cent Store, a men's haberdashery, a grocery store, a meat market, a bakery, a ladies dress shop and a beauty parlor. Down the block was a barbershop, a dentist's office, and a couple of lawyer's offices (to take care of clients who had business at the court house). Off on the side streets were a couple of funeral parlors, a small but well cared for hospital, an assortment of churches (there were over a dozen different denominations in that small town, all vying with one another in the scramble for religious adherents). There were a couple of car dealerships, auto repair shops, an old-fashioned black-smith shop, and the usual appliance stores, etc. The consolidated school was a few blocks farther out on Main Street. It was a typical small mid-western town of about 2,000 souls with a larger population living on farms and cattle ranches in the outlying countryside.

Cherokee County is located in the farthest southeast corner of the Jay Hawk State of Kansas, at the conjunction where the Kansas State line meets the abutting corners of Missouri, Oklahoma and Arkansas. There are lead and zinc hard-rock mines in the area. There are also scattered oil wells and an oil refinery nearby; and wheat is the main crop planted and harvested by the Kansas farmers; and there are some cattle and other kinds of agriculture which have historically been the main industry in the region.

*   *   *

It was Matt Oceanbeam's custom to walk from the boarding house, in which he rented a room, up the two or three blocks to the court house square where he would find a bench upon which to sit and while away the day by swapping yarns about the good ol' days with some of his elderly retired cronies. As a small boy Matt had traveled westward in a covered wagon with his pioneer parents from Pennsylvania. They had crossed the wide Missouri River at St. Louis and made their way to Kansas where his family had homesteaded. He and his cohorts would share stories about the days when the Cherokee and other Indian tribes roamed the hills and plains and when life on the frontier was still rough and tumble when even in the growing towns things were still quite primitive. Everybody in town knew Matt Oceanbeam, and the word began to spread that the young preacher at the Pentecostal Church had prayed for Matt and God had healed him of his cataracts and from his cancer. The curious began to drop in on Sunday mornings just to see for themselves what the new preacher was like. One by one the little congregation began to grow, and soon the little church house became crowded to the gunnels.

Someone had strung two parallel wires from side to side about ten feet high across the church's nave, and the ladies had made tan colored curtains which were pulled from the sides across to the center isle to provide two partitions of sorts to make four "class rooms." The Adult Sunday School Class was on one side in the front pews, and across the isle was a "young adult" Sunday School Class. There was a class for teenagers behind the adult class, and across the isle from them was a class for elementary school children. The pre-schoolers sat up behind the piano on little wooden chairs, making five classes in all. Each of the Sunday School teachers competed with the others to be heard above the voices from behind the piano of the little children chattering and giggling and singing their tiny-tots' choruses. It was one big noisy bedlam that grew worse with each passing week as new faces showed up in the children's classes and new families began attending. There was no baby nursery, and there were no inside restrooms; so anyone who needed to do so had to walk outside and use the outhouse in back of the parsonage. There was no inside plumbing in the parsonage either, except for a single spigot in a small kitchen sink; so the parson's family also used the outhouse. There was a big pot-bellied wood burning stove on the left-hand side of the chapel, and in the cold winter months when the temperature dropped below zero, those sitting close to the old stove would swelter from heat while those on the other side of the church huddled up and kept their winter coats and hats on to keep warm. It was truly primitive by modern standards, but nobody seemed to mind since that was the way it had been from the time they were small children. When the number of rowdy elementary school boys increased to the point where it was determined that the boys needed to be separated from the elementary school girls class, there was no place to accommodate the Boys Sunday School Class except in the parsonage living room.

The parsonage, too, was typical of many of the earlier houses in this small Midwestern town. It was a small four room clapboard bungalow that was not fully insulated except for the old newspapers that someone had stuffed between some of the studs in the walls. The windows were not well glazed and the house was like an oven in the hot summer sun when the temperature would reach into the 120s in the shade. During the winter months when the temperature would drop below 0 degrees Fahrenheit it was like trying to heat a sieve and it was difficult to keep warm even with long underwear and heavy sweaters. The house had never been properly wired and was lighted by a single bare light bulb that hung from the middle of the ceiling in each of the four rooms. There was no bathroom, so when members of the parson's family wanted to take a bath, water was heated in a tea kettle on the small kitchen stove and poured into a round metal wash tub. The tub was placed in the middle of the small kitchen floor, and for privacy sheets would be hung over the window above the kitchen sink and the back porch door and the door between the dining room and the kitchen. Baths were hurried affairs, especially in the winter. Clothes were scrubbed on a wash board on the back porch and hung on a line in the back yard, advertising to all passersby the size bra and panties of the parson's wife and the color of the parson's shorts. Modesty was subject to the primitive necessities of life.

During our first winter there, we realized that the outhouse was not a viable alternative, especially during the dark of night. It was really dangerous because instead of just a hole in a board, someone had installed a metal toilet seat on the stool in the outhouse. The problem was that when the temperature dropped below sub-freezing, if contact by one's skin was made with the frozen metal it was likely that their flesh would become almost instantly frozen to the metal and it was next to impossible to get free without the aid of hot scalding water and some painful skinning of the posterior. So I found an old chair with a woven caned seat. I cut the caned bottom out of the chair and purchased a porcelain pot with a lid on it which was placed under the bottomless chair. The only place to put it was in a corner of the bedroom, and in order to provide some semblance of privacy, I hung a piece of green cloth around the privy chair. The only problem was that the green cloth could not hide the noise nor the odor associated with that pot, even though we poured creosote into the bottom of the privy pail to keep the foul odor down until we could carry the pot outside and dump it in the outhouse. It may be hard for this modern generation to imagine, but the out-house was a common thing on farms and even in small towns back in those days, and it was a step up from the common "Turkish Toilets" still in use in primitive third-world countries today.

There was one good thing that the outhouse provided. On the back side of the outhouse I built a series of rabbit hutches, and during all but the hottest months of summer we were able to raise rabbits which I would kill and skin to augment our meat rations. We also made a trip to the local farmers co-op (a grain elevator company), which gave out six baby chicks to the children of the town at Easter each year. I bought some chicken wire at the co-op and we were able to raise chickens in the parsonage's backyard.

Between our chickens and rabbits and a small vegetable garden, and through the gifts of fresh vegetables and fruit from the gardens of our parishioners and with left-over handouts from Mrs. Margaret Edwards who was the cook at the local Criterion Restaurant on Main Street, we managed to survive. We were young and living on love, and grateful for every gift we received. However, Mrs. Edwards would bring us left-over soup in a #10 metal can from the restaurant kitchen, and when I became sick from ptomaine poison after eating left-over soup from that tin can, thereafter we would always take care to thank Mrs. Edwards for her gifts of food, but the soup and anything else that was delivered to us in a tin can was disposed of down the hole in the parsonage outhouse.

Because there was only a bed frame and an old mattress in the bedroom, and we did not have the money with which to buy furniture, I improvised. I managed to get two orange crates from the back of the local grocery store and a nail keg from the local lumber yard. I put a beaver board top across the two orange crates and tacked a piece of yellow cloth around the crates to craft a make-do dressing table for Mary. I found an empty nail keg at the local lumber yard and took some cotton batting and covered it with Naugahyde for a dressing table seat; and I tacked a matching piece of the yellow cloth around the keg to dress it up a bit. On the wall above the orange-crate dressing table I hung a round glass mirror I had purchased at the local 5 & 10 cent store, and draped another piece of yellow cloth around it just for show. Mary Elizabeth was a real trooper and seemed to be grateful for her little dressing table into which she tucked her powder and perfume, her hair brush and whatever else its four small shelves would hold.

There was no study/office for the parson, so our dining room table became my desk. But I needed a bookcase and a file cabinet of some sort. I made a couple more trips to the back of the local grocery store where I scavenged five more orange crates. I nailed the crates together to form file cabinet shelves and made two doors from a sheet of Masonite pressed particle board nailed onto 1" x 2" wooden frames that were fastened to the orange crates with a couple pairs of small brass hinges. The file cabinet doors were adorned with a couple of wooden button handles purchased for a few pennies from the local lumberyard. And I managed to hammer together a small bookcase to hold the few but precious volumes I had acquired at college. I painted the file cabinet and bookcase with a couple coats of faux-mahogany maroon paint, and considered myself fortunate to have a semblance of a study. When we had company we used the top of the bookcase as a serving stand and made do with what we had.

*　*　*

After the miracles of healing that God granted to Matt Oceanbeam, in my naivety and ignorance I assumed that because our prayers had been answered before, therefore, every time I prayed God would keep His promise that "the fervent prayers of a righteous man would avail much." In Pentecostal fashion and following the example of some of the older ministers who seemed always to pray loud and long, I reasoned that the correct way to pray was "fervently," i.e., loud and long. When one of the elderly women of our congregation was taken to the hospital stricken with kidney failure, I was asked to go to the hospital and to pray for her. The hospital was on the next corner up the block from our church, so I walked up to the hospital and found the room where our parishioner was lying in bed yellow with jaundice and in a terminal condition. I anointed her with oil from the bottle of consecrated oil I had take from the pulpit, and I began to pray . . . "fervently" and loudly. It had never crossed my mind that this was the community hospital, until the nurses came running into the room and admonished me that I had to be quiet in the hospital. Surprised at my own stupidity but confident that God could hear me if I just whispered a pray, I continued, remembering the gospel hymn "whisper a prayer in the morning, whisper a prayer at noon, whisper a prayer in the evening, keeping your heart in tune." Yes, "God answers prayer in the morning, God answers prayer at noon, God answers prayer in the evening, so keep your heart in tune." I was certain that God would heal this woman just like he had healed Matt Oceanbeam, so I left the hospital thinking that I had done my pastoral duty and now God would surely do His part and heal my parishioner. I was really shocked when I learned shortly thereafter that she had died; and when I was not asked by her family to conduct the funeral I thought that for some reason I couldn't fathom, God had let me down. Maybe it was to teach me a lesson not to be so cock sure and vain as to think that all I had to do was snap my fingers and God would step in and miraculously intervene and do whatever I asked of Him. After all, hadn't Jesus said, "Whatever you ask the Heavenly Father in my name, He will do it?"

"Lord," I wondered, what have I done wrong? Where have I failed? Have I somehow misunderstood or misrepresented You? Forgive me Lord for not trusting you enough."

*   *   *

The financial arrangement by which we subsisted in that first parish was based upon the long standing custom that the minister received the Sunday morning offering as his monetary stipend; and the offerings from the Sunday evening evangelistic service and the mid-week Bible Study went to pay the utility bills for the church house lights, the natural gas bill, Sunday School supplies, etc. A second-hand gas heater was finally installed to replace the old pot bellied stove which had become a fire hazard. When the old wood-burning stove would be fired up it would become red hot and threatened to scorch anyone who got too close. The metal floor pad beneath it was in danger of overheating. The metal chimney stack that was stuck through the side wall of the church and jutted up above the eves on the side of the building would allow smoke to blow back inside the church during a high wind. The gas heater was placed along the left-hand wall, so there was still the problem of unequal heat distribution in the winter, but it was far better than the old pot-bellied wood-burning stove with its wood box and a pail for ashes.

The first couple of years, I was lucky if the Sunday morning offering from those poor folks would average six or seven dollars a week. I honestly don't know how we ever managed to make ends meet. We lived very simply and frugally. Mary sewed her own clothes and made some of my shirts from material and patterns purchased at the yard goods department of the local 5 & 10 cent store. During the summer we ate a lot of tomato sandwiches, and in the winter we ate a lot of oatmeal, homemade corn scrapple, eggs, chicken, rabbits and vegetable soup. Gasoline was only 15 cents a gallon. We had an icebox on the back porch and bought ice from the local ice house. In the cold weather of winter the ice chest was packed with snow to keep food from spoiling. Mary was a good cook, a faithful and devoted wife and companion, and my partner in the ministry. She was also a real prayer warrior and trusted God to supply our needs and to help us stretch what little we had—like when Jesus had multiplied the loaves and fishes with which he fed the multitude.

NOTES:

[1] I never told anyone in my first pastorate how young I was and yet the good people in that congregation always treated me with respect. No one ever called me by my first name but I was addressed as Brother Jones, Pastor Jones or Reverend Jones. Back in those days it was not uncommon for Bishops to recruit whomever they could find including college boys to fill small rural churches when no fully ordained ministers were available. Bishop Fredrick Wertz of the Baltimore-Washington conference was appointed as a "lay pastor" to his first small rural church in Pennsylvania when he was only 16 years of age, and I have known several clergy colleagues who like myself were only teenage boys when we were sent out to do a man's job in the pulpit. But then we were not without a sound Biblical precedent, because it was a teenage shepherd boy David whom God sent out to do battle with the Philistine giant Goliath.

Clarence Oliver "Ted" Slover

CHAPTER 1

CLARENCE OLIVER "TED" SLOVER

"TED" SLOVER had the biggest forearms of any man I had ever met.[1] His forearms were like those of the cartoon character Popeye the sailor man but, unlike Popeye whose biceps appear in contrast to his forearms as being exaggeratedly slim, Ted's biceps were large and in good proportion to the rest of his muscular upper torso. He was not a tall man, standing only about 5 feet 9 inches tall, making his stature appear all the more strong and powerful. He was a man's man, a hardworking, highly skilled and likeable fellow. He reminded me of the cartoon characters that used to appear in the Hastings Piston Rings ads which always depicted a strong rugged muscular man doing something kind like tying a bandage on the wounded paw of a little puppy, and the caption under each illustration was "Tough but oh so gentle!" That was Ted Slover—tough, but oh so gentle especially in his relationships to small children, ladies and the elderly. Ted Slover was also a godly man and the lay leader of the **First Assemblies of God Church, Columbus, Kansas**.

Ted was a journeyman electrician/plumber/HVAC mechanic, who spent his days working with monkey wrenches, pipe die-cutters, electrical conduits, metal ductwork, pulling wires and lifting heavy heating units into place, which explains how he came to develop such extraordinarily large forearms and strong muscles. Engaged as he was in the building trades, he had also mastered several other construction trades including carpentry and cement/masonry work. His skills and his devotion to our little church were a God-send to our congregation when it came time for us to construct a new brick church building on the corner of Sycamore and Minnesota Streets in the small mid-western town of Columbus, Kansas. In order to help the reader understand better the circumstances and the magnitude of Ted Slover's invaluable financial assistance, encouragement and friendship, the following vignettes are intended not as a nostalgic autobiographical narrative but rather to provide the backdrop setting by which to highlight and underscore the critically important contributions that Mr. Slover made to our very survival and to the success and growth of our congregation.

*   *   *

After the Sunday evening services, Ted and Margie Slover would invite Mary and me over to their house for homemade pie and ice cream. During the summer the days were long and hot, and after the air cooled down a bit in the evenings it was a pleasant thing to sit out on the front porch swing or rocking chairs and visit. We would pass away the time chatting about the events and news of the previous week, discussing local and national politics, and once in a while talking about some profound mystery of life or the Christian faith. Television was just in its infancy and even for those few homes that had a TV the network channels were few and the program offerings were limited. The local newspaper, the *Saturday Evening Post*, the *Reader's Digest* and books from the local library were sources of evening entertainment, but just plain ol' yarn telling and conversation were a welcome and cherished way to pass a quiet Sunday evening.

*   *   *

Shortly after I began my pastoral ministry in Columbus, Marjorie Slover died. I was asked to conduct the funeral. I really can't remember anything about Marjorie's death, except that she left Ted Slover with a teenage daughter, Imogene, who really needed a mother; and it was obvious even to us that Ted had dearly loved Marjorie and missed her terribly. I can understand now that which I was too immature and poorly trained and insensitive to more fully comprehend then about what it means to lose a spouse. It was only after Mary Elizabeth died nearly twenty years later that I came to grasp with more understanding, insight and empathy what Ted Slover felt at Marjorie's passing. He was at peace knowing that Marjorie, who was a sweet and devout woman and a devoted wife and mother, was at "home" in heaven; but that knowledge alone could not fill the void in Ted's aching and grieving heart.

*   *   *

The following summer of 1952 we learned that Mary Elizabeth was pregnant. The congregation was delighted at the news that there would be a baby in their parsonage. But something would have to be done to make the parsonage more habitable for the baby.

Ted Slover who was a master electrician volunteered to rewire the parsonage, to install electrical outlets in each of the four rooms, to hang new light fixtures in the ceilings, and to install a new safe circuit-breaker box by the electric meter on the back porch. It was when the wires were being pulled for the electric outlets that we discovered that old newspapers dating back to the civil war days had been stuffed between some of the studs in the walls for insulation, but there was no insulation above the ceiling. Some of the ladies in the congregation who knew how to wallpaper volunteered to wallpaper the living room, dining room, bedroom, and kitchen. I painted all the woodwork white, and Mary bought new curtains and shades for the windows. Mrs. Edwards donated a washing machine which we placed on the back porch. This made it much easier for Mary since she would no longer have to wash all of our clothes and the baby's diapers on an old fashioned scrub board.

There was also the problem of refrigeration. We would need a decent refrigerator in which to keep the baby's formula and baby food. We drove to Joplin, Missouri which was the closest town that had a Sears & Roebuck store that handled appliances. We found a refrigerator that would serve our purposes, but when I sought to purchase a new refrigerator "on time" and to make monthly payments I was turned down because I was not "of age." I was only 20 years old at the time and I wouldn't turn 21 until November, just a few weeks before the new arrival was expected to be born. Not knowing what else to do, I confided in the pastor of the local Church of God (the Anderson, Indiana branch of the Church of God). He was a kindly and godly man who took pity on me. He was the only person in town to whom I ever revealed my age. He agreed to co-sign the purchase contract with me, and it was through his kindness that we were able to make that vitally important purchase, though we were not certain just how we would pay the monthly bill.

Ted Slover became a much beloved friend and the first among that group of men who would become to me the trusted allies and comrades-at-arms that King David's Mighty Men became to him. After Marjorie's death, Ted's days were filled with his work, and because of his superb craftsmanship he was always in demand as an electrician, plumber and HVAC technician. But the nights were long and lonely, and even though he loved and cared for Imogene, doting on her without spoiling her, there was still that empty void left by Marjorie's passing. We didn't understand at first why it was that almost every Sunday after the evening evangelistic service, Ted Slover would stay around praying at the altar and visiting with the other parishioners until every one else had left and gone home.

Ted would volunteer to help us tidy up the church, making sure that all the hymnals were carefully put back in their racks on the back of the pews, that all the trash was picked up, and checked to see that the gas furnace was turned down, all the lights were turned off and the church doors were all carefully locked and secure. Then, invariably he would ask us, "Would you like to go for a little ride?"

Of course we would like to go for a ride. We didn't have any TV and we seldom played our little radio which would crackle with static. We had already read the local weekly paper from cover to cover. But after teaching a Sunday School Class, preaching the Sunday morning sermon, conducting a service at one of the convalescent homes or at the county jail in the afternoon, conducting the Christ's Ambassadors youth service for an hour prior to the evening evangelistic service, singing and preaching again in the evening, I was ready to unwind by going for a little ride.

We were never certain where Ted would take us. It might be to one of the neighboring communities, to Ft. Scott or Oswego or one of the other towns north or west in Kansas, or it could be to across the Missouri line to Joplin, or down into Oklahoma, to the town of Commerce, which was the home of Mickey Mantle, or to some other place. One evening we were driving along aimlessly in Oklahoma, and when we came to a cross roads, Ted said "Let's follow that car and see where it's going." It turned out that we drove and drove, mile after mile, until we were on the outskirts of Tulsa before we realized where we were. But wherever we went there was the inevitable stop at some drive-in restaurant for a hamburger or a hotdog and a big milkshake or ice cream sundae. When we would finally arrive back home, he would reach out his big beefy hand to shake our hand good-bye, and he would often pass from his hand to ours a $5 or $10 bill. Ted was our head usher and he knew how little was in the offering plate sometimes on a Sunday morning. Out of his great big magnanimous and generous heart he was determined to see to it that his pastor's family would not go without because the offerings were inadequately small. Ted knew that we lived on the proverbial "shoestring," and he knew how grateful we were for his largess.

*   *   *

Our first child, Daniel Stephen, was born on December 29, 1952, a belated Christmas present for us.[2] Since Ted Slover had no son of his own, it seemed as if he adopted Danny as his own "grandson." On Danny's first Christmas

Ted gave to him a little pair of bib overalls and a red American Flyer wagon, and he doted other gifts upon Danny on his birthday and whenever there was an occasion to do so.

*　　*　　*

Four times during the first couple of years of my pastorate in Columbus we were confronted by what were for me terribly disheartening and discouraging challenges by charlatan unethical clergy and wannabe lay preachers. The first time was when a self-styled female evangelist named Mrs. King from somewhere in Oklahoma blew into town and attempted to take over the Pentecostal Oneness Church.[3] Mrs. King was a short stout woman who fancied herself as the next Aimee Semple McPherson. She made open and aggressive attempts to recruit my wife and me as guest musicians for her evangelistic crusade and when we explained the error of the Oneness heresies she became very indignant and spoke ill of us in her public meetings. That was in the early 1950s before the advent of TV and the Internet; and any bizarre religious huckster, however convoluted his brand of religion might be, was a welcomed entertainment and diversion from the monotony and boredom of a small town. In less than two weeks Mrs. King brazenly announced that she was going to change the name of her host's church and institute her own whimsically devised reforms, but to her surprise and dismay, the women who held the keys to the church doors had the locks changed and locked her out!

*　　*　　*

The second threat that was made to split our small congregation was initiated by a Pentecostal Church of God home missions church planter who moved a portable Quonset-hut building onto a rented vacant lot a couple of blocks east of us on the same street as our church. His intent was to found a new Pentecostal congregation by recruiting undiscerning people whom he would steal from our congregation and other local churches. Because ours was the only active Pentecostal church in town, this "church rustler" and his wife and children would occupy a pew in our church on Sunday mornings. When I would stand at the door of the church to shake hands with departing parishioners at the close of the service, he would stand across from me and greet everyone and invite them to come to his services on Sunday afternoon and evening and to help him build a new congregation that would preach the "full gospel" (as if we and the other ministers in town were not preaching the whole Word of God). His blatant efforts to split our congregation were so transparent that even a young novice such as I could see what he was trying to do toward enticing and entrapping our members to join with his group thus splitting our congregation. Mary and I invited him and his wife to our home and served them cherry pie and ice cream and coffee at our dining room table where I confronted him with his being a "wolf-in-sheep's clothing" and charged him with attempting to steal our flock. I asked him to never return to our church.

Since our small but growing congregation was a "home mission" congregation that had never been "set in order," I distributed membership cards to everyone who was a member of our Sunday School and who attended our church regularly. I invited the "Bishop," Rev. Victor Greissen, to be our pulpit guest on a Sunday morning, with the intent that he would officiate at the ritual of receiving members and constituting our congregation as a church in full connection with voting privileges at the District (Conference) meetings. Inexperienced neophyte pastor that as I was, I did not have the good sense to have the parishioners sign and submit their membership application cards ahead of time, but naively expected them to bring them forward and present them to Bishop Greissen on the morning he would preach and officiate in the "setting in order" of our congregation. When Rev. Greissen invited those who wished to become members to come forward to the altar, not a single soul responded! I was caught totally by surprise and humiliated beyond all limits. Neither Rev. Greissen nor I could figure out what had happened. Later, upon inquiry of our parishioners, it was disclosed that when I had publicly announced that the Bishop was coming and would receive members into our congregation, word of that event had been carried by gullible people to the Pentecostal Church of God minister and he had immediately announced that on the very afternoon of Bishop Greissen's visit he would receive members into his Quonset hut church! Not wanting to do the wrong thing, and wanting to continue as members of our Sunday School and congregation, but also wanting to be part of establishing a brand new church to the honor and glory of God, those poor innocent and simple but gullible folks had talked among themselves and decided not to join any church. Some of them, like Frank Burton and his wife, decided that they didn't want to join any church where they would be expected to tithe. When I visited the Burtons to inquire why they did not join our congregation, they said quite matter-of-factly and without any apparent shame that they had decided to use their tithe money to buy a new gas range for their kitchen. The Pentecostal Church of God charlatan minister had tried to entrap Mr. Burton into being their Sunday School Superintendent, but when Mr. Burton was confronted with the dilemma of having to choose between our church and the Quonset hut church, he recanted and refused the position of Sunday School Superintendent at the other church.

I was so shocked, disappointed, disheartened and discouraged at what I felt was a public betrayal by our congregation when Bishop Greissen came, that I sat down at my little Underwood typewriter and wrote out my official resignation from the pastorate and from the ministry. That was one of the very lowest points in my entire ministerial career. But as I sat at the dining room table typing that letter something came over me—there arose in my spirit a righteous indignation not at the people or even at my own stupidity but at Satan who is the perpetual adversary of our souls. I suddenly realized that what had happened was that Satan had used my inexperience, and the simple-minded lack of spiritual maturity on the part of our parishioners, and the unethical behavior of the Pentecostal Church of God minister to try to destroy God's work in the life of our congregation and to crush out my own service to Christ. You may call it righteous indignation or whatever you wish, but it seemed that the Holy Spirit came upon me and I tore from my typewriter the piece of paper upon which I had written my resignation, and with a red lead pencil I wrote across the face of that letter the words, "If every last soul forsakes the church, Lord, help me and I will remain faithful." Somewhere among my files I believe I still have that declaration of faith and of faithfulness to the ministry to which Christ has called me. Whenever I have felt tempted to walk away from the pastorate, I have recalled that incident in my first pastorate and I have by the grace of God reaffirmed my commitment to Him and to the pastoral ministry.

*   *   *

That was not the only disappointment that confronted me, however. Our little church conducted a revival campaign at the Cherokee County Fair Grounds featuring the Rev. Warren Litzman from Waco, Texas who was a well-known Pentecostal evangelist throughout the central and southwestern states. Litzman was a fiery, eloquent preacher (in the oral tradition of Pentecostal evangelists,) a prolific author and a gifted young man who showed aspirations of becoming another Oral Roberts. That campaign was a true venture in faith for us—it was also a bitter learning experience in the politics of the institutional church. Another evangelist from Texas had held an areawide healing revival campaign under a large circus tent in the nearby town of Joplin, Missouri which had gained a large audience. I had joined the other Pentecostal ministers sitting on the platform and at the close of each service praying with people at the mourners' benches below the elevated stage. Every pastor in the area wanted to sit on that stage and gain visibility and vicariously to benefit from the public endorsement derived by association with this understudy of Oral Roberts.

It seemed to me to be a great idea for our church to sponsor an area wide revival campaign in our county seat which had easy access along the famous Route 66 that connects towns between St. Louis, Missouri all the way to Santa Fe, New Mexico. In my naivety and blind zeal I had made the rounds visiting all of the Pentecostal pastors in the surrounding towns within a 50-mile radius and had believed that they would support our campaign with Warren Litzman not only with their prayers but also by their attendance and with their generous offerings.

Ted Slover had caught my enthusiasm and jumped in to help us by managing to borrow a truck from one of his friends to help us transport an old up-right piano, a little rented Hammond electronic organ, wooden pews and benches, and folding chairs from wherever we could beg or borrow them. We worked like beavers cleaning the large main pavilion at the county fair grounds. We set up seating and spread bales of straw over the dirt aisles and Ted and some of his friends helped us string light bulbs, install some spot lights in the parking lot, and make whatever other arrangements were necessary to meet public safety and sanitary requirements. For our small handful of volunteers it was a tremendous undertaking, but being young and zealous, full of energy and lacking in know-how, experience and better judgment, we plowed full-steam ahead.

Flyers were printed, ads run in the local papers, phone calls made, and prayer vigils scheduled. Having no organist in our little congregation, we hired the wife of a local county court judge to play the organ for our Litzman campaign. I knew that JoAnn Litzman could play the piano and make it *sing* because at college she had often accompanied our Keynote Saxophone Trio: I knew that JoAnn was a truly accomplished pianist with an "evangelistic flair" who could have wowed Lawrence Welk's audiences.

When on the opening night of the campaign only a handful of physically worn-out folks from our little congregation gathered in the big pavilion, and not a single neighboring pastor showed up, it was apparent even to me that something was terribly wrong. I had envisioned a packed house. Litzman demanded to know: "Where is everybody? Where are all the neighboring pastors that you had promised were in support of this campaign?" I was befuddled and dumfounded, and all I could say was: "I don't know!"

The next day Litzman and I drove a couple hundred miles making the rounds to visit all of the pastors we could find at home in the four-state area within a fifty-mile radius of Columbus. When Litzman and I confronted my fellow pastors, their response was, "Sure, Jones, we told you that we would support your campaign with our prayers, but we never meant that we would be in attendance to sit on the platform with you or that we would haul our congregations over to Columbus. After all, our people are hard-working folks and after a day working in their wheat fields or on their oil rigs and refineries or in the lead and zinc mines or at whatever else it is that they do to carve out a living, most of our people just don't have the energy to drag themselves way over to Columbus and sit on a hard board bench for a couple of hours and then drive all the way home again late at night and get up and go back to work again the next morning. What do you hope, man?"

I was speechless, but Litzman held nothing back in shaming those older ministers for their phony piety and their lame excuses. If they and their parishioners could make it night after night to attend an Oral Roberts tent meeting or a Jack Texan's revival campaign, there was no excuse for their failing to honor their word and not supporting the Litzman campaign in Columbus. Litzman's *hellfire and brimstone* approach seemed to have built a fire under some of those not-so-conscientious ministers, because one-by-one they began to show up for the services; and since it was summer and the days were long and daylight lasted until after nine o'clock in the evening, it was not such a terrible thing for people to take a little drive and enjoy an evening of gospel singing and Litzman's preaching. Somehow we managed to get through the two-week campaign, and in the process we won some local notoriety and gained for our membership an exceptionally fine and lovely woman, Mrs. Edington, who became one of our Sunday School teachers, VBS workers and an active leader in our WMC (Women's Missionary Circle) group.

*　*　*

The Columbus AG Congregation began to grow and when the little one-room church house was packed to the gunnels, we moved the elementary school boys' class over to the living room of the parsonage. However, as could be expected, the rambunctious and energetic boys took a toll on our already threadbare furniture, and we knew that something must be done to find more suitable quarters for the growing congregation. Ted Slover became the prime mover in encouraging us to dream and pray for a new church. I had taken mechanical drawing in the ninth grade at Langley Junior High School in Washington, D.C. Our teacher in that vocational education class was a retired WW II Seabee who really knew his business, and I had enjoyed that class a great deal. I still had my mechanical drawing T-square and my drawing tools tucked away in a little black case. I bought a roll of drafting parchment paper, found a piece of plywood to use as a drawing board and began drawing the basic blueprints for a new church building. I adapted the design of the new Assemblies of God Church in Coffeeville, Kansas where the Reverend Everett Ewing was the pastor, but I downsized that large-scale edifice to meet the needs of our small but growing congregation.

It was **Ted Slover** who suggested that we might build using an "SCR" large size brick that could be laid up as a single wall with fasteners embedded in the mortar onto which furring-strips could be nailed and insulation and sheet-rock attached at a later date. It was an inexpensive way to construct a building within our limited financial means. I designed trusses which were bolted together with split-rings for added strength. The trusses sat on brick pilasters spaced at 10' intervals, and a cupola with a spire was added to sit on top of the roof. The building was 50' by 80' giving us 4,000 sq. ft. of space or over twice the size of the original small frame structure one-room church. Ted Slover gave me the name of a structural engineer who took my blueprints and amended them to meet all of the structural and standard building code requirements.

Ted was invaluable to the success of our do-it-yourselves building program. He recommended a local brickyard where we negotiated the purchase of 88,000 bricks that were shipped via the Santa Fe Railroad directly from the kilns of the brickyard to a railroad siding in our town. Ted helped us arrange with the local co-op grain elevator for free use of their trucks to transfer the railroad carloads of bricks to our building site. And then he helped us negotiate the free use of the grain elevator's trucks to haul several hundred yards of gravel one of the lead and zinc mines just over the Kansas State line in Oklahoma. The men from the church—Ted Slover, Wayne Wixon and a couple of others including the pastor loaded those large 30-yard dump trucks by hand, pitching the gravel from the huge piles sitting around above the mines into the truck beds, and then driving back and unloading the trucks on the church site.

With Ted's guidance and the help of the local lumber yard, we ordered a railroad carload of roofing—about 50 squares of shingles. And we also ordered a railroad car load of Portland cement for the footings and floor slab and also masonry cement for the brick mortar. Again we borrowed a truck from the grain elevator to transfer the roofing shingles and the cement to a storage site located in the back of the storefront that the congregation rented just off the town square where we held worship services during the time we were constructing the new church building.

When the townspeople learned that the members of the Assemblies of God Church were planning to build a new church, they were curious and wondered how in the world we would ever manage such a large undertaking with such a small handful of members. Some offered encouragement and others just took pity on us, but we forged ahead with enthusiasm and made do with what we had, and somehow we managed to survive that transitional interim period between the time when we sold and moved the old church and when the new church was completed. It was a hardy and loyal band of Gideon-like warriors.

Ted used some of the lumber for the trusses and rigged up a string of 300-watt bulbs all around the periphery of the building site. Later, as the walls went up and the roof was covered, Ted strung up temporary interior lights as well. The men worked at their regular jobs all day; grabbed a bite to eat and then showed up at the church's building site to work until 9 or 10 o'clock night after night. We did not have access to a backhoe, so all of the ditches for the footings and foundation walls were dug by hand using picks and shovels. Ted scrounged up an old *Sears & Roebuck* cement mixer, and we mixed all of the concrete for the footings, floors, and mortar in that little mixer. It was my job to get up early and have the bricks stacked and the mortar in place on the mortar boards for the two masons by the time they arrived for work. I toiled from morning 'til night carrying hod and bricks for the masons and helped with erecting the scaffolding and keeping trash picked up around the construction site. It was a good thing that I was young and in excellent physical shape. During the summer of 1950 to earn money for my college tuition I had worked in the Kidder Slope coal mines in Wilkes-Barre, Pennsylvania, and I was physically strong and full of energy and zeal.

*   *   *

It was during the early part of the construction of our new church, as the masons were laying up the outside walls which had reached the height of about 4 to 5 feet, as I was working at the task of mixing mortar and hauling bricks, that my peripheral vision caught the image of an elderly man hurriedly coming down the alley behind our parsonage and church construction site. It was old Mr. Frank Burton who was in his late eighties. He was all out of breath, huffing and puffing when he reached the area where I was working. He proceeded to tell me what had occurred at the county fair grounds on the previous night.

Once again it seemed as if Satan had attacked our congregation, this time through a former Assemblies of God Presbyter from Enid, Oklahoma, a Reverend Shackelford. When he had been the senior pastor of the First Assemblies of God Church in Enid, Shackelford had been like a dog-in-the-manger ruthlessly guarding his personal "turf," objecting to and thwarting attempts by other young Assemblies of God ministers to establish new congregations on the other side of town or in the surrounding countryside. When things went sour for him in his Enid church, Shackelford decided he would hit the evangelistic trail. He had heard that our little church had conducted a revival campaign at the Cherokee County Fair Grounds featuring the Rev. Warren Litzman from Waco, Texas. Litzman's campaigns were widely advertised, and I suppose Shackelford figured that if our congregation could manage to engage Warren Litzman, our town might be a good place to stage his entrance to the arena of tent revivals and evangelistic campaigns. What Shackelford did not know was that while I was at CBC in Springfield I had dated JoAnn Towe who later became Litzman's wife. In retrospect, I have an idea that JoAnn may have had something to do with Litzman's consenting to accept our invitation for him to conduct an area wide revival campaign under the sponsorship of my congregation.

Like the Pentecostal Oneness woman evangelist and the Pentecostal Church of God "sheep-stealer," Shackelford intended to establish a beachhead for a satellite congregation over which he would preside in our town. He would unashamedly proselyte members from any church from which he could recruit members for his new "pioneer" church. He had rented the county fairgrounds and was in the second week of what he had planned to develop into an extended series of revival meetings reaching toward the formation of a core group and the renting of a storefront in which to launch another congregation in our town. When I had been asked to participate and support Shackelford's campaign, my response was that which Nehemiah had given to his neighboring Arab enemies:

> *When word came to Sanballat, Tobiah, Geshem the Arab and the rest of our enemies that I had rebuilt the wall and not a gap was left in it—though up to that time I had not set the doors in the gates—Sanballat and Geshem sent me this message: "Come, let us meet together in one of the villages on the plain of Ono." But they were scheming to harm me, so I sent messengers to them with the reply: "I am carrying on a great project and cannot go down. Why should the work stop while I leave it and go down to you?"—Nehemiah 6:1-3 ff.*

I had decided that if David Jones would take care of David, God would take care of Saul and of Sanballat and Tobiah and any others whom Satan might send to destroy the work we had undertaken.

Shakelford and his co-workers had been praying for the sick in the hope that, on an outside chance, some miracle of healing might occur which would give impetus to his efforts to establish another church in our town. Throughout his evangelistic campaign, during the daytime Shackelford and his associates were canvassing the area around town and the outlying countryside visiting in the homes of anyone whose name had been given them by someone attending their meetings. One afternoon a man and two women visited in the home of a man and woman who had attended our church and for whom I had been asked to offer prayers for their healing. They were elderly and suffered from the chronic rheumatoid ailments common among old folks. The man and one of the women had entered the home of the couple and had anointed the homeowner's wife with olive oil and, laying his hands upon her, had offered prayers for her deliverance from her aches and pains. After praying the visitors hurriedly left the house and quickly drove off leaving a trail of dust in their wake. The elderly woman arose from the sofa upon which she had been reclining and realized that her apron was askew and her clothes seemed a bit ruffled up. As she straightened her garments she suddenly realized that she had been frisked and the departing associates of the Rev. Mr. Shackelford had made off with their life's savings which she had kept pinned in a little pocket inside her apron.

Having lived through the crash of the banks in 1929 and the aftermath of the great depression, like many of the farm folk in the Midwest and elsewhere, they no longer trusted the banks, so they hid their money in jars and buried it in the ground, stuffed it under or inside of the mattresses, or carried it on their persons as this woman had done.

Immediately the elderly couple phoned the county Sheriff and an all-points bulletin was issued by the police for the apprehension and arrest of the guilty culprits. Shackelford's campaign was shut down by the authorities and he pulled stakes and left town. But even without the long arm of the law, Shackelford and his bunch were through in our town where word traveled like lightening via the phone lines and the back-yard over-the-fence gossip grapevines. Even though it was the county seat, Columbus was by all standards even back then a relatively small town of around only 2,000 souls, and gossip traveled very swiftly.

When old Brother Burton asked me what I thought about Shackelford and about the thievery and what I was going to do about it, I looked him in the eye for a long minute and finally said to him: "Nothing!" "I'm not going to do anything at all!" I reminded him that I had warned the members of our congregation not to be led off by pied pipers or wolves in sheep's clothing and that if they persisted in running after every religious charlatan who passed through our town, then whatever happened to them would serve them right and could be a deserved punishment from the Lord for their wandering waywardness. That seemed to put the fear of God into some of our parishioners . . . but not all of them had learned yet. One more similar incident still lay ahead of us.

We continued with the construction of the new church without allowing ourselves to become sidetracked again. After the beams were covered with roof sheeting and tarpaper, we tackled the task of installing the 50-odd squares of roofing shingles. Eventually the cupola and spire were added to the front gable of the roof; the outside work on the church was completed and our attention was finally focused on finishing and decorating the interior of the new church building.

*   *   *

Ted Slover eventually became our Sunday School Superintendent and we established a goal to set a new enrollment and attendance record. On a Sunday in the spring of 1954 we dedicated the new church. Dr. Carlson, President of Central Bible College, Springfield, Missouri, was the guest speaker, and Bishop Victor Greissen officiated at the consecration ceremonies for the new building. The ladies of the church prepared a "fellowship dinner" for the visiting guests from the community and neighboring churches in our District. The church was packed, and not long after the consecration of the new church we set a new attendance record of 125. Considering that on my first Sunday in that pastorate there were only 31 souls counting Mary Elizabeth and myself, that new record attendance was a considerable achievement, nearly quadrupling the membership.

In the Baptist fashion of baptism by immersion, we had built a pool about four feet wide and seven feet long and four feet deep in the back center of the Sanctuary Chancel. The baptismal pool was constructed out of cement blocks and waterproofed with Thoroseal. We had installed a foot high plate-glass "window" on the top front side so the water in the pool came up high enough that worshippers in the congregation could actually see the baptized candidates as they were "dunked" under the water in the symbolism of Christ's burial and resurrection (Romans 6:4 KJV). We had installed an "overflow" pipe at one end of the baptismal tank; but what we had not anticipated was what would happen if a really large person entered the tank. One of the baptismal candidates was a very large woman who must have weighed close to 300 pounds. I was not worried about drowning her because I reasoned that she would float. But when she entered the baptismal pool the water ran over the top of the glass window and spilled down the wall onto the chancel carpet. Immediately I unscrewed the overflow pipe to let more of the water drain out, but after I had baptized her, I could not get the overflow pipe back into its socket. I still had to baptize her six-foot tall husband, but the water kept flowing out so by the time I finally got around to baptizing him I practically had to lay him down on the bottom of the pool where there were only about two feet of water left in the tank and that was rapidly disappearing!

*   *   *

Things seemed to be going along fairly smoothly when there was another—a fourth—attempt by Satan to stir up a division in our congregation: this time it was instigated by a woman who lived on the other side of Sycamore Street in the second house in the next block south from where our church stood. We could see her house from the parsonage, but we had no idea about the mischief that she was planning. She had a son in his late forties who worked at the nearby oil refinery; but she fancied that her son should become a minister. He had neither a college nor a seminary education, but he apparently had the "preacher's itch" that, with his mother's prodding, he decided to scratch. She convinced some of the older women that their young minister was not as spiritual as she thought he should be, and that there were not as many *messages in tongues* and *interpretations of tongues* as she understood St. Paul to have allowed in his letter to the Corinthians. She and others had arrived at the conclusion that there ought to be as many as three messages in tongues and interpretations of ecstatic prophetic utterances in every public service as St. Paul permitted. [4] People in town thought that the Pentecostal "holy rollers" were crazy enough as it was without our parading *glossolalia* as a litmus test in every service. She managed to goad a group of her friends into holding clandestine "cottage prayer meetings" in their homes around the parish with the idea that her son would take the place of the pastor in these séance-like meetings. Mary and I sensed that in spite of our new building project and the growing attendance, something just wasn't quite right. Body language, chuckling, the exchanging of private insider's jokes, cliquishness, snide muffled remarks, etc. were all signs that something was going on behind the pastor's back.

One Sunday morning I accidentally happened to overhear a conversation between a couple of women who exchanged the time and place of the next clandestine "cottage prayer meeting," which was to take place the following Thursday evening in the home of Mrs. Nettie Osborn. I talked it over with Mary Elizabeth and we began to put the pieces together. We were not certain about what was afoot, but whatever it was we would try to cut it off at the pass. I decided to pay a pastoral visit to the home of Mr. and Mrs. Osborn and asked Mary Elizabeth to go with me. We would go about 5:30, right after the Osborns' usual supper hour. We would just drop in unannounced for a friendly chat and to check up on Mr. Osborne whose health was failing. When we arrived Mr. Osborn, who was a quiet elderly gentleman, greeted us warmly and invited us into their living room. The longer we stayed the more uneasy and fidgety Nettie became. Then there was a knock on the front door and one of our other parishioners happened by. Soon another member arrived and then another and another. Mary and I acted totally innocent and greeted each person cordially and expressed our delight that they had stopped by while were there. "That way I can visit with all of you at once," I cajoled them. As still others began to arrive, finally with a red face filled with embarrassment Nettie couldn't hold her shame any longer and blurted out, "Well, we might as well 'fess up, 'cause the Pastor can see that this isn't any accidental gathering—he knows something is going on here so we might as well admit to him that we are having a cottage prayer meeting."

"Wonderful," I said; "My father is an Assemblies of God minister and I attended cottage prayer meetings with my parents from the time I was just a toddler and throughout my early childhood days. We will be delighted to stay and pray with you." What could they do? We had caught them flat-footed and red-handed in their little splinter conspiracy, so they reluctantly but courteously invited us to stay. As might have been expected, our neighbor's over-grown son attempted to lead the group in one song and chorus after another and then he asked everyone present to give a testimony and several read various and sundry Scripture passages and their favorite memory verses, and then the neighbor's son began embarrassedly to mumble some random thoughts in a feeble and fumbling attempt to preach a sermonette. By that time I had had about enough of this charade, so I held up my hand and said, "May I ask a question?"

"Yes, Pastor, what is it?"

"Pardon me," I protested, "but I thought the purpose of this meeting was to offer prayers of thanksgiving, intercession and supplication, not to hold a community hymn sing or a Sunday evening evangelistic service. If we are here to pray, then let's get at it and begin to pray! And if we truly believe that God answers prayer, then let's anoint with olive oil Mr. Osborn and any other persons who are ill and trust God to grant them a miracle of healing. The effectual fervent prayer of a righteous man availeth much and the prayer of faith shall save the sick as St. James promises us in his epistle. Let's see if God will hear *your* prayers and heal Mr. Osborn."

All of a sudden it got very quiet. Not only was their cover blown but they were exposed by their own behavior and their guilty consciences for the hypocritical way in which they were behaving. Whether by that time they felt like it or not they began to offer prayers almost as if in desperation until by and by they were exhausted and "prayed out." And they were ready for refreshments—the usual coffee, lemonade and home-baked cake and cookies.

Before anyone left, I asked when and where they planned to hold their next cottage prayer meeting and stated that I would be glad to announce it the following Sunday so everyone who wanted to pray could come and join in.

There was a hesitation and a stammering and stuttering and an acknowledgement that no time or place had yet been decided upon. We all knew that this was a confession that the ring leader and her son had not yet co-opted anyone else to be the host or hostess for their next meeting and that, in any case, it could no longer remain a clandestine meeting but would have to be thrown open to anyone who wanted attend. That, in itself, would impose an improbable problem since most of the homes of our parishioners were small and limited as to how many people could comfortably be crammed into a tight space.

The hold that the neighbor woman and her son had upon this kind but gullible group of our parishioners was broken and we never heard any more about cottage prayer meetings. The woman and her son stopped attending our church and we noticed after a while that we no longer saw the neighbor woman out in her yard or walking about town. When I asked about them, my inquiry was met with a comical but pathetic response: "Oh, Pastor, didn't you know that your neighbor lady lost her mind and has been sent to an insane asylum and her son has been taken ill . . . because they went behind your back and tried to split our congregation!" As far as these unsophisticated Midwesterners were concerned, God had visited His judgment upon those who had thought to do despite to his servant David Jones. That was the last time in my tenure as pastor of the AG Church in Columbus, KS, that the congregation suffered a dissident distraction that threatened its unity and its growth. We know that Satan is a relentless foe but that in the end he is a defeated enemy of Christ and he will not prevail.

*　　*　　*

As far as I know, **Ted Slover** never participated in or condoned any of the four episodes that involved some of the other members of our congregation in any of the divisive or proselytizing attempts made by unscrupulous persons in an effort to divide and destroy our congregation. Throughout my ministry in Columbus, Ted remained our closest and most loyal supporter and friend. Without his invaluable help and generosity we would never have been able to achieve the measure of growth and success that the congregation experienced.

Over the following months Ted Slover cautiously began courting the widow Mrs. Lula Coble. Her husband, Roy Coble had been a successful wheat farmer, raising bumper crops. Her mother-in-law, Mrs. Mattie Coble was a good and godly woman, who like Dwight Eisenhower had come from an Anabaptist plain folks (like the Mennonites) religious background, and had never been baptized. Mattie Coble was among the first baptismal class that I baptized in the new baptismal pool in the new church. However, her son Roy was not religiously inclined. It may be that he resented the strict upbringing in which his parents had reared him and he may have been ashamed of his mother's religious zeal and her involvement with a Pentecostal congregation. One day I drove out into one of his fields where Roy and his eldest son were plowing, to speak with him about his soul. He didn't even get down off his tractor to talk with me but in a crude and rude manner he declared that he didn't care if he died and went to hell, and ordered me off of his property. It was just a few days later that I received a phone call informing me that Roy had suddenly died of a heart attack, and I was requested to officiate at his funeral service. Later on his wife stated that although she had loved Roy, she realized that had he lived he would have set a very bad example before his children and it isn't likely that any of the family would have come to know Jesus as their Savior. Lula was an excellent cook and a hardy farmer's wife who endeavored to keep operating their farm and to raise her children in the Christian faith. Mary Elizabeth and Danny and I were often invited to the Coble farm for a hearty home-cooked country dinner, and quite often Ted Slover and his daughter Imogene were also invited. Eventually Ted and Lula were married. Each one of their children grew in the Christian faith and their oldest son became a Christian minister.

*   *   *

There were several other men in that congregation about whom I have vivid memories. Old Mr. Homer Wilson had a big pocket watch and every time I would stand in the pulpit and begin to preach he would take out his big gold pocket watch and wind it as if to let me know that he was timing me to see how long-winded I would be.

And there was old Mr. William Newberry who smoked Prince Albert tobacco in his pipe. His pipe was his best friend, but after I preached about how our bodies are the "temple" of the Holy Spirit and we ought not to do anything that would harm our bodies, and that tobacco was known to be a carcinogen and a deadly contributor to both mouth and lung cancer, Mr. Newberry struggled with his tobacco habit. He spoke to me about his struggle with his tobacco addiction and asked me to pray with him that the Lord would deliver him from that bad habit. I visited him in his room at the boardinghouse where he lived, and he took his can of Prince Albert tobacco and his pipe out to the garbage can in the alley. After I left Mr. Newberry's room, I drove my car around the block and walked back to the garbage can and removed the can of tobacco and Bill's pipe and took them down to the city dump where I scattered the tobacco on the ground and took the pipe apart and threw the bowl in one direction and the stem in another direction as far as I could toss them. I knew that Bill Newberry would probably have second thoughts and might go back to the garbage can to retrieve his beloved pipe and tobacco, so I thought I would remove the temptation from him. I never knew him to smoke a pipe again after that.

There was an old retired Baptist minister by the name of Rev. Workman who with his wife regularly worshipped with us, though I felt that he didn't think much of Pentecostal churches. Nevertheless, he seemed to tolerate my attempt at homiletics and exercised a great deal of patience to put up with my ineptness in the pulpit. On occasion I would ask him to lead us in prayer or to offer the benediction; and now I wish that I had honored him in a more significant way as a senior minister of the Gospel.

Mr. Wayne Wixon who worked at a nearby oil refinery came second only to Ted Slover in the number of long hours of donated labor, financial sacrifice and assistance that he gave to the construction of the new church. One of the young men, Fred Bridges, also gave hours of volunteer labor as did other men from the congregation and the community. There was also a faithful band of women whose faces I can still see in my mind's eye but whose names elude me now more than half a century later. All of these good Christian people are part of that elite group of warriors of the faith who in that very first pastorate were to me as King David's mighty men were to him. I give thanks to God for each one of those dear souls who were not only my parishioners but who were also my friends and mentors as I began my career as a Christian minister. I owe to each one of them, and to the others whose names appear in this book, a debt of gratitude that I cannot overstate. May God Himself reward and bless each one of them. I look forward to seeing all of them again some day.

NOTES:

1. I never knew that Ted Slover's name was actually Clarence Oliver Slover until I wrote this book and his step-daughter, Patty Coble White, surprised me by telling me Ted's full name! To me he will always be "Ted" Slover.

2. It was my privilege to be in the delivery room when he uttered his first plaintive cry. Many times I have thought that if God had given me drawing paper and a pencil and asked me to design the little boy I wanted, I would not have changed a single thing—Danny was everything and all I ever wanted in a son. Fortunately for both of us, Dan and I have enjoyed a close bond and camaraderie throughout his childhood, high school, college days and his adult life.

3. Oneness Pentecostalism is a blend of Modalism (Sabellianism), Nestorianism, Arianism, Monatism and 20th century beliefs not found in any corresponding ancient Christian sects. Jesus Only cult which holds the ancient heresy of modalism. -- From Wikipedia http://en.wikipedia.org/wiki/Oneness_Pentecostal,

4. I Corinthians 14:26-33

Donald Reincke, ThB

CHAPTER 2

REVEREND DONALD REINCKE

DONALD REINCKE, ThB, was a close friend, an esteemed colleague in the ministry and the best fishing buddy I ever had.

Don was a tall six-foot plus handsome well-built blond haired descendant of German ancestors. He had served in the U.S. Navy, and before he became a Christian he, like many of his friends, enjoyed sloshing back a couple of beers at the local tavern and was ready to mix it up in a barroom brawl with the best of 'em. He was a likable man's man, a real he-man.

Then he met Marquita Engemone, the pretty and vivacious daughter of a staunch Norwegian couple who lived in Tacoma, Washington. When Marquita was very young she became seriously ill with a crippling infirmity that threatened her life. Her parents who were Lutherans heard about a Pentecostal Revival campaign at the **First Assemblies of God Church in Tacoma, WA,** where the evangelist prayed for the sick and reportedly a number of miracles of divine healing occurred in these meetings. Marquita's parents took their little girl to the revival meetings and, in answer to their request that prayers be offered for their daughter, Marquita was miraculously healed and made physically whole and well. She grew up to be a very pretty and vivacious young woman who loved the Lord God with all her heart.

Marquita's father, Clayton Engemone, was the comptroller of the giant Weyerhaeuser Timber Company, then headquartered in Tacoma, Washington. It was through him that I acquired a complimentary membership in the Weyerhaeuser Golf and Country Club in Enumclaw, WA. Clayton was so embarrassed over the ante-diluvian set of old wooden-shank golf clubs and the tattered old canvas golf bag that I had purchased at a second-hand store in Joplin, Missouri when I was pastoring in Kansas, that he offered to sell to me for only $50.00 his matched set of MacGregor golf clubs for which he had paid a fortune; and he prodded me to purchase an inexpensive golf cart, a decent leather golf bag, and a pair of fancy golf shoes so he would not need to be ashamed of me when he took me golfing with him. Clayton would take Mary Elizabeth and me golfing at the Enumclaw Golf Club and would challenge Mary Elizabeth by promising her that if she could beat our scores he would take us to dinner. Mary was a south-paw who played a very competitive game with a set of left-handed clubs we rented for her from the club's pro shop. Invariably Mary would beat the socks off of Clayton and me (though he probably could easily have won hands down if he really wanted to) and he would treat us to a fine dinner afterward. He was a good and generous man, and being good-hearted in his joking Norwegian way he "forgave" me for being partly Swedish.

It was through Marquita's Christian testimony that Don eventually became a Christian and the couple became active in the South Tacoma Presbyterian Church where Don served as an elder on the congregation's Session (ruling elders) and was a delegate to the local Presbytery and Synod. Occasionally they would attend the evening evangelistic services at the First Assembly of God Church where Marquita's parents had become members.[1] It was in September of 1954 that I had accepted the call to become the Assistant Pastor (the *de facto* "assistant to the pastor") of that church. It was there that I met Don and Marquita Reincke.

The Reinckes owned and operated a thriving egg business: they purchased all the eggs they could find from local farmers who would deliver their eggs to the Reinckes' warehouse. The Reinckes and their staff washed, candled, sorted and processed thousands of eggs every week and sold them to grocery stores, restaurants, bakeries, etc. through their own large distribution network. They owned a beautiful new home in South Tacoma and were "sitting on top of the world."

Mary Elizabeth and I envied them and looked forward to the day when instead of living in a "company-owned" parsonage, we might be able to own a home of our own. At that time we were living in a make-do "apartment" in the education building of the Tacoma AG Church, which was far from being ideal living quarters: we had little privacy and there was no bedroom for our son Danny, so we were forced to place his crib in a Sunday School room next to our bedroom on the second floor of the educational wing; and on Sunday morning we had to remove his crib to make way for a class of youngsters who carried all of their coughing and cold-germs into our living quarters. Don and Marquita took pity on us and often invited us to be guests in their home. Having no children of their own, they "adopted" Danny as if he were theirs and doted gifts of clothing and little toys upon him. In a short period of time there developed between the Reinckes and us a strong bond of friendship which later extended into our professional careers.

Although they were prosperous and their business was growing and promised an expanded future, Don felt the call of God upon his life to study for the ministry. Marquita managed the business while Don pursued pre-seminary and then post-graduate theological studies at Northwest University. He earned his B.A. and then a Th.B. degree, managing to gain a grasp of the theological disciplines including the Koine Greek language of the New Testament, etc. After graduation Don was called to pastor the Hartline Assemblies of God Church in eastern Washington, where Don served faithfully and with distinction. Then they returned to the western part of the state where Don served for a number of years as pastor of the Assemblies of God Church on Bainbridge Island which is located in Puget Sound between Seattle and the Olympic Peninsula. The only direct way to reach the island was via the ferry boats that run between Seattle and Bainbridge's port docks.

Even though it was an expensive proposition, the Reinckes would often catch a ferry boat after their church service on Sunday evenings and travel to Seattle to spend a couple of hours commiserating with us. We would engage in what my colleague Dr. James D. Glass refers to in his book *Putting It Together In The Parish* as "bitch/brag" sessions where we would compare notes about our respective parishes and blow off steam either expressing our gratefulness or our angst over the events of the day and past weeks since we had last met to console or cajole each other.

*　　*　　*

It was during this period of time that Don introduced me to salmon fishing. All the fishing I had ever done before was for sunfish perch in Chautauqua Lake, NY where my Grandmother Hallin took me to fish off the dock at the Celeron amusement park not far from Lucille Ball's home. I had fished for Chad in the Susquehanna River below the Conowingo Dam in Maryland, and for rainbow trout with Rev. Manlius Davidson in one of the streams around Wrightsville, PA. I had also fished for ocean perch in the Potomac River when visiting my Uncle Paul and Aunt Orpha Steinmetz in their riverside cottage near Leonardtown, Maryland. But I really didn't know what fishing was until Don Reincke took me saltwater fishing for king salmon.

Don owned a boat trailer and a 16' wooden hull fishing boat with a 50 hp Evinrude outboard engine and a smaller 15 hp outboard engine for trolling. He had acquired an accompanying assortment of typical salt-water rods and reels, nets and other necessary gear, and he knew how to use it! He also had a tent and propane cook-stove, lanterns, ice chest, portable charcoal grill, thermos bottles and the rest to go with it. He was a serious fisherman as well as being a capable *fisher-of-men*. Though his methods were not the same as the fishermen of Capernaum whom Jesus called to follow him, Don had followed Jesus' call as had Peter, James, John, Jude and the others. And like them, when he experienced the frustrations that sometimes accompany pastoral ministry, Don found rejuvenation by returning to his boat and fishing where he could spend quiet time in reflection and pray while waiting for the fish to bite.

I shall never forget the memorable expeditions we made to the salt-water fishing grounds where the Pacific salmon ran up the Strait of Juan de Fuca into the Inland Passage through the San Juan Islands chain in Puget Sound. The first time Don took me salmon fishing was a summer weekend in 1955. We loaded his boat and trailer with our gear, and took a Puget Sound ferry from Seattle to Bremerton. Then we drove north on the Olympic Peninsula to Pillar Point on the south shore of the Strait of Juan de Fuca across from Vancouver Island, British Columbia. It was around 2 o'clock in the morning when we arrived at the campsite where we pitched our tent in the dark, stowed our gear, and crawled into our sleeping bags to catch a couple of hours' sleep.

At around 5 AM Don rousted me out of the sack and ordered: "Come on, Jones, let's get going." He already had an enameled pot of coffee brewing and Canadian bacon and eggs frying on the camp stove, and toast was made over an open burner. In the chilly wind blowing off the salt-water, that he-man breakfast tasted mighty good. We hurriedly packed our camping gear into the tent and wheeled the boat trailer out into the cold saltwater where we launched the boat into the shallow tidal waters of an extended salt flat that stretched out into the straits. Don had on his hip-high waders but I only had a pair of knee-high Wellies. Before we had waded out very far I stepped into a gooey duck hole (gooey ducks are giant clams that grow in the waters of the Pacific Northwest) and first one boot and then the other was filled with freezing salt-water. We continued to push the boat out for over a half-mile or more before the flat bottom along the shore around Pillar Point became deep enough in the low tide for us to climb into the boat and start the outboard engine. That was the beginning of what would be the most miserable six hours I have ever endured in my entire life!

My feet were freezing in the saltwater that was pickling my feet inside my boots. We make homemade ice cream in metal cans submerged in a tub of salt-water. Think about it. My feet felt like they were in a hand-cranked ice cream freezer. I had removed my boots and dumped out the ice-cold saltwater, but my socks were soaked. Even though I wrung them out as best I could, they were sopping wet as were my boots, and my body heat was not near hot enough to dry out those wet socks and boots. Don didn't have time to think about my wet feet; and he probably thought that I deserved my saltwater foot-bath for not having the good sense to have obtained a pair of hip waders before we started out. He probably never gave it a second thought. He was busy rigging our saltwater fishing poles and cutting the herring bait. He patiently showed me how to run two tri-point hooks through the herring and to use either a whole herring or to cut the head off at an angle and make what is called a "plug herring." When using a whole herring he would place a little brass clamp over the mouth of the bait to keep it from dragging awkwardly as it was trolled through the water. He demonstrated how to tie on a white or silver metal plate called a "flasher," and how to select and tie on the proper lead weight or sinkers, depending upon the swiftness of the current when we were "mooching" or just running with the current and the tide, and what weight would be needed depending upon the speed at which we would be trolling. Don knew every trick in the book, and he knew how to tell when his bait had been nudged by a fish who was testing it; and he knew if the fish had taken the bait and just when and how to jerk on the pole to tighten the line and set the hook.

Don had brought along a big thermos of hot coffee and a mug for me (he drank out of the cup that screwed onto the top of the thermos to cap it). Even though my feet were tormenting me with the freezing cold of my saltwater soaked wool socks and Wellington boots, the hot black coffee was not enough to stop my continuous shivering and trembling. But I never dared to complain to Don about my physical agony. I did not want to compound the fact that I was a greenhorn landlubber and a novice who knew absolutely nothing about salmon fishing; but what would have been even worse would have been to have Don think that I was a complaining sissy. So I said nothing during that whole six hours between 6 AM and noon when we came back to shore for lunch and a short nap. Once back on shore I took off my boots and hung them upside down to dry out and I put on a clean dry pair of wool socks inside my Docksider boating shoes.

We had fished all morning, getting several strikes to let us know that there were salmon all around us, but we hadn't caught anything yet.

After about an hour's snooze Don was up and rarin' to go again. I put my partially dried out Wellies back on again and once more we shoved off, but this time the tide had come in and we didn't need to go so far out on the sand-flats before we could climb aboard and start the engine again. Later that afternoon Don caught a whopping 60-pound king salmon and I managed to land a 30 pounder. That fish was longer than our little 20-month-old son Danny was tall and it weighed more than he did at that time. I don't remember what else we caught, probably a couple of flounder and a red snapper or two and a couple of sea bass; but you really haven't experienced what it is to really fish until you land a king salmon or one of the larger saltwater game fish. Over the years since that first initiation I have had the thrill of catching other kinds of Pacific salmon and other fish (including sand sharks, rat fish, a large octopus and an assortment of bottom fish, and on one occasion caught we around 45 white fish within a single hour—almost as fast as we could bait the hooks and haul them in—but no fishing trip exceeds the thrill of landing that 30-pounder on my first fishing expedition with Don as my fishing guide, buddy and my friend!

At dusk we pulled the boat ashore, packed up our gear and began the long drive homeward. Don claims that I slept and snored all the way home, and perhaps I did since I was completely exhausted from the physical exertion and the adrenalin drain from all the excitement and thrill of that exhilarating adventure.

One of our other favorite salmon fishing locales was in the Pacific Ocean waters off the Quillauyte Indian Reservation at Lapush, Washington along the western seaward shores of the Olympic Peninsula. We would follow the same regime getting to our fishing site, usually arriving in the pitch black of night and digging out of the sack long before the break of dawn, fishing all day long except for a short break to catch a bite of food around noon. Sometimes Don would pack a dinner bucket and we'd eat sandwiches and an apple in the boat rather than to take the time to interrupt our fishing time, thereby shortening our chances of catching the big ones.

Lapush presented a different set of challenges. The site on the Indian Reservation where we pitched our tent was upriver by the reservation lodge and general store. We would launch the boat at a dock along the river near our campsite and float or motor down the river to where it opened into the great Pacific Ocean. Depending upon the time and flow of the tide, we would have to navigate the breaking waves that crashed ashore where the onrushing waters of the river collided with the incoming waves from the ocean. Don would try to time our crossing of the bar so that it would be at slack tide when the water was its quietest and least turbulent. Even then, if there were a stiff wind blowing in off the ocean, the waters would churn and it could be tricky business that required sound seamanship and the careful handling of the tiller to keep the boat from being swamped or overturned by the incoming waves. What always amazed us was the way the native Indians would fearlessly glide their long narrow canoes through the breakers with only a few inches of freeboard between them and the swirling waters of both the river and the sea. It was not uncommon for our boat to completely disappear in the troughs between the 10' to 20' swells and whitecaps that rolled in from the ocean. It was riding a never-ending roller-coaster and was certainly no place for anyone who is prone to seasickness. Fortunately, I never needed to take Dramamine or anything else to fight the green monster of seasickness. There was no "potty" aboard, so if we need to relieve ourselves we just hung over the side of the boat and fed the fish just like the Indians and other fishermen did. It was part of roughing it that goes with the sport when fishing from a small boat. Those fishing trips with my fishing buddy Don Reincke were some of my most memorable experiences, and I am especially grateful for Don's friendship and camaraderie.

After we purchased our little yacht the *Marilynne I* (a 21' Owens cruiser) and later the *Marilynne II* (a 26' Sabercraft cruiser), we did a lot of salmon fishing and cruised the American and the Canadian San Juan Islands from the southern tip of Puget Sound to the Canadian Straits of Georgia and Victoria Island. But that's a story for another chapter.

* * *

Don and Marquita Riencke's friendship meant a great deal to both Mary Elizabeth and to me for many reasons other than fishing. My tenure at the First Assemblies of God Church in Tacoma turned out to be a terrible disappointment to me as no doubt it was to Pastor Everett Ewing. I had met Rev. Ewing when he pastored the First Assemblies of God Church in Coffeyville, Kansas. He took me under his wing and became a mentor and esteemed friend, as did many of the other pastors in the Kansas District/Conference of the Assemblies of God. The new church that we built in Columbus, KS, though constructed on a smaller scale, was patterned after the design of Rev. Ewing's church in Coffeyville. He and the men of his congregation traveled to Columbus and assisted our congregation by giving generously of their volunteer labor in the building of our new edifice. Rev. Ewing served as our District Presbyter and his wife and the ladies of the District Women's Missionary Circles pooled their funds to purchase a wardrobe for Mary Elizabeth. They were good to us and gave a baby shower for Danny when he was born. It was a great compliment to me that when Rev. Ewing accepted the call to be the senior pastor of the Tacoma church, he selected me as the young minister of his personal choice to receive the call to be his Assistant Pastor. We were well received by the congregation which purchased new furnishings for our apartment in the Education Building. We were graciously entertained in their homes and my ministry was appreciated by many of the parishioners who treated us cordially.

Almost from the very beginning, however, it became apparent that there was a problem that none of us had anticipated and, perhaps had I been more mature and circumstances had been different, things might have worked out far better. Upon my very arrival I encountered what was the first "red flag" which indicated to me that I had not understood the nature of the position to which I had been called. After having served as the pastor of the church in Columbus, KS and having experienced a measure of success in the growth of that congregation and the building of the new church, I had become accustomed to preaching at both the morning and evening services on Sunday and again at a midweek Bible Study. I had been accepted as "Pastor Jones" and in my first pastorate not a single soul ever addressed me by my first name. But the very first time I walked into the church office in Tacoma the secretary whom I had never before met, Mrs. Mary Bermark, cheerily greeted me: "Hello, Cal! Welcome to Tacoma."

It hit me like a ton of bricks when I realized that to that congregation I would never be more than "Cal"—the office flunky and gofer for the senior pastor. I was never regarded as Rev. Jones or as Pastor Jones, but I was just "Cal," the church office clerk and errand boy! I was invited to preach only once—on my first Sunday evening in Tacoma, but never again during the six months that I served the Lord in that congregation was I ever again invited to "preach"—not even at either the Tuesday evening or the Thursday evening Bible Study meetings. Perhaps my first sermon was such a terrible fiasco that Rev. Ewing was directed by the Deacon Board to never set me loose in that august pulpit again. I was confined to preparing and running off on the office mimeograph machine the weekly Sunday bulletin, typing an occasional letter for the senior pastor, running errands, and serving as the night watchman to police the grounds and make sure that all the doors were locked after the last soul departed the premises, which was often well after midnight. I was to be up bright and early every morning to open up the building, man the office, visit Sunday School first-timers and chaperone the youth group. It was a thankless job and I felt betrayed for having been sucked into a situation that was a far cry from what I had expected an assistant pastor's role to be in a congregation of over 1,000 members.

One of the prominent members, the mother of the well-known Rev. Thomas Skinner, requested that I visit one of her neighbors; and on that occasion I met Rev. Skinner's father who, although he was antagonistic toward senior ministers, for some unexpected reason took a liking toward me. When Mrs. Skinner brought glowing reports to the women's circles that the new assistant pastor had been well received by her unconverted husband, apparently a spark of unwarranted jealousy was ignited in Rev. Ewing's mind and heart, just as jealousy had reared its ugly head in the heart of King Saul against the shepherd boy David. Then, an occasion arose when the senior minister was unavailable: I was called to the hospital to minister to a parishioner who had been entered into the hospital emergency ward, and it infuriated the senior pastor that I got to the hospital before he did. He commanded me to never again visit in any of the homes of *his* parishioners or to ever make another hospital call without first getting his "permission" regardless of any emergency or other mitigating circumstances. From then on, my relationship with the senior pastor deteriorated at an accelerating pace and finally culminated in my being summoned to his office the week before Christmas 1954 where he and three of his hand-chosen deacons informed me that my services as Assistant Pastor were no longer desired![2]

I was stranded 2,000 miles away from my home on the East Coast with a wife and an 11 month old baby and nowhere to go. What was I to do? I prayed and trusted God for his providential guidance and blessing, which He granted by opening for me a door of ministry as pastor of the First Assemblies of God Church in Buckley, Washington.

* * *

Don and Marquita had become aware of the totally unwarranted envious spirit of their senior pastor and his adversarial posture toward me. They were appalled, as were other members of the congregation, but the die had been cast and I was history. During this period of what was for me a dreadful dilemma, Don and Marquita and others offered their prayers and their support to me and to Mary Elizabeth, and their friendship toward us deepened and continued unwaveringly. Don was much more than just my best fishing buddy, he was a real friend and confidant.

When our daughter Deborah Marilynne was born, Don and Marquita adopted her into their hearts as well. Our friendship continued and grew over the years, so much so that after Don died, Marquita made a trip by herself to visit our daughter Debbie and her family in Cleveland, Georgia where Debbie's husband Jeff was pastoring a church, and we continued to correspond until Marquita went to be with the Lord a few years ago.

After serving for several years as the pastor of the Bainbridge Island Assemblies of God Church, Don eventually became the Chaplain at a large hospital in Seattle and continued in that much appreciated and fruitful ministry until his retirement. Don and Marquita adopted a beautiful little Quinault Indian girl who is now a grown woman with her own family. Often, whether at home or in a restaurant when I am enjoying a salmon dinner, I will think of those happy days fishing and commiserating with my friend and best fishing buddy, the Reverend Don Reincke.

NOTES:

[1] First Assemblies of God Church of Tacoma is now known as a Christian *Life Center*: to learn about the church's history visit its website at: **http://www.life-center.org/ AboutLC/LCHistory/tabid/93/Default.aspx**

[2] One of the things I learned in that parish was something about the political dynamics that prevail in every congregation and especially in large congregations with manifold constituencies. When these influential groups within a congregation become factious it can lead to chaos and sometimes results in church splits, the destruction of the congregation, and the forfeiture of its Christian witness in the community; but when they work together it is wonderful and rewarding and provides a powerful witness to the genuine love of Christ working within the lives of His people.

Nels Russell Wasell

CHAPTER 3

NELS RUSSELL WASELL

NELS RUSSELL WASELL offered to me his friendship both as a parishioner and as a hunting buddy. He gave me support as his pastor, and he showed me how to track and hunt big game.

*　　*　　*

On the first Christmas after we were married in 1951, among other things Mary Elizabeth gave to me was a Mossberg 16 gauge bolt action shotgun that held three shells in the clip and one in the barrel chamber. As a boy I had never done any hunting. Mary's father, who was a Cherokee Indian entitled to a head-right in the Oklahoma Cherokee Nation and whose ancestors had survived that ignominious "Trail of Tears," was, like his Indian brothers, a hunter and crack-shot. He could bring down a rabbit on the run with a single-shot 22 rifle and preferred the rifle over a shotgun. After Mary Elizabeth gave me the shotgun, I hunted with her father and later with other friends and eventually got good enough at it that even with a bolt action I could get several shots off at a running varmint or a bird on the wing. But it wasn't until we moved to the great Pacific Northwest that I had an opportunity to hunt big game. It was Russ Wasell who became my hunting guide and mentor introducing me to hunting in the big timber of Douglas fir forests in the Cascade Mountains of Washington State.

*　　*　　*

When I was asked by the pastor and deacons of the church in Tacoma to seek another appointment, I spent many hours on my knees begging God to provide for me an open door of ministry somewhere in His harvest field. I had no idea where else to turn than to the Lord, and I had no inkling whatsoever as to how or where God would lead me. Then unexpectedly I receive a phone call from the Tacoma District Presbyter who had taken a liking toward me and Mary and Danny. He asked me if I could fill the vacant pulpit of the **First Assembly of God Church in Buckley, Washington.** He explained that the Buckley congregation was "trying out" candidates in the process of seeking a new pastor for their church. The previous pastor, a Reverend Wesley Banta, had enjoyed a good ministry and several miracles of divine healing had been reported under his preaching and intercessory prayers; but unfortunately he had become embroiled in sexual misconduct and became a disgrace and a reproach to the church. The parishioners were being extra careful in their search for someone who could help hold their congregation together and live down the reproach that had been brought upon it. They had already had five ministers preach as pastoral candidates, including a former district presbyter and a former veteran missionary, but though the candidates were all good and well qualified men, the board of deacons just didn't feel that they had yet found the right person. I was merely to substitute in their pulpit that next Sunday morning and give them an opportunity to line up additional pastoral candidates. Because I was so young, they had not thought of considering me as a possible candidate. I accepted the substitute preaching assignment, but I still had no idea where I would end up.

I do not remember what I preached about, but I have an idea that it might have been along the lines of my first sermon back in Columbus, Kansas—*"faith is the substance of things hoped for and the evidence of things not seen!"* I wasn't even hoping that I might be considered as a candidate, but to my amazement and happy surprise, following that Sunday morning service the Deacon Board had met together in a special consultation and they were unanimous in their decision to extend a call to me to be their new pastor! I was surprised, and as much as I wanted a place to preach and a parsonage roof over my head, I was sincere when my response to them was that "I would pray about it and seek the Lord's will regarding their call." I think that my response to their invitation surprised them as much as it shocked me! That evening I preached again, Mary and I sang a couple of duets accompanied by Mary playing her accordion, and I played an instrumental offertory, led the congregation in a "testimony time," preached an evangelistic sermon, gave an altar call invitation and led the congregation in a period of intercessory prayers at the communion rail/altar which curved around the chancel platform.

The church had originally been a Methodist house of worship constructed after the widely used Akron Plan which placed the congregation in a semi-circle closer to the chancel than permitted by a design with a long narrow nave. At the back of the nave was a set of large folding doors that opened to a large multi-purpose parish hall that could be used for overflow seating. When the doors were closed it could be used as a fellowship hall or as room for multiple Sunday School classrooms. There were also Sunday School classrooms, a restroom, and a large coal-fed furnace in the basement.

On February 22nd, George Washington's birthday, the deacons convened a special meeting of the congregation and announced their unanimous recommendation of Calvin David Jones for election as their new minister. To the happy relief of both the congregation and their candidate, I received an overwhelming majority affirmation with only four members abstaining or voting negatively, probably because they may have considered me too young to step into the serious situation with which they had been confronted due to my predecessor's unprofessional behavior.

We moved into the little five-room parsonage on Cedar Street and began what turned out to be a two-year tenure that was one of the happiest and most productive pastorates it was my privilege to serve. The congregation began to grow and we were soon surrounded by an enthusiastic group of young people, including some who came from other churches in town where they continued their membership even though they became active participants in our Christ's Ambassadors youth group.

The teenagers all fell in love with little Danny and vied to be his baby sitter. Before long we had thirty-plus voices in our robed youth choir, and an hour-long Sunday afternoon live radio program aired from the nearby radio station in the Puyallup Valley town of Sumner, Washington. The group entered two floats in the annual 4th of July parade, one advertising the summer Vacation Bible School and another float promoting the congregation and its youth program. It was my privilege to baptize by immersion, in the melted snow waters off Mt. Rainier that flowed down into Lake Tapps, several of the youth who dedicated their lives to Jesus Christ as their Savior.

*   *   *

Russell Wasell and his pretty wife Jolene served as youth counselors. Jolene, who was the mother of two active little boys, also served as a Sunday School and VBS teacher. The Wasells lived in a company-owned house available to Weyerhaeuser supervisors and employees at the company's Enumclaw lumber mill located west of Enumclaw, Washington, where Russell worked as a mill foreman. Russ was a tall lanky handsome fellow who knew his way around the big timber forests surrounding the mill. Weyerhaeuser Timber Company owns thousands of acres of tall Douglas fir trees in the Cascade Mountains and in the foothills around the monumental and perpetually snow-clad Mount Rainier.

These woods are full of white-tail deer and elk and an occasional moose, bear, cougar and other big and small game, (and some also say Sasquatches).[1]

I have vivid memories of my first deer-hunting venture into the forest of giant Douglas fir and the dense underbrush beneath those huge trees. Russ led me along a trail that ran north into the hills behind the Weyerhaeuser Mill. After about a half-mile or more Russ pointed to a ridge and instructed me to climb the ridge and continue along its crest and he would hunt the draw on the east side of the ridge in the hope that he might be able to flush a deer out of the bottom of the draw and force it to climb the ridge where I could intercept it and get a clear shot. As I mounted the ridge and started moving along its spine, I heard stomping and loud snorting back in the brush to my left. The hair literally stood up on the back of my neck and I burst out into a heavy sweat, not so much from the exercise of the climb, but from being surprised by the noise of deer stomping in the brush. Apparently I had startled a couple of bucks who could see me, even though I didn't have the slightest notion where they were located. Then as I looked around me, all of the woods seemed to me to look the same. Although I was carrying a compass, matches and a candle with which to start a campfire, a canteen full of fresh water, a hunting knife strapped to my belt, and a holster slung on my hip in which I was carrying a 22 caliber pistol with nine bullets in the revolver, I felt lost and frightened not knowing how to find my way back to the mill. My heart was pounding in my chest so hard that I could feel it beating clear through my Woolrich hunting jacket. I knew that I needed to get a grip on myself and a handle on my sense of panic. I sat down on a large stump and looked all around me. I heard the deer that were hiding in the brush stomp off and suddenly everything became quiet as a morgue. I WAS LOST! It is a terribly frightening feeling to be lost in the deep woods knowing that there are wild animals all around. I felt like the proverbial sitting duck with a big target bull's-eye painted on my back. I called out several times for Russ but he could not hear me since my voice was carried away by the wind and it did not reach him in the draw down below. Out of desperation I fired three .30-06 bullets into the air in the hope that he would hear the shots. Shortly after I fired Russ came panting up the side of the ridge and when he saw me the first thing he asked me was, "Where's your deer?" When with a red face and painful embarrassment, I explained to him that I thought I was lost, and that I had heard the deer stomping and snorting in the brush close by, Russ laughed 'till tears came to his eyes, and he never let me live down that first hunting fiasco.

With Russ's patient encouragement, little by little I began to catch on and followed his good example as he taught me how to read the wildlife signs, to distinguish the white tailed deer from the larger elk tracks, and to differentiate between bear signs and the tracks of wolves, cougars and other critters in the woods. Eventually I felt comfortable enough and at home in the timber stands around the mill to venture into the woods by myself, and often jumped deer and other creatures. Once I stumbled upon a little pond deep in the woods and was surprised to see a magnificently adorned male Wood Duck swimming silently about. I saw a lot of elk tracks and droppings and wondered how those large animals with their huge racks of antlers could manage to wend their way through the thick brush, and I wondered what I would do if an elk or wapiti stag in rut were to charge out of the brush at me.

On one of our hunts it was Russell who became lost in the thick underbrush not very far from his house. The area was thick with deer signs but the brush was so thick that Russ became turned around and could not find his way out of the maze. He hollered for me: "Pastor, I'm lost in here; if you can hear me, shout at me so I can find my way out and come to you." We shouted back and forth to each other until Russell finally worked his way out of the dense thicket, and we continued our hunt. Russ shot a deer and knowing that his bullet had found its mark, he began to track its trail of blood through the woods. When he saw the deer standing back in the woods, he fired another shot and dropped his deer where it had stood. As he moved toward the fallen buck he came across another dying deer and realized that this was the first buck he had shot and that the last deer was his second bag of the day—not quite two birds with one stone but two deer on a single tracking.[2]

*   *   *

The tower over the main entrance of the Buckley AG Church either had its spire blown off or it had never had one. When, at my urging, the Board of Trustees agreed to permit me to build a spire to cap the church's tower, Russ Wasell was one of the younger men who climbed up on the roof and helped me nail down the cupola and its spire. We had given the cupola and spire several coats of paint before we hauled it up with heavy ropes and a lot of muscle and grunting. The older men may have had their misgivings about either the necessity or the wisdom of my architectural ambition to place a spire on the church, but good-naturedly they suppressed their reservations, and with a strong group effort, we finally managed to get the spire structure firmly anchored atop the tower roof. It was no small accomplishment for this young novice church builder and his volunteer crew; and to our relief the spire managed to withstand the strong winds that blew in from the Pacific and down from the higher mountain ranges to the east. It was as much a psychological victory as it was an achievement in volunteer church construction. Without Russ's invaluable construction knowledge and his brawn, the project would never have gotten "off the ground."

*   *   *

It was while we were still living in Buckley that our daughter, Deborah Marilynne, was born in the nearby Enumclaw Hospital. There were a number of young couples in the Buckley church, like the Wasells, who also had young children, and the congregation was happy to have a baby girl join their minister's family. However, two weeks after Debbie's birth we packed and moved to Seattle, WA where Debbie grew up and attended elementary and junior high school; but that's part of the story for the next chapter.[3]

*   *   *

Although Russ was kept busy with his work at the Weyerhaeuser timber mill, he made time to serve on our Board of Trustees and to offer his physical muscle when we needed him. Sometimes, especially in the winter when the roads were treacherous even with chains on the tires, it was easier for the Wasells to stay home on a Sunday morning, but the encouragement and friendship of Russ was an invaluable morale support and a great help to this young pastor and to the small congregation.

There were several other men who also were among "David's mighty men" in that small logging community tucked into the foothills of the high Cascade Mountains. Mr. Glenn Grant was a widower who lived in a small cottage at the end of the black topped road that wound its way from Buckley to the old coal mining town of Carbonado, Washington. Mr. Grant was one of the Deacon/Trustees who faithfully made the drive down the dirt road from Carbonado and on into Buckley to regularly attend our worship services. His close friend, Fred MacDonald, who ran a giant logging crane for the St. Regis Lumber Company, was another of the faithful Deacon/Trustees who unstintingly gave of his time and energy and tithes in support of the church. In each of the churches that I pastored, there were also, as in the Buckley congregation, faithful women like Abigail who joined with David's faithful warriors to support their king. These women were also "soldiers of the Cross," who were loyal to their pastor and more particularly loyal and faithful in their obedience and service to Christ our King. Among such women there were in the Buckley Congregation Mrs. Violet MacDonald, Mrs. Stella Olsen, Mrs. Helen Brown, Mrs. Criswell, Mrs. Rhode, Ms. Etta Baker, Mrs. Evans and several others. To all of these wonderful people I am everlasting grateful.

NOTES:

[1]   Sasquatch, also known as Bigfoot, is an alleged ape-like creature purportedly inhabiting forests, mainly in the Pacific Northwest region of North America. Bigfoot is usually described as a large, hairy, bipedal humanoid. Many believers in its existence contend

that the same or similar creatures are found around the world under different regional names, most prominently the Yeti of the Himalayas. There have been numerous sightings and a growing body of evidence of their existence—*Vide:* **Bigfoot - Wikipedia**, *the free encyclopedia*; Cf., for a fascinating read see Frank Peretti's book **Monster**. Nashville, WestBow Press, 2005.

2   When our son Danny was almost five years old, I bought a little Daisy BB gun for him and took him hunting with me. I showed him how to recognize deer tracks and droppings and rubbing signs and occasionally we would actually flush a deer out of its hiding place. Later when Dan was in college and after he was married we enjoyed bow hunting and rifle hunting, yachting, golfing, and just being in the great outdoors together. It's not what we're doing but it's the companionship that really counts.

3   Although very little is said in this book about Debbie, she was a darling little girl whom we referred to as our *Pixie* because she was always bursting with energy and innocent mischievousness. She too, like her brother, was a delight and a joy in our lives. Today she is happily married to a minister, the Rev. Jeffrey W. Howard, who is the pastor of a United Methodist Church in LaGrange, GA. Their son Joshua is studying at Oxford University, England and their daughter Hannah is a high school junior who is looking forward to a career in journalism.

George Alvin Jendresen

CHAPTER 4

GEORGE ALVIN JENDRESEN

GEORGE JENDRESEN was a true cowboy who was reared on a succession of small ranches owned by his parents near Whitehall, Montana. Of all the men I have ever met, he is the best friend I ever had. He was also a dedicated Christian layman and the President of the Administrative Council of the **Brighton/Trinity Assemblies of God Church, Seattle, Washington**.

Maybe it's unfair to all of the other fine and noble men whom it has been my privilege to know over the past seven decades for me to single George out from among the other men who have been to me as David's mighty men were to their young shepherd king. Yet even King David ranked one man above all of the others among the *37 mighty men of valor* who formed his elite personal guard and Delta fighting force of special ops warriors. These men were fierce and fearless heroes whose exploits were incredible and their loyalty to David was total and unwavering even unto the very death. Seldom in human history has a monarch had such a valiant group of men who gladly would lay down their lives for their king. They were called *David's Mighty Men*—they were the most heroic and loyal men in David's army:

> "**The first** was Josheb-basshebeth from Tah-chemon, known also as Adino, the Eznite. He once killed eight hundred men in one battle. The next in rank was . . . "—2 Samuel 23:8, 9 ff. LBP

Although David's elite guard were ranked in military order of command according to their deeds of valor on the battlefield and also on the basis of their wisdom and strength of character, it would be very difficult for me to attempt to rank in any order of superiority the men who are listed in this book since of all of these men were *straight-arrows* of exemplary Christian character and integrity with whom I count it my privilege to have shared strong bonds of camaraderie. Yet it is George Jendresen who stands out in my mind and heart as the man whom I trusted the most and toward whom I held the strongest bond of friendship in our common commitment to Jesus Christ our Lord.

George had consecrated his life to Christ when as a teenager, through the providence of God, he met the young Assemblies of God pastor, Rev. Gene E. Peretti and Gene's charming Canadian wife, Joyce Snider Peretti. When the Perettis returned from Whitehall to the Seattle area, George followed them and found work first as a warehouseman at Ernst Hardware Company and then as a mechanic at the Boeing Company. Gene and Joyce resumed worshipping in their home congregation, the Brighton Gospel Tabernacle, an Assemblies of God Church, located in the Brighton neighborhood of Southeast Seattle. Gene's older brother Jack, Jr. had married a girl from California, Eva, and it was Eva's sister Ruth who caught George's eye and captured his heart. George, whose ancestors were Danish, could refer to the Perettis as *slakting* or "shirt-tail" relatives as Scandinavians would call them. The Peretti family, following the pattern of their Italian heritage, is a large and close-knit clan which formed a significant part of the core group in the Brighton AG Church and which fostered in that congregation a high level of commitment, talent, and leadership that was vital to the success and growth of their church.

*　　*　　*

My first Sunday as pastor of the Brighton congregation was the Sunday after Easter which is traditionally called "Low Sunday" but on that day, to my great surprise, the Sunday School attendance reached an all-time high of 323 surpassing the Easter Sunday attendance of 320! As I walked through the church that Sunday morning I observed to my astonishment that the church building looked like the nursery rhyme place of "The Old Woman Who Lived In a Shoe—she had so many children she didn't know what to do!" The building was veritably bursting at the seams with children crammed into every nook and cranny. Every Sunday School room in the basement was filled to capacity. There were Sunday school classes in what had been the temporary living quarters of the former pastor's basement apartment, in the living room, the kitchen, the laundry room, and even in the furnace room where an elementary boy's class met with Harvey Sanderson as their teacher. There were adult classes and teenage classes in un-partitioned areas of the main floor nave and in the "prayer room" behind the chancel. What was even more amazing to me was that the overflow crowd had required that the two large Sunday School busses had to be commandeered as make-shift classrooms as well. Under the leadership of my predecessor, the Rev. Dr. David Aasen, and the aggressive canvassing of the Holly Park public housing development and the surrounding neighborhoods, the Sunday School staff had managed to attract a growing overflow crowd of subdivision children whose parents were glad to have the church take their kids off their hands for an hour on Sunday morning so the parents could sleep in or have a few minutes of peace and quiet while our Sunday School teachers were babysitting and entertaining these rambunctious children with Bible stories, action choruses and simple handcraft projects.

What was an equal surprise to me was that immediately after Sunday School was over the hoard of happy and energy-charged children and their chaperone teachers were loaded back into the two Sunday School busses for the trip back to their homes throughout the Holly Park housing development. Only a relatively small handful of adults and only a few children were in attendance at the Sunday Morning Worship service: around 30 persons counting the preacher's family, or less than 10% of the Sunday School attendees!

Several things became immediately apparent to me on that "Low Sunday" morning: (1) because of the lack of sufficient space and the absence of adequate off-street parking space, the congregation would be unable to sustain the sudden and marked growth it had experienced through the outstanding visitation efforts Dr. Aasen had promoted; (2) even if there had been adequate space within the building and if there had been adequate parking available, it was unlikely that the small contingent of dedicated adults could absorb and deal with any additional growth. In time, without the influx of a significant number of adult members, the present small staff would simply suffer burn-out and its effectiveness and limited resources would inevitably dissipate. Moreover, (3) the financial requirements and labor-demanding burden of maintaining the two Sunday School busses would continue to pose a drain on the limited financial resources of the small adult membership. The added burden of increasing operating costs for additional printed Sunday School materials and VBS materials would further compound that financial burden.

*   *   *

George Jendresen had acquired a respectable knowledge of auto mechanics in high school and through the work required on the family's ranch. It was George who, with the help of a couple of other volunteers, had managed to maintain the two busses in operating condition. George, Burton Gibson, Tom Prichet, and a couple of other volunteers also served as bus drivers and chaperones, and in that capacity were removed from participating in any significant portion of the Sunday morning worship services, thus cutting down the size of the Sunday morning congregation. Even at their best, especially during the cold winter months, the Sunday School busses could not provide a satisfactory substitute for the much needed additional Sunday School and office space necessary for a growing congregation.

It was unmistakably obvious that if the Brighton congregation were going to maintain and advance the growth of its membership, its Sunday School, its Christian outreach into the surrounding community and fulfill its missions responsibility abroad, the existing building would have to be significantly remodeled and enlarged and more adequate off-street parking would have to be provided.

It was with that urgent need confronting us that I began almost immediately to make inquiries regarding the particular building codes and requirements imposed by the city of Seattle requisite to enlarging the present church facility. The corner lot upon which the original building was constructed included a fairly large vacant area immediately to the east side of the structure. However, an investigation of the off-street parking and other building code requirements revealed that the City of Seattle had adopted the U.S. Uniform Building Code and would demand off-street parking for approximately one car for every five fixed seats in the nave. That meant that if a new sanctuary nave and balcony would seat 500 people, the church would be required to provide off-street parking for 100 cars. The new building code was scheduled to become effective and binding on July 1st of that year! The paramount problem was that there simply were neither lots nor space available anywhere in the immediate neighborhood to meet the new off-street parking requirements. If the congregation were going to do anything at all, it would need to develop building plans and blueprints immediately and to file a building permit application with the city of Seattle and King County on or before July 1st!

The young families of the congregation were all so busy working and raising their families and caught up in the demanding task of surviving in the ever-increasing pace of daily life that, amidst the thrill of growing a large and promising program of Sunday School evangelism, no one had stopped to consider where the church was going in the immediate or distant future.

Even though I had arrived on the scene only a few short weeks earlier, I called a special meeting of the Board of Trustees and laid before them the challenge with which their congregation was confronted. I urged them to authorize the immediate retention of a church architect who could be commissioned to make it a time-sensitive number-one priority to develop preliminary design drawings which had to be completed within a time crunch of about six weeks for presentation to the City of Seattle for a building permit! That in itself seemed almost impossible to accomplish in such a short time frame.

Not fully realizing what that might mean to the future of the Brighton congregation, but faced with the stark reality that if the church ever wanted to grow on that site and in that neighborhood, it had little if any alternative other than to begin a concerted search for an alternate building site. The six-man Board of Trustees reluctantly agreed to search for an architect, contingent upon the cost of obtaining preliminary blueprints and the availability of the necessary funds to pay for the drawings. Realizing the urgency and the dilemma with which the congregation was faced, I volunteered to personally cover any shortfall of funds necessary to cover an architect's initial fees—I felt that if I could borrow the money to buy a car I could certainly borrow the money to help the church insure the possibility of its future growth and expansion.

A very fine architect was retained. He had also designed the edifice of the Calvary Assemblies of God Church which was the parent church that, under the leadership of its Pastor, Rev. Henry Ness, had purchased, owned and constructed the building in which the Brighton Congregation met. Unbeknown to the Brighton congregation, Calvary Temple had used the Brighton Church property as collateral against is mortgage on their large and handsome new edifice along the Seattle freeway in the northern part of the city. It was Ness's plan to establish Brighton and a number of other satellite Sunday Schools around the city with the expectation that the adult members would continue to consider Calvary Temple as their "church home" and would attend and support the "mother church" with their tithes and offerings. As the city grew and travel time and expense increased over the years, these satellite Sunday Schools grew into congregations with their own membership rosters and a demand that they be recognized as full-fledged and separately incorporated congregational bodies in their own right. It was something of a reality check and a shock when the Brighton congregation suddenly was reminded that they did not actually own the building for which they had paid and in which they had worshipped for the previous eighteen years. The Brighton congregation petitioned the parent church for the privilege of purchasing the building which many of the members had mistakenly believed that they already owned. With some measure of reluctance, the Calvary Temple congregation conceded, and an arrangement was made whereby the Brighton Church would be granted a mortgage that would require regular monthly payments until the mortgage was satisfied.

Nobody had the slightest idea where the money would come from! They could hardly pay their pastor's stipend and the utility bills and operating expenses, let alone absorb the costs of mortgage payments and then on top of that find the wherewithal to construct a new church building even if their architect were able to meet the deadlines in time for the congregation to obtain the necessary building permits. When an examination of the financial records revealed that the stipend of the pastor and his family averaged less than $30 a week, some of the younger members of the Trustee Board who were making two and three times that amount at their manual jobs at Boeing or elsewhere around the city supported a motion that the pastor's weekly salary be set at a minimum of $35 a week. For the small congregation that was a reach of faith, though based upon the aggregate incomes of the members it was well within the capability of the combined membership. The undertaking of a major building program, however, was truly a tremendous venture of sheer faith, even if that faith were only as tiny as the proverbial mustard seed.

When the Chairman of the Board was relocated by the Boeing Company to Florida, the mantel of the church's Presidency was passed to George Jendresen, who was a superb choice for that position.

*   *   *

Among the members of our Brighton Church congregation was a Norwegian master boatwright, Mr. Emerald Baunsgard, who owned and operated the *Shabaun* yacht works which abutted his home in West Seattle. Em Baunsgard and his wife showed to their Pastor and his family a kindness and a friendship that were greatly appreciated by us. When Em completed building and outfitting in his boatyard shop a truly beautiful 56' *Shabaun* yacht, I had the privilege of being in attendance when that vessel was first launched and christened at a marina on Union Bay. When the craft was lifted from a large flatbed trailer and lowered by a crane into the water, Em's trained eye saw immediately that the boat rode about three inches to four inches low in the stern because of the extra equipment that his cousin, who was his partner, had insisted upon cramming below the aft deck. Below the aft fishing cockpit were large twin diesel engines, a good-sized electrical generator, the water tank, and refrigerated ice chests to hold a large catch of fish and other seafood. The original design had allowed for the heavy diesel engines and water tank, but did not take into account the weight of the other heavy equipment that was added by the owner's change orders as work on the vessel progressed. Em Baunsgard was such an exacting and precise craftsman that he had the boat hauled out of the water and trailered back to his boatyard where he proceeded to strip off the stern transom and added an additional 4' to the length of the yacht. It was a major structural refitting of the yacht but Em's pride of craftsmanship required (for his own personal integrity and his commitment to the high quality and performance standards to which he held himself, and at his own expense and hard work) that he make the necessary changes to the hull and decks. These changes were sufficient to give the yacht the necessary draft, beam and length to carry not only the additional marine equipment but also to support on an even keel the body weight of the crew and guests who would gather in the stern to enjoy a cruise and to fish along the way. When the boat was once again lowered into the water, the craft rode on a perfectly balanced hull that when running at cruising speed enabled that beautifully designed yacht to glide over the water in the fashion of the best custom built yachts anywhere in the world.

Em phoned me and said, "Pastor, we are going to take the newest *Shabaun* yacht for a shake-down cruise north through the San Juan Islands of Puget Sound and up into the Canadian waters of the Inland Passage through the Straits of Georgia. Would you and Mrs. Jones and Danny and Debbie like to come along with us?" I had some vacation time coming, and was able to turn the Sunday morning pulpit over one of our Assistant Pastors, so we packed our bags and climbed aboard for what was one of the most delightful experiences it was ever our privilege to enjoy.

The yacht could sleep ten in forward, aft and mid-ship cabins. Em had thoughtfully brought along some fishing gear so we and our children could fish when we were at anchor. The captain found anchorages where we were able to gather oysters, clams and crabs and where the bottom fishing would give us red snapper, flounder, sea bass, an occasional sand shark and an assortment of other aquatic creatures. When we were able to find a sandy beach we could go swimming, but the sea water in that northern region was cold even during the hottest days of summer, so we didn't stay in the water very long. Em and his cousin who was along for this maiden voyage were both gracious hosts and on occasions when we were cruising in open water where there were not a lot other boats around, they allowed me to take the helm. They patiently mentored me and taught me how to handle the wheel and that just the slightest turn of the helm was sufficient to keep us on a straight course. At first I had jerked the helm to starboard and then to portside, back and forth—back and forth, causing the stern to "fish-tail" and roll from side to side; but eventually I got the knack of steering; and with their tutelage I learned how to read the binnacle compass and to navigate following the nautical charts. I was thoroughly hooked on yachting! With a name like *Davy Jones* it was natural for me to feel at home on the water, and I silently hoped that someday we might have our own little yacht which could become a getaway for our family and a haven away from the telephone and the responsibilities of a busy and growing parish!

* * *

After we returned to Seattle following that cruise, I began to make the rounds of the marinas in the area in search of a small yacht that we might be able to afford. Finally, at the Seacrest Marina (where scenes from the movie "Sleepless in Seattle" were later filmed) just south of Alki Beach at the north end of the West Seattle Peninsula, I found a little 21' Owens cruiser sitting all covered with dust and cobwebs tucked in among the other boats in a large storage barn. It was the smallest cruiser in the marina's inventory and it had been sitting in dry-dock for quite a while. When I inquired about its price, I discovered that it was available for only $2,800 but for me at that time, half a century ago, it was a small fortune. When I received my tax refund from IRS that year it was around $285, just enough for me to make a 10% down-payment on our little dream boat.

After I had completed my pastoral duties and my college studies, in my "free time" I worked at the marina for a couple or hours each day for several weeks, scrubbing, sanding and varnishing the hull, and cleaning the "covered wagon" style canvas that enclosed the cockpit area. The marina's mechanics serviced the engine and we were ready for the beginning of our maritime adventures.

I made inquiry regarding the possibility of our gaining a membership in the Rainier Beach Yacht Club, which was originally sponsored by the Seattle Yacht Club with which it shared reciprocity. To our happy surprise, we were welcomed with open arms by the yachting fraternity members who "adopted" our family and treated us royally. I was named the Club's official *Chaplain* and given the traditional Chaplain's ensign to fly from our masthead. As far as I was able to ascertain, I was the only ordained Chaplain on Puget Sound other than the U.S. Navy Chaplains stationed at the Navy's Pier 90/91 on the Seattle waterfront. We knew one of the Navy Chaplains, Lieutenant Ronald DeBock, a fellow alumnus from Northwest University who gave me a copy of the Navy Chaplain's Prayer Book, *Prayers at Sea*, which I still have and cherish, and which I later used while conducting a memorial service for Captain Hayes, USN Retired in the U.S. Naval Academy Chapel in Annapolis, MD, and for his interment in Arlington National Cemetery in Virginia.

It became my duty to offer the table grace at our yacht club dinners and upon other special occasions; and I was introduced to the sport of Predicted Log yacht racing and served as an official observer aboard several large and handsome yachts during a number of competitive race events on Puget Sound. Although our family was the youngest in the yacht club and we had the smallest little cruiser, the members voted us the "Yachting Family of the Year," and they served as knowledgeable and trusted mentors who tutored us in the ways of the sea.

* * *

George and Ruth Jendresen and their daughter Carol and their son Johnny (who is now an Assemblies of God pastor in Oregon) were often guests in our home and aboard our yachts. Mary Elizabeth was my "First Mate" and George became my boatswain, chief engineer and mechanic. On several occasions I had problems with the battery. On numerous occasions I had run the battery down trying to get a damp engine started. George saw my dilemma, took pity on me and offered to install twin batteries in the *Marilynn's* engine compartment. He also taught me how to remove the carburetor filter and give a shot of quick-start ether vapor directly into the carburetor for an easy start to an engine that has a buildup of the condensation which sometimes forms due to the changing heat and cold and fog, especially around waterfront areas. George is a first-class mechanic and easily designed and installed a neat twin battery hookup whereby I could switch on either of the single batteries or both of them at the same time to provide a hot charge that would kick over the engine and give a quick re-charge to the batteries. Once under way, I could switch off one or the other of the batteries and alternate between them to keep them both fully charged. It was not long after the installation of the dual batteries that I came to fully appreciate George's mechanical skill and his innovative twin battery installation.

*   *   *

Shortly after George had installed the dual batteries, I decided to take our family on our first week-long extended cruise to Canada. I purchased the required Canadian Maple Leaf courtesy flag to fly from our boat's mast upon entering Canadian waters; we stocked the galley, took along our Sunday-go-to-meeting dress clothes, our swimming suits, fishing gear, etc. and set out northward through Puget Sound. We followed the same route we had taken on our maiden voyage with the Baunsgards aboard the *Shabaun* yacht, traveling through the Inland Passage to the leeward side of Camano Island and passing north of Shaw Island through Mosquito Pass to Roach Harbor and then back south darting across the Strait of Georgia to Victoria Harbor at the south end of Victoria Island. Dan and Mary Elizabeth spelled me off at the helm while I read the navigational charts and with the binoculars followed the lighthouse beacons and buoy markers to our destination. It was a two-day cruise each way in our little cruiser, and the first night we tied up to the dock at a marina resort near Rosario. When we motored over the international waterway into Victoria Harbor the next day we tied up at the civic dock across from the Queen Victoria Hotel. I donned my Captain's hat and walked up the waterfront sidewalk to the Canadian Customs House to report in. A handsome young Canadian customs officer escorted me back to the dock and asked me where our "yacht" was moored. He was used to boarding 100' plus seagoing pleasure yachts, and when I pointed to our little 21' Owens a surprised look came over his face and he exclaimed: "You mean to tell me that you came all the way from Seattle in *that* little thing?" He shook his head in disbelief but allowed us to come ashore in Canada anyway!

We passed a couple of happy days exploring and shopping in Victoria, but on our return voyage from Vancouver Island back to Seattle we discovered a serious problem with the generator bushings and an oil leak developed around the engine shaft. By God's mercy we managed to make it southward as far as Edmonds, Washington where we crawled into the Edmonds harbor and maneuvered the *Marilynne I* into a vacant space at the city dock. From the Edmonds Marina's chandlery I telephoned Emerald Baunsgard and explained to him our dilemma. "Don't worry, Pastor," Em assured me, "just sit tight right where you are and we'll come and get you with the *Shabaun.*" Fortunately for us, Em still had possession of the yacht upon which he was finishing up some final refinements for the new owner.

After awhile the *Shabaun* appeared on the horizon and eventually the Baunsgards turned the bow of their yacht into the Edmond's Harbor and had no trouble finding us tied up at the end of one of the inside docks along the breakwater channel. They threw a tow rope to us that I tied onto the main central bow cleat atop our boat's forward deck and they fastened their end of the line to the stern of their vessel. After we cleared the harbor we transferred our family to their yacht for the cruise back to Seattle. As soon as we were past the 6 mph no-wake zone around the harbor area, Em shoved the *Shabaun's* twin throttles forward and the big diesel engines churned up the waves as we accelerated speed. At first I was afraid that the force generated by those big engines would pull the bow cleat right off the deck of the little *Marilynne,* but it held fast and our little cruiser rose out of the waves and planed along behind as we motored the twenty nautical miles south through Elliot Bay to Seacrest Marine.

When George Jendresen learned about our mechanical problems with the old generator, he volunteered to replace it with a new alternator. I rented a boat trailer, loaded on the *Marilynne* and hauled it out to the Jendresen's ranch southeast of Seattle. Having been raised on a ranch in big-sky country, George wanted to get out of the city so he and his wife Ruth bought a small acreage out in the rural area of Maple Valley and named it the *Lazy J 4* Ranch. George acquired a non-descript rogue horse that he named Babe, planted a sizeable garden, bought a small second-hand Caterpillar tractor which he used to clear his land, and had a decent shop in one of the out-buildings on their small ranch. Using his mechanical skills and creative ingeniousness he somehow found the time to do a credible job of fitting and installing the alternator and taking care of a few other minor mechanical repairs that, if I had taken the boat to a marina, would have cost me a sizeable chunk of money. For George it was just another challenge that to him was a break from the aerospace world where he and Ruth worked at Boeing. To me he was a God-send.

Later, in the summer of 1964 when we traded the *Marilynne I* in for a 26' Sabercraft cruiser, we purchased a new unsinkable Nelson fiberglass 8' sailing dinghy which we mounted upon brackets affixed to the stern transom.[1] We christened the larger yacht the *Marilynne II* and enjoyed that cruiser and its sailing dinghy immensely, and George learned how to sail the dinghy.

Over the months and years that passed, Mary Elizabeth, Dan, Debbie and I had the privilege of being guests at the Jendresens' dinner table on many weekends and holidays. Our families went camping together at Corral Pass in the high Cascade Mountains, in the wind-blown Sun Lakes campsites of Eastern Washington, at the Pacific Ocean beaches around Gray's Harbor and around Puget Sound. One of our favorite camping sites was Birch Bay State Park south of Olympia at the southern end of Puget Sound. The Jendresens owned a mid-size camping trailer which they would pull to the campsite and locate it close to a boat launch area. Our family would cruise down Puget Sound and drop anchor or tie up at a mooring dock in the park. That way we had the best of both worlds—on land and on the water. We would take our two families aboard the *Marilynne I* and later aboard the *Marilynne II*, and we would explore the shore lines, fish, go clamming, and hunt oysters. We could heat coffee and soup and fix sandwiches in the little galley aboard the *Marilynne I* when we were out on the water. Then we would cruise back to the campsite where it was easier to clean our catch of fish and clams. It was also easier to prepare meals on shore where we could use both a portable barbecue as well as portable camp stoves and the kitchenette in the Jendresens' trailer. The kids would trade off their sleeping arrangements: Debbie would invite Carol Jendresen to bring her sleeping bag and sleep aboard our boat, and Dan would bunk with Johnny Jendresen in their trailer one night and the next night they would reverse their sleeping locations.

One of our favorite anchorages for a Sunday afternoon cruise from the dock of our Lake Washington waterfront home was the short cruise to Seward Park. It was a good place for the kids to swim and a great place for George to sail our dinghy.

* * *

Each of our families had its own tent and camping gear. However, whether we were camping in the mountains or at the ocean shores, it was always more fun when we camped together; and the young families of our church did a lot of weekend and holiday camping throughout the year. It was truly a great time for all of the young families of our congregation, and we used our group campouts as occasions to bring new families into the fellowship of our congregation—it proved to be a great means of doing what we called "fellowship evangelism." You can learn a lot about people when you spend time camping and fraternizing together. After sunset in the evening we would tuck the kids into their sleeping bags and then we adults would sit around the campfire and sing hymns, gospel choruses, and fun songs, after which we would share our personal testimonies about God's goodness in our individual lives. It was a wonderful way to forge strong friendships and to foster Christian ideals about family and our vocations and about living righteous lives and the meaning of loyalty to Christ and to the church. For our families those were truly happy times with many happy and fond memories.

*   *   *

George Jendresen was a real outdoorsman and an excellent hunter. He had a pickup truck with a homemade camper that he could load into the truck-bed. It wasn't fancy, but it was great for hunting. Several fellows from the Brighton Church were deer hunters and we sometimes hunted in foursomes or pairs. On one hunting trip to the Saddleback Mountains in Eastern Washington I jumped a buck and flushed him out of a ravine. It ran up the other side of the gulley and just stood there on a ledge looking back at me while I fired six shots that blew up puffs of dust all around the buck. I didn't have a scope on my Remington semi-automatic .30-06 rifle and the buckhorn site on my gun just wasn't accurate enough for me to make that shot across the ravine. I knew that by the time I re-loaded my rifle the buck would most likely have run off. Don O'Leary and Gene Peretti were along on that hunt and it was Don who bagged the buck with a clean 200 plus yard dead-eye shot, but I never lived down the frantic fusillade that I fired off that afternoon. I wasn't used to hiking as far as we did on that hunt and I was bushed when after sun-down we climbed into George's pickup truck and headed back across the mountains toward Seattle. I laid down in a sleeping bag the back of the truck and slept all the way home; but when I went to get up I suffered severe leg cramps that were my payback for sleeping while the other fellows road in the truck cab and gabbed on the trip back. Gerry Hilldall and Delbert Eibey hunted with us up in the Cascade Mountains around Corral Pass and we usually managed to flush a deer or two. We didn't always bring venison home with us, but it didn't seem to matter since, as most hunters will agree, it's just being outdoors in the great tall timber country of the Pacific Northwest or wherever men hunt and fish and enjoy the camaraderie of good friends that is what is really important.

*   *   *

George not only gave excellent leadership as the President of our congregation's Administrative Board, but both he and Ruth also taught Sunday School classes and served as counselors for the Christ's Ambassadors youth society. George joined with the other men of the church serving as an adult leader for our church's Boy Scout troop, and Ruth was one of the adult leaders of the girls' Missionettes (like Girl Scouts) organization. Like many of the other men of our congregation, George gave hundreds of man-hours of volunteer labor on evenings and weekends during the extended eight-year—long period that it took to complete the major building program during which the old building was remodeled into a Parish Hall, a new Sanctuary, offices, classrooms, prayer chapel, and tower were added to provide a handsome and modern church facility. George was active in the Men's Fellowship and Ruth was active in the Women's Missionary Society as well as the Brighton Ladies Guild. Ruth also sang in the choir, and there was very little that happened in the congregation in which the Jendresen family did not actively participate. Even though their Lazy J 4 Ranch was the furthest distance away from the church of any of our member's homes, the Jendresens were generally early and among the first to arrive, and whenever the church doors were open the Jendresens were often among the last to leave.

After we moved on and I entered the ministry of the United Methodist Church, we continued to enjoy the friendship of the Jendresen family. So highly did we regard, love and trust George and Ruth that when we learned that Mary Elizabeth was terminally ill with cancer, we requested that George and Ruth serve as our proxies and become the guardians of our children if we were both to die before Dan and Debbie became of age, and they consented to accept that responsibility should they be called upon to do so. When Mary died just two days before Christmas in 1970, George served as one of the pallbearers at her memorial service on the morning of Christmas Eve. Following Mary's death, the Jendresens were among those of our closest family and friends who provided to Dan and Debbie and to me their prayers and their moral and spiritual support.

The Jendresen family became so closely bonded with our family that Carol and Johnny became like our own children or at least like a niece and nephew in our hearts, and George and Ruth were truly a brother and a sister in Christ to Mary Elizabeth and to me. If you were to ask George who his best friend is he would probably refer to one of his *slakting* shirt-tail relatives or someone else, and being the modest fellow that he is, he is probably a bit embarrassed when I tell him that I regard him as the best friend I ever had. It's been over a half-century since we first met and I still feel that way about this good and godly man for whose friendship, trust and loyalty I will be everlastingly grateful.

NOTES:

[1]   In the summer of 2008, I completely refurbished the Nelson sailing dinghy and gave it, as well as the 3.7 hp Mercury outboard (which I had kept like new), and a smaller electric trolling motor to my grandson Joshua Howard to use for fishing and sailing. Joshua's Uncle Dan transported the dinghy and its motors, oars, anchors, and gear to Joshua's home in the waterfront community of North Pointe on West Point Lake near LaGrange, Georgia where Joshua's mother, Debbie Jones Howard lives with her husband, The Rev. Jeffrey W. Howard and their daughter Hannah Elizabeth Howard. That little dinghy brings back many happy memories for Debbie and her brother Dan, and hopefully will have good memories for Debbie's children also.

James Kirkman

CHAPTER 5

JAMES KIRKMAN

JAMES KIRKMAN was a developer and master builder and also served as the Chairman of our Administrative Council at the **Kennydale United Methodist Church, Renton, Washington**. Not only was he a capable leader in our congregation, but through an unexpected serendipity he became an esteemed personal friend and a trusted business partner.

*   *   *

After having served for nearly two decades as an Assemblies of God pastor and having served over half of that time as the senior pastor of the Brighton/ Trinity Assemblies of God Church in Southeast Seattle, it became apparent that God in His providence had another direction in which He would lead me along my Christian pilgrimage. My immediate predecessor at Brighton, Dr. David L. Aasen had transferred his clergy credentials to the Methodist Church, and he and other clergy colleagues who knew me through my role as the Secretary of the Seattle Council of Churches encouraged me to find another denominational affiliation. Dr. Aasen had invited me to be his guest at several of the Pacific Northwest Methodist Annual Conferences, and urged me to submit my name as a candidate for appointment in that denomination.

On Easter Sunday, 1967, I tendered my resignation from the Brighton pastorate which was to become effective the following June 30[th.] After having earned my B.A. and M.A. in Theology degrees from Northwest University and my B.Ed. degree from Seattle University and receiving certification as a public school teacher in 1965, in addition to continuing my pastoral responsibilities as the senior pastor of the Brighton Church, from 1965 through 1967 I also taught English, Social Studies, World History and U.S. History at Rainier Beach Jr.-Sr. High School in Southeast Seattle. In the absence of a pastoral call or appointment, my plans were to continue to pursue that teaching vocation. However, when Dr. Aasen related my plans to Dr. Joseph Harding who was the Superintendent of the Methodist Seattle District, I was offered an appointment to the South Park Methodist Church located adjacent to Boeing Field in a transitional area that was quickly becoming heavily industrialized. I knew that the South Park Church was a dying church with little if any chance of meaningful growth and survival. I affirmed my desire to affiliate with the Methodist denomination, but stated that I would wait until the Bishop could offer me an appointment where the congregation had a potential for growth. Perhaps Dr. Harding and Bishop Everett W. Palmer decided that I was worth something better than standing at a funeral wake over the South Park congregation, so they offered me the pastorate of the Kennydale Methodist Church.

Kennydale was a small residential community of lakeside cottages tucked in between Interstate Highway 405 and Lake Washington near Renton, Washington. The Kennydale Church was a small Tudor style building on a corner lot overlooking the south end of the lake. The parishioners were a fine group of people who gave evidence of a loyal commitment to Jesus Christ and to their church. It was a good appointment and an excellent entree for me into the Methodist denomination.

Since Mary Elizabeth and I owned our own waterfront home along the south end of Lake Washington not far from the Kennydale church, we were permitted to continue to live in our own house. The Kennydale parsonage was rented out as an apartment, but the church retained access to a basement "family room" with its own outside entrance and I was able to renovate that space and turn it into my pastor's study. My office had a cozy fireplace, room along the walls for my growing library, for my desk and also for a counseling area. Not long after my arrival the congregation hired Jim Kirkman's construction company to build two Sunday School annexes with two classrooms in each building, cater-corner across the intersection from the church. The basement was also remodeled and redecorated, and little by little the congregation began to grow. We reached out to a nearby home for disadvantaged boys and became active in the local ministerial association and I served as one of the chaplains at the local hospital. When it looked as though the Kenneydale congregation might outgrow its small chapel, the idea of relocating to a more suitable site was explored, and among the options that were considered was the possibility of establishing an "ecumenical" cooperative parish where several denominations would share a common campus, a larger sanctuary with three multiple chancels constructed on a large turntable designed to accommodate several different ecclesiastical/liturgical configurations, and a separate office building, classrooms and fellowship hall facilities, recreational areas, etc. that are common to most denominations.

A 40-acre parcel of high ground overlooking the eastern shore of Lake Washington was located in the proximity of Lake Boren. The property was owned by a defunct coal mining company and it was believed that the property might be obtained at a discount or as an outright gift from the owners as a tax write-off for their company. Several denominations were called together by the Washington State Council of Churches which controlled the *comity* allocations throughout the greater Seattle area and across the state. Funds were advanced as a pilot venture to obtain the services of a prominent architectural firm, surveys were made by site engineers, and preliminary plans were drawn and a three-dimensional scale model was made showing the possibilities and advantages of such a shared project. One denomination, the Seventh Day Christian Church (not to be confused with Seventh Day Adventists) actually approved the allocation of several thousand dollars to launch the joint venture and begin the process of acquiring the property and erecting the chapel as the first phase of the site development.[1]

In the 1960s ecumenism was the "in" thing among the mainline churches, but in spite of the measured successes of ecumenical experiments like that undertaken at the model community of Columbia, Maryland which was strategically located mid-way between the cities of Washington, DC, Annapolis and Baltimore, Maryland, history would prove that denominational ecumenism as embodied by the Council of Churches Uniting (COCU) was little more than wishful thinking and ecclesiastical window-dressing. Although all publicly agreed that the idea of a full-fledged ecumenical cooperative parish made sense from the standpoint of good stewardship, sound churchmanship, and especially as a powerful Christian witness to our unity and oneness in Christ, every denomination except the Advent Christian Church made flimsy and superficial excuses to justify their non-participation and the ventured died a still birth!

The Methodist Church, which was in the process of absorbing the smaller Evangelical United Brethren denomination, won the comity allocation for the development of establishing a new Methodist church within the upscale Fairwood Golf & Country Club under construction by the Bell & Valdez Development Company. To my happy surprise, Bishop Palmer appointed me to be the "organizing pastor" of the proposed new church at Fairwood! Dr. Harding had seen the new Brighton Assemblies of God Church which I had served when it was being built, and he had observed my leadership in creating and advocating the Lake Boren Ecumenical Parish; so when the Fairwood comity allocation was assigned to the United Methodist Church, I was chosen to be the pioneering pastor in undertaking the establishment of the new congregation.

*   *   *

As our Administrative Council Chairman, **Jim Kirkman** had participated in the exploration and advancement of the Lake Boren Ecumenical Parish project in which the Kennydale congregation would have had a major stake. When Jim recognized the political dynamics that undermined the Lake Boren project and learned that the Bishop had appointed me as the pastor of the new Fairwood congregation (which became part of a two-point charge with the Kennydale Church), Jim must have seen something that prompted him to extend an invitation to me to have lunch with him one day. He picked me up early at my church office and said that before we stopped for lunch he wanted to show me what he did for a living. At that time he had a major housing development of four-plex and six-plex units under construction in the neighboring community of Kent, Washington south of Renton. It was an impressive apartment complex. He also showed me several of the upscale custom homes that he had built around the Seattle-Tacoma area. Then over lunch he explained that his partner was retiring and moving to California and Jim was looking for a new business partner. He knew that I had experience in the construction industry through my involvement in the building of the church in Columbus, Kansas and more recently the construction of the Brighton church. He asked me if I would consider going into business with him—he made me an offer that I could hardly refuse: he would split all of our net profits with me 50/50% right across the board! When he told me what the combined net earnings of his corporation had been the previous year, I could hardly believe my ears—it was more money than I had ever dreamed of earning as a poor preacher! I told him that I was flattered by his offer and that I would talk it over with my wife; we would pray about it and I would give him my answer within the week. I explained to Jim that full-time United Methodist pastors were not permitted to engage in any other part-time employment that would in any way interfere with their pastoral duties and that I would first have to meet with the Bishop to gain his approval before I could enter into any such business arrangement.

When I met with Bishop Palmer, he was most gracious and kind to me. He said, "Brother Jones, I know that you are a hard-working pastor and that you have had to start over at the bottom of the totem pole when you transferred into the Methodist denomination. I realize that your income is minimal and that you have withdrawn from your former high school teaching position to devote full time to your two-point charge. I know that you give well beyond the normal 40-hour standard work week. What you do with your free time is your own private business. Some pastors golf, some fish, some have other hobbies, and some just plain loaf. If you want to engage in some sort of business arrangement with one of your parishioners, I trust your judgment and your personal integrity that you will not do anything that would supplant or supersede your pastoral responsibility to your congregation. So long as the Pastor-Parish-Relations

Committee and the Administrative Council of your congregation approve of your going into partnership with Mr. Kirkman, I have no problem with that and you and Jim have my blessing!"

Jim and his wife Pauline invited Mary Elizabeth and me over to their home for coffee to discuss the possibilities of our business joint venture. Jim drew up a simple partnership agreement which in essence stipulated that as he had originally proposed we would share 50/50 any and all profits and liabilities, and that we would never proceed with any business venture or transaction unless we were both in full agreement. That last provision proved to be the genius and the key to our success. Jim would be responsible for structural safety and meeting or exceeding the Uniform Building Code Standards, and I would be responsible for site acquisitions, design and marketing.

We began with a suitable building site for our first joint venture. We found a 3½ acre parcel in the city of Puyallup, Washington near the city of Tacoma. We could purchase the property for a small down payment of only $7,000 and on the strength of Jim's fine reputation as a developer/builder we were able to finance the rest of the project through one of the local Puyallup banks. I didn't have any extra money lying around, but my parents agreed to lend me $3,000 at the going interest rate of 7 ¼ % (I was able to pay back that loan upon the rental of our first duplex.)

Jim's wife, Pauline, was an excellent designer and drew the preliminary layout on that site for the construction of six duplex apartment units. On the front of the property there was an old chicken coop and Jim asked me what I thought we should do with it. I asked him if he thought we could salvage it and remodel it into two one-bedroom apartments. The building had been erected on a slab foundation and appeared to be structurally sound and was deemed worth the investment. With the conversion of that structure we wound up with seven duplexes giving us fourteen apartment units.

As our business partnership progressed and our first project grew, it became prudent for us to incorporate, so our partnership became *Investment Builders, Inc.* Jim asked me to serve as the president and he would serve as the vice president, Mary Elizabeth served as our corporate secretary and Pauline served as our corporate treasurer. We hired an architectural firm (Zanoni and Associates), retained a corporate attorney, and hired a local CPA as our accounting firm. We hired one of his staff to be our company's bookkeeper. Jim also had a superb construction foreman Bob Lathe, and between them Jim and Bob had the building skills to handle almost any part of the job; and Jim had the knowledge and wisdom to hire the best subcontractors and suppliers in the area. We paid our sub-contractors the going union rates for their various specializations: concrete & foundations, plumbing, electrical, HVAC, roofers, etc., and Jim hired whatever extra carpenters the project might need. Jim and Bob were both hard workers and I often saw them literally running from place to place in order to complete a particular operation on time and in proper sequence. Once the footings were poured and the foundation blocks were laid up, it would take less than a week for Jim and our own construction crew to get a duplex building under roof provided there were no delays due to bad weather. We used Jim's construction trailer as our construction office, and the back section of the trailer was our "tool crib." Because we were careful, frugal and used our resources of men and materials wisely, we were able to run a tight operation with low overhead and a high productivity ratio that contributed to our success.

When Jim asked about choosing a name for our first apartment complex, I suggested "GLENN COURT" in honor of my father, the Reverend Glenn D. Jones. To my delight, Jim and Pauline and Mary endorsed the suggestion, and we ordered a sign shop to design and make a handsome sign which was mounted in the masonry wall flanking the roadway at the main entrance. I contacted the Buckley Nursery owners with whom I was well acquainted and they provided the landscaping for each of our building projects.

Our next venture was a single four-plex located on a corner lot along one of the main thoroughfares in Puyallup. The building's design was adapted to a Spanish motif with a stucco exterior and a tile roof. I commissioned a local artist to cast a statue of a monk which we placed under a canopy frame to give the building the look of a Spanish mission, and we named the apartments THE EL CASTILIAN. Eventually I ended up owning the El Castilian and hired a manager to handle the rental collections and any needed repairs: those four units paid for themselves and accumulated an equity that helped me buy a new waterfront home on Chesapeake Bay when I later moved to the Baltimore area in 1977.

We incorporated into all of our apartment complexes a couple of signature features that set our developments apart as a bit upscale from the run-of-the mill developments in the area. We decided to include Heatilator wood-burning fireplaces in the living room of each unit, and in the master bedrooms we installed a circular baffle four feet in diameter that was suspended by brass chains under the light fixture in the center of the room: the baffles, which were painted with the popular popcorn vermiculite texture that matched the ceilings, provided an inexpensive novel indirect lighting source that was controlled by a dimmer switch to provide a more "romantic" setting. Everything else in the apartments was pretty much standard *boiler-plate*, but the finish carpentry, paint jobs and floor coverings were of a high quality that gave our apartments an "above average" upscale appearance and contributed to our excellent high occupancy rate when other builders' units sat empty. We also found that a specified but limited area of exterior brick or stone masonry work, together with carefully designed landscaping, helped give our developments a "curb appeal" that made them desirable living units.

At Glenn Court we set aside a little area for a small but well equipped playground for pre-school children; and in the center of the area we placed a little used dinghy which I rigged complete with twin masts and sails to make it look like a little schooner in which the children loved to play. With a simple sandbox and a swing and sliding board, the children and their mothers were happy. In the center of the development we also created a mound of earth 15 feet in diameter upon which we built a series of three recirculating waterfalls that flowed from the top pond to each of the lower ponds that were surrounded by colorful and sturdy landscaping. We wanted to create an inviting and pleasant environment for our tenants and for the eventual buyers to whom the developments would be sold after a five-year period of maturity and appreciation.

Our third development was WILLOW HEIGHTS, a larger development planned for 254 apartment units covering a 10-acre site with a 900 foot commercial frontage strip along the main highway leading from Puyallup toward South Tacoma, McChord U.S. Air Force Base, and the U.S. Army's Fort Lewis. We had completed the rough layout for the development and had completed selective logging to clear the roadways and the sites for the three major multiple-apartment buildings. We planned to incorporate a carefully determined mix of two and three bedroom units, an office and club house building with a pool and tennis courts. Toward the front of the complex there would be a separate apartment building with its own swimming pool and recreation area which would be designated for single tenants only. Our architectural firm had completed preliminary drawings and we had hired a professional consultant to assist us in completing a comprehensive feasibility study. We had just filed an application with the Bank of California for the $3,000,000 project when the economic bottom dropped out of the entire greater Seattle/Tacoma area.

The Boeing Company had amassed the largest and finest team of aero-space engineers, technicians, and manufacturing facilities in the world and had submitted what everyone believed was a shoo-in to guarantee for Boeing the government contract to build the experimental TFX fighter plane for the U.S. Air Force. However, the Lyndon Johnson Administration played dirty pork-barrel politics and handed the coveted contract to a non-existent aerospace company that was hastily thrown together in the Houston, Texas area. In that debacle the Seattle/Tacoma area suffered a mass exodus of over 500,000 people whose jobs suddenly evaporated into thin air. Many families just took their car and whatever they could pack into the trunk and fled the area: they just walked away from their empty houses, pleasure boats and whatever other luxuries they may have acquired. The housing market throughout the entire area was glutted with home foreclosures and empty dwellings. Realtors, real estate entrepreneurs, developers and builders, and many small businesses and aerospace supporting industries in the area declared bankruptcy and closed their operations. Out of disgust, the Boeing Company turned its attention away from the fickle market of government military contracts and focused its expertise upon the development of the 707 commercial airplanes and ultimately the giant 747 planes which changed the nature of that industry.

We put the Willow Heights development on hold and later, after the dust had settled and the Alaskan North Slope Oil boom began, we managed to sell the property for the recovery of our initial investment and a small profit on top of it.

SQUIRE ESTATES, a series of five duplexes or ten apartment units directly across the road from Olympia Golf & Country Club, was our last major development project, and turned out to be a success, probably because Olympia was the Washington State Capital and its major business was state government rather than the single-focused aero-space industry upon which a major part of the Seattle area had depended.

While we were still completing the Glenn Court apartment complex, Mary Elizabeth became terminally ill and died two days before Christmas in 1970. Jim and Pauline and our parishioners at the Kennydale United Methodist Church and many of our former parishioners from the Brighton AG Congregation were wonderful to Dan and Debbie and to me, and surrounded us with their love and encouragement. Jim served as one of the pallbearers at Mary's funeral which was held at the Bellevue United Methodist Church where Mary and I attended following my tenure at Kennydale. Jim and Pauline never hesitated to grant me a temporary "leave of absence" from my duties as President of Investment Builders. Immediately following Mary Elizabeth's funeral service Mary's brother Rev. Jonathan M. Hollis of Wichita, Kansas drove us to Sea-Tac Airport where we boarded a Boeing jet and flew to the East Coast to spend Christmas Eve and the holidays with my parents and family. Both Jim and I drew fixed salaries of $1,000 per month plus money to cover our company-related expenses, and we shared on a 50/50 basis the net gains from the eventual sales of our business holdings. Jim never questioned my right to my salary during the month that I was away in Pennsylvania following Mary's death. At the end of January we flew back to Seattle and Dan and I resumed our work on the Squire Estates project which was completed later that summer.[2]

It is my hope that the reader will understand that the purpose of relating my involvement with Jim Kirkman in our joint business ventures is not to brag about our success, but it is to demonstrate that the relationship that Jim and I had was more than simply that of a pastor and a parishioner. We were engaged in the serious business of jointly operating a development & construction company that involved all of the facets related to the designing, building, financing, marketing, and management of apartment complexes. Though the projects were not large by some standards, they nonetheless demanded that we meet all the local city, county, state and federal regulations governing such a business. It was Jim Kirkman's skill as a master builder and his impeccable personal integrity that made it such a rewarding joy for me to be not only his pastor but also his business partner.

When I accepted an appointment to pastor the First United Methodist Church in Canton, Pennsylvania, Jim and Pauline were supportive of my decision. I returned to full-time ministry in my home Conference where my father and my brother, Rev. Everett W. Jones, had also served as pastors. It was formerly the Susquehanna Conference of the Evangelical United Brethren Church which during that year merged with the Methodist Church to form the United Methodist Church. For two years after I moved to Canton, I continued in absentia to hold the office of President of Investment Builders, Inc. and Jim and Pauline faithfully mailed to me the monthly financial statements and consulted with me via phone on the management of the properties our company owned. Eventually we recognized the inevitable, and Jim and Pauline bought out my interests in the company; and Jim found a new partner with whom he was able to successfully continue the company's business until his eventual retirement.

Jim Kirkman proved not only to be an exemplary churchman (as his name suggests), but he and his wife proved to be true and loyal friends and trusted business partners when I needed them most. Jim and Pauline were devout Christians and were faithful leaders in the Kenneydale United Methodist Church. It was, however, their business partnership which provided to me and my family the economic stability we needed during the year prior to Mary Elizabeth's death. I had taken a supernumerary leave of absence from full-time pastoral ministry in order to be able to have the necessary time to take care of Mary during the last months of her fight against cancer. When Mary and I and our children needed their help and encouragement, Jim and Pauline were there for us. When I needed business partners whom I could trust, they were there for me. They were not just "Sunday Christians," but Jim was an honest, reliable and ethical man on the job, and his workmanship and stewardship in our business enterprises were invaluable. I count it a privilege to have been able to serve as their pastor and to have had the privilege of working with them in what was for all of us a worthy and profitable business relationship.

NOTES:

[1]   The Seventh Day Christian Church denomination is not to be confused with the Seventh Day Adventist denomination. For information about the Seventh Day Christian Church denomination, see their website at: http://seventhdaychristianchurch.org/

[2]   When we began the Squire Estates project, Jim hired our son Dan as an apprentice and taught him some of the "tricks of the trade" associated with the construction industry. Jim worked our employees hard but fairly, and he required of Dan that if he wanted a man's pay he would have to do a man's work. Dan had graduated from high school at the end of his junior year, and spent the following year working for our company. In the fall of 1971 Dan entered Lycoming College, graduated with honors, and has had a good career. He and his wife Judy are both engaged in the real estate business in the Atlanta, GA area.

Gary Patrick, MEd

CHAPTER 6

GARY PATRICK

G **ARY PATRICK, MEd** was the Principal of the Fairwood Elementary School and was the Chairman of the Administrative Council of the brand new **Fairwood Community United Methodist Church, Renton, Washington.**

*   *   *

When the Washington State Council of Churches allocated to the United Methodist denomination the comity agreement for the sponsoring and development of a new church within the Fairwood Golf & Country Club, Bishop Everett Palmer appointed C. David Jones, pastor of the Kennydale United Methodist Church to be its first and "organizing" pastor, thus forming a two-point pastoral charge. I suppose it seemed to be a "natural" appointment inasmuch as there was no parsonage for the as yet unformed Fairwood Church, so our family would continue to live in our own home along Rainier Beach, and I was to divide my time and energies between the two congregations. There would be no increase in my salary, but my workload was more than doubled. Moreover, it was expected that I would resign my position as a teacher at the Rainier Beach Jr.-Sr. High School where I had been on the faculty for the previous three years. And yet the prospect of pioneering a new congregation appealed to me.

When I made inquiry about the proposed Fairwood UM Church project, my first discovery was that the Pacific Northwest Conference had purchased a five-acre parcel of wooded land off the main road up a dirt road that passed a goat farm with the rusting hulks of abandoned junker cars and worn-out farm implements scattered around the field. The Conference had paid $30,000 for this isolated parcel of land, which was the most that the Conference had ever paid for a new church building site. Even at that, the property was located about three miles south of the new up-scale Fairwood Golf and Country Club subdivision that was rapidly being developed by the Bell & Valdez Corporation. The Conference had attempted to acquire property for a church building site within the boundaries of the Fairwood Community, but all such efforts were rudely rebuffed by the corporate sales office whose agents made it clear that the developers didn't want any religious folks bothering their residents or their prospective property owners with any solicitations or high-pressure religious crusading or proselytizing. The Conference officials and volunteer personnel had scoured the surrounding countryside for a suitable and affordable building site and the dirt-road property was the very best that they could find.

I knew that even if the Conference forged ahead and expended the funds first to clear and level the site, then to bring in electrical power, natural gas, phone and TV cable lines, and either drill a well and dig a septic system or else pay an exorbitant fee to bring public utilities a mile from the highway up the dirt road to the property; and even if a modern new church were erected on that site, the residents from the Fairwood Country Club Community were not likely to bring their new cars up that dirt road to attend church. That was a lost cause from the start. However, that suited the Rev. Earl Dean, senior pastor of the First United Methodist Church in the nearby city of Renton, Washington, just fine! Although he had been appointed as the Chairman of the Committee assigned with the responsibility for assisting with the plans for the founding of the new church, Rev. Dean feared that if the new Fairwood church actually turned out to be a success, his congregation would most likely lose a significant number of families to the new congregation. That possibility would impose a serious diminishment upon the ability of the Renton UM Church to pay their apportionment assessments or to register enough growth in the near future to make up for the gap that would occur as a result of the loss of members. These combined factors posed a significant threat to any possibility of success for the establishment of the proposed Fairwood church.

Realizing that the combined factors described above resulted in a deck stacked against the success of the proposed Fairwood church development project, I asked the District Superintendent, Rev. Joe Harding, for his permission to allow me to make a property search on my own. "Good luck, David; go to it," he said to me. He probably knew that I was going to need a lot more than just good luck to achieve what others who had tried before me had failed to accomplish.

It was at this very point that my twenty years of experience trusting God in faith ventures as a Pentecostal pastor in the Assemblies of God denomination may have given me a bit of an edge. Like David, I had met a bear and a lion and a giant or two, and the same God who had given me victories then was still the same God whom I served now as a United Methodist pastor. I dressed in a pair of gray slacks, a white shirt and tie and my yacht club blue blazer, and made a trip out to the Fairwood sales office. When I arrived, I introduced myself as Rev. C. David Jones, a United Methodist minister, and explained that on behalf of my denomination I was enquiring to determine what building sites might be available upon which to build a new church within the Fairwood Community. The sales representative abruptly took me by the arm and escorted me to the door giving to me a rude rebuff that the Bell and Valdez developers didn't want any churches within their new up-scale Fairwood Golf and Country Club premises.

I returned home and knelt in prayer and offered to God my supplication which went something like this: "Lord, the church is not mine—it is yours. I can't do anything by myself, but if you will go before me and stand with me, I know that you can open doors that no man can open and you can close doors that no man can close. If you want a new Methodist church to be established within the Fairwood Country Club community, then Lord, please open the door; and if I must choose a building site please guide me by closing any doors that might not be in your will for this new congregation. This I pray in the Holy Name of Jesus Christ our Lord. Amen."

The very next day I donned my clerical collar and my new summer serge suite, hung a silver pectoral cross around my neck and drove back out to the Fairwood sales office. It is hard even now for me to grasp what happened when I walked through the door!

The very same salesman who had forcibly shown me to the door the day before was the person who greeted me when I entered the sales office. "Good morning, Father," he greeted me as he stuck out his hand and shook mine with an enthusiastic cordiality, "What can I do for you, Father?"

The sales agent did not recognize me at all. It was as if he was blinded to my identity just as God had blinded the eyes of the soldiers of the King of Syria when they came to capture the prophet Elisha at the ancient city of Dothan (*Vide* 2 Kings 6:18, 19ff). I learned later that the sales agent was an avid Episcopalian who had a great respect for his own priest and others wearing a clerical collar. Apparently when he saw me wearing my clerical collar and my pectoral cross he must have thought that I was a bona fide and credible clergyman and not just some Bible-thumping fundamentalist preacher. The same man who the day before had given me the bum's rush and shoved me out the door, on this day treated me with the utmost respect and courtesy. I knew that this was God's doing. I explained to the sales agent exactly as I had the day before who I was and that my mission was to locate a suitable building site for a new church to be erected by the United Methodist Church under the comity commitment of the Washington State Council of Churches. After I had once again explained my purpose, to my utter amazement the salesman said, "Well, Father, we have three excellent building sites that have been designated for commercial purposes by the developers. Let me show you the developer's plats and then I will take you around and show you the actual sites, all of which are approximately five acres in size." When he showed me the plats of the three parcels, I immediately knew in my heart which one would be the most ideal—the perfect site for the new church; but I asked him to show the three sites to me so I could make an informed choice.

The first building site abutted the location upon which the new Fairwood Elementary School was being constructed. The second site, which abutted the boundary of the subdivision, was a corner location outside of the subdivision proper and had no access or egress directly to or from the Fairwood County Club residential area. It was an out-parcel that would be an ideal location for a small shopping center for the surrounding area, but the intersection would be heavily traveled and would lend itself more to some commercial development other than a church. The third site was not yet developed and the roads and infrastructures of water mains, sewer lines, and underground electrical, phone and TV cable lines were in the very beginning stages and the site work by heavy earthmoving equipment had just started. We walked through the dust and dirt about a quarter-mile to this last site, which had been set aside by the developers for the erection of high-rise apartment buildings. The property's frontage extended for 1,004 feet along the main divided boulevard that ran through the length of the Fairwood community. At the back of the property was the 14th Fairway and along the east side of the property lay the 15th fairway. Across the boulevard was the 16th fairway, so no houses would ever be built across the street from this particular property. There were a couple of natural springs on the acreage which would lend themselves to provide a constant water source for a series of architecturally enhancing ponds that could be incorporated into the landscaping around the church property. It was the choicest piece of property in the entire development and it hadn't even been placed on the market yet by the developers.

I knew instinctively that the moment the Bell & Valdez sales office were to announce to local builders and apartment entrepreneurs the availability of this five acre parcel of land, it would be instantly snapped up by the first bidder. When we arrived back at the sales office, the real estate agent asked me if I had seen anything that I liked that might suit our purposes for a new church site. Trying to hide my growing excitement over this special piece of property, I inquired about the price of each parcel and when he stated that the site in which I was so keenly interested would be placed on the market for $75,000 my heart skipped a beat. That was nearly three times what the Conference had paid for the five acres up the dirt road past the unsightly goat farm. I knew that the property was undoubtedly worth every cent that the developers were asking for it and that it would be a bargain for some high-rise apartment developer. If a builder were to construct as few as 25 apartments on the site, it would bring the land cost per unit down to a mere $3,000 per unit as opposed to $50,000 or more for each single residence building lot. I said that I had decided to take the boulevard parcel and would like to sign an earnest money agreement to bind the purchase contract. When I asked him if he would accept my personal note in the amount of $7,500 (10% of the purchase cost), he quickly agreed and wrote out the contract papers. The only contingency that I requested was that the purchase would require the approval of the Pacific Northwest Conference of the United Methodist Church. I had been careful to write on my note that "This note will be due and payable upon the exercise by the Pacific Northwest Conference of the UMC of the option appertaining thereto." To my amazement and enormous relief, the sales agent accepted my personal note and handed me two copies of the earnest money agreement (one for me and one for the UMC Conference Office). I left the Fairwood sales office that day with a signed and notarized contract for the purchase of a beautiful site upon which to build the new church.

The only problem was that I had no idea whether or not the Conference Board of Missions and the Conference Committee on Stewardship and Finance would ever agree to pay that much for this choice piece of land, or if they would just abandon the whole idea and look elsewhere.

I drove to the Skyway United Methodist Church and located the pastor, Rev. David Ernst, who was a good man and a close friend and colleague who grew up in a spiritual Evangelical Church and knew how to pray. I asked him if he had time to go with me to look at the property I had just bought for the new Fairwood church site! When I told him about the events related to my purchase of the site, he was as amazed as I was. We drove back out to Fairwood and walked along the golf course fairways until we reached the 14th fairway. We stood on the hill overlooking the site for the new church and the boulevard that stretched out below us. I reminded Dave of the promise of Jesus, "*That if two of you shall agree on earth as touching any thing that they shall ask, it shall be done for them of my Father which is in heaven*" (St. Matthew 18:19 KJV). We joined our hands and our hearts in prayer and claimed the promise of our Lord for the acquisition of this special piece of ground upon which we stood for the purpose of erecting upon it the new Fairwood Community United Methodist Church.

*   *   *

The next day I drove to Tacoma, Washington and knocked on the door of the parsonage of the First United Methodist Church in that city. The young pastor of that congregation was the Chairman of the Conference Committee on Missions and Evangelism, and it was his committee that would decide whether on not to sell the old dirt road site and to exercise the newly acquired option to purchase the new building site now available to the Conference. When the minister, a Rev. Norman Lawson, answered the door, I introduced myself to him and related to him the commission that had been given to me by Bishop Palmer and Dr. Harding, and I gave him an account of my search for a suitable building site within the boundaries of the Fairwood Country Club. I was disappointed but not surprised by his abrupt and arrogant reaction when I handed him a copy of the earnest money contract. He looked it over and challenged me: "Who gave you the authority to purchase this five-acre parcel for $75,000 dollars? Don't you understand that nobody has the authority to make such a purchase without the prior approval of me and my committee? How dare you to go around me and act unilaterally on your own. Maybe you could pull a stunt like that in the Assemblies of God, but now that you are a Methodist you need to follow *our* rules."

I looked him straight in the eye and said boldly, "If I were to have waited until your committee meets in October, that property would have been long gone and the opportunity to secure this choice church site would have been forever lost. I did what I believe is in the best interest of the Conference and which I believe I was authorized to do by the Bishop and my District Superintendent." Since it was already the middle of July, Rev. Dean and many of the other clergy were away on their summer vacations. I reminded this arrogant man that the Fairwood church was scheduled to be launched on Worldwide Communion Sunday, the first Sunday in October, and the congregation didn't even have an available place in which to meet! Nobody else seemed to be in any particular hurry to get on with the task, but each passing day drew us closer to the start-up day without any prospects or idea of how or where that would take place.

The pompous Rev. Lawson continued to berate me for not having met first with his committee members and receiving their approval, and again he insulted me and tried to intimidate me by insisting that I had to follow the rules of the *Discipline* or else! I felt that I did not deserve his abusive and demeaning remarks since I had exercised initiative, faith, and responsible action in locating a suitable building site.

I stared at him and further angered him and wounded his pride when I said with undisguised disgust, "You want to force me to wear Saul's armor, but like my namesake David, I find your fancy armor to be an encumbrance that would only weigh me down and cripple me—I prefer to take my *shepherd's sling and five smooth stones* from the brook when I go out to do battle with the giants who are the enemies of the church."

In a fit of anger and wounded pride because a former Pentecostal pastor who, in good faith, had accomplished what he and his committee had failed to do, the mean-spirited man threatened me with a warning meant to intimidate me. He declared that unless I followed the Methodist *Discipline* to the very letter of the law, I would eventually be "broken on the rocks" of that institution and its ecclesiastical rules. Throughout my four decades of ministry within the United Methodist Church I have honored and kept the *Discipline* but where the *Discipline* falls short, like most human instruments do, I have sought by God's help to find a way around the encumbrances and roadblocks thrown up by apostate churchmen who themselves increasingly appear to disregard their own rules and laws whenever it suits them and their personal agendas.

I was called by the Rev. Lawson to appear before the Conference's Chancellor who was a young and pompous attorney who was all full of himself and a false notion of his own importance. He interrogated me and asked what I would do if the Conference rejected the option to purchase the Fairwood site—how would I pay the personal note that I had signed?" He mocked me and grinned at me as if I were some stupid school boy. I told him that I could sell the option to any one of a number of builders who would be glad to pay me a finder's premium in order for them to gain access and control of that choice parcel of land. Surprised at my answer, he asked me what I thought the Conference should do with the five acres they had purchased up the dirt road. He was surprised and dumfounded when I told him that my partner, Jim Kirkman, and I owned and operated Investment Builders, Inc., and that, as a courtesy to take it off the Conference's hands, we might consider buying the property at the same price for which it had been originally purchased and that we probably would develop it into a small subdivision of country homes. I learned later that the attorney and his colleagues on Rev. Lawson's committee were afraid that Jim Kirkman and I might just make some money on the development of the property, so on the feigned grounds that there might be an ethical problem inasmuch as we could then have a vested interest in the whole transaction, they decided not to sell the property to us. I really didn't want the old dirt-road property; but when I shamed them because of their lack of entrepreneurial creativity, and because they recognized the new piece of property on Fairway Boulevard for the enviable prime location and valuable site that it was, they voted to purchase it after all! So in the end my faith and judgment were vindicated, and the Bishop and other clergy colleagues thanked me and congratulated me for my courage and action.

*   *   *

As the new owners of the church building site, the church could now claim a membership status in the Fairwood Golf & Country Club Property Owners

Association, and as such we would have a membership access to the Country Club's facilities and the golf course.

Because the large and attractive Club House had a bar connected to its dining room and dance floor area on the main floor and the Club wanted to protect its liquor license, the main Club House was off-limits to minors under twenty-one years of age. Wisely, the B&V developers had constructed a relatively large separate Club House designed and dedicated especially for the youth of the Fairwood Community. The Youth Club House, which in the summer time doubled as a bath house for the adjacent Olympic size swimming pool and tennis courts, sat empty during the winter months and was idle even in the summer because of the lack of an adult chaperone or official Youth Director (that was not in the Association's budget but would be added later as the development was built out and completed).

I approached the manager of the Country Club and requested the use of the vacant Youth Club House as a temporary office quarters and worship center for our fledgling congregation. In exchange I proposed the possibility that the Conference might assist us in hiring a Youth Director for our Church's youth activities and that our activities would be open to all of the teenagers in the community regardless of their church affiliation. My proposal was brought before the Country Club's Board of Directors and with the concurrence of the B&V developers my proposal was accepted. It was a win-win situation for everyone.

*   *   *

Now that we had secured a site for our new church, we needed to gather a congregation! Much to the credit of the Pacific Northwest Conference and especially to the credit of Bishop Palmer, Dr. Harding and other members of the Bishop's Cabinet who provided superb spiritual and administrative leadership, every possible effort and resource was made available to ensure the success of the new Fairwood church. The Bishop and his colleagues knew that it was an impossible task for a single pastor to achieve without significant help from others. The General Conference Board of Missions and Evangelism was contacted, and the services of the Rev. Al Wilson were obtained for a short six-week period for the specific purpose of launching a concerted canvas of the area within a five-mile radius surrounding the new Fairwood Community. That was a major undertaking and it proved to be a key to the success of the entire enterprise.

I had known Al Wilson and had worked with him on the Board of Directors of the Greater Seattle Council of Churches, which represented over 900 churches in Seattle and the surrounding suburbs. Al was the Treasurer and I was the Secretary of the GSCC. We had worked together on interdenominational and interchurch projects for several years, and I considered Al as a good and esteemed colleague and friend. He had been a very successful new-church pioneer and planter, having served as the "organizing pastor" of the Bellevue United Methodist Church. His success there led to his being recruited as a new church development consultant by the UMC General Board of Missions & Evangelism in Nashville, Tennessee. It was a natural thing to call Al back to the Seattle area to assist us in carrying out the essential canvas mission. Al and his wife arrived in mid-July. We only had a few weeks to plan and carry out the proposed canvas. Al obtained reverse directories from the local telephone companies in the surrounding area. Using the reverse directories, he had prepared 3x5 inch cards with the name, address and phone number of every resident within the wide five-mile area which we planned to canvas. Dr. Harding recruited the cooperation of every pastor and two lay persons from each of the thirty-five United Methodist Churches within the Seattle District. The second Sunday afternoon in September was chosen for the day of the canvas. Over a hundred pastors and laypersons gathered in the Fairwood Club House hall which we had reserved for that afternoon, and the group was divided into teams of two persons, each of whom were handed an area map, a packet of address cards and a bundle of brochures which I had designed and had printed advertising the new Fairwood Church. Over the next four hours the volunteers knocked on the doors of over a thousand homes within our target area and returned with nearly a thousand survey cards.

Because of the rapid growth of the Seattle area following World War II and with the construction of residential housing developments throughout the suburban areas, there was a constant influx of new families moving into the area. Most of these newcomers to the area had not established any church affiliation even though many of them had been active in their home churches from which they had come. Among these new families were many young couples with pre-school, elementary school, and teenage children. Most of those who were moving into the Fairwood community were well educated and affluent people as were many of the families living in the nearby subdivisions. The denominational churches were having a difficult time trying to keep pace with the rapid growth, which made the mutually cooperative comity arrangements so vital to the evangelization of the area. From the one thousand survey cards, we were able to cull out over five hundred families who had expressed an interest in visiting and possibly joining our new Fairwood congregation! Those prospective-member cards were a veritable gold mine!

I realized it would be humanly impossible for me to personally visit in each of the homes of those prospective members in time to make an impact sufficient to launch the new Fairwood congregation by the first Sunday in October. I begged Dr. Harding to find a way for us to retain Al Wilson not just for the initial short six-week period but, if at all possible, for us to somehow retain Al at least for the next six months. Again the Bishop and the Conference leaders came through and found the funds necessary for us to keep Al Wilson as part of our team. Al Wilson had a God-given gift and a knack of being able to knock on a door "cold-turkey;" when a door was opened, he would greet the homeowner with a big smile and genuine warmth of personality that would make a total stranger feel like they had known Al forever. He and I began making the rounds of each of the neighboring subdivisions and we followed up on every one of those prospective member cards. Al was absolutely fearless and didn't seem to mind the real threat from neighborhood dogs with a strong territorial imperative and a native instinct to protect their master's and also their master's property. Even when he was bitten occasionally by an aggressive guard dog in the more rural areas, Al was nonflappable and he bravely and eagerly forged ahead. It was his special talent as much as anything else we did that contributed to the rapid growth and success of the new church. As the membership began to grow Al also helped in the formation of our Administrative Council and the organizing of several of the congregation's working committees.

Together with our concerted program of follow-up visitation we ran newspaper articles and ads in the local newspapers and placed posters wherever we could announcing the opening day which was scheduled for the first Sunday in October. Over the next nine months the church's membership grew from zero to two hundred ninety-seven baptized, confirmed and communicant members, and our total constituency swelled to over five hundred people. It was an incredible success!

Although we had a place in which to worship and space for a parish office, we didn't have one stick of office furniture nor a single piece of office equipment or supplies. When I briefed Dr. Harding about our dilemma, he said, "David, I still have about $3,000 dollars in our District contingency fund: you can have all of it, but please just use it wisely." I shopped the used office furniture and equipment outlets in the downtown Seattle area and was able to purchase office desks, chairs, file cabinets, an electric IBM typewriter, a mimeograph, a folding machine, stationary, staplers, paper punches, and everything else we needed to establish a working parish office. We had phone lines run into the offices and were ready for business. But we still didn't have a parish secretary nor did we yet have a Youth Director for our parish and the community. I discussed with Joe Harding and with some of the new members our need to hire a parish secretary and a youth director. We believed that the tithes and offerings we were receiving in our Sunday worship services would permit us to fill these positions with part-time staff personnel. Dr. Harding recommended to us a pre-seminarian who was a senior student at the University of Washington, David Heather. Dave, who was a bright young man full of energy, enthusiasm and a genuine commitment to Christ, brought his fiancé with him and together they became a great team as our Youth Director and Youth Counselor.

When I announced in the Sunday services that we were seeking someone to work part-time as our Parish Secretary, we were fortunate to have Mrs. Doris Hoagland apply for the position. Doris had been the private secretary to the CEO of one of the large steel companies in New Jersey and was a highly skilled woman who had exceptional skills as an administrative assistant and secretary. She and her husband had purchased a beautiful home in Fairwood and like many of the other members they were good golfers. Her husband, Stan Hoagland, was a products representative for the steel company for which both he and Doris worked in the East, a company that specialized in titanium and other exotic metals used in the aerospace industry. Almost overnight we had been able to bring together a viable parish staff and arrange what turned out to be an excellent interim facility for our fledgling church.

* * *

Gary Patrick and his family became regular worshippers and active participants in the new church from the very beginning and were among the first persons to become Charter Members. Gary was a gregarious and enthusiastic supporter of our start-up efforts and it was not surprising that the congregation elected him to be the first Chairman of its Administrative Council. As educators, he and his wife Madeline, who was also a school teacher, gave leadership to the formation of the Sunday School, summer Vacation Bible School, and Adult Christian Education programs of the congregation. Dr. Jerry Zimmerman, who was the Superintendent of public schools in the Kent, Washington area and his wife Verna had served a short term as vocational missionary educators: they were able teachers and also helped foster an interest in both foreign and home missions.

Among the members were an impressive number of well-educated and competent professional persons, which gave to this new congregation an exceptionally bright and gifted group of lay leaders. The choir director was a circuit court judge. The organist was the editor of the Renton Newspaper's Society pages and knew everyone in town. She managed to obtain a front-page full-color story about the new Fairwood Church. The full-page color photo showed Pastor Jones engaged in a "dialogue sermon" with the teenage artist who had created a wall-to-wall symbolic psychedelic painting depicting the world of teenagers in the late sixties and showing the contribution that faith in Christ makes in the formation of their adult lives. One of the young couples in the church owned and operated the local roller skating rink and opened their establishment to the Youth Fellowship. The Patricks' teenage daughter Colleen and her two brothers, Brian and Kyle, were active participants in the Church sponsored youth activities.

Gary Patrick and his whole family were active in the social life of the community and were excellent recruiters for our new church. They brought their friends and neighbors with them to church. Gary and his family became good friends with the Pastor's family and it was our privilege to entertain them in our home. It was Gary's enthusiasm, his high level of energy, his gregarious personality, and his commitment to Jesus Christ and our new congregation that made him such a valuable member of the Fairwood congregation.

Like many of the church's members, Gary was also a good golfer, had a fair handicap, and was friends with the golf pro at the Fairwood Golf Club. One of the pros joined our congregation, and I was invited to have my own locker at the club and to keep my own golf clubs at the Club House.

Knowing about the perks that I enjoyed through the church's membership as property owners in the Fairwood Community, some of the other pastors were understandably envious. I realized very keenly that without the help of the other pastors and their parishioners who assisted with our initial canvas of the area, we would never have been able to get off to the good start that they helped to facilitate. Each of the pastors in the Seattle District had a vested interest in the new Fairwood UM church. In a concerted effort to make them feel part "owners" in the new church, I systematically began to invite each of the pastors to be my guest for lunch at the Country Club and after lunch I would introduce them to the golf club pros and treat each of the pastors to a bucket of golf balls for the driving range and to try their golfing skill at the practice putting green. That was one of the best PR things I could have done, and it helped foster a stronger spirit of collegiality and camaraderie between those pastors and me. Our success was, after all, the result of a real team effort.

When the Fairwood congregation outgrew its quarters in the Youth Club House, it was Gary Patrick who helped negotiate the arrangement whereby the Fairwood Congregation was able to rent the auditorium and class rooms of the Fairwood Elementary School to use for its Sunday worship services and Sunday School. As the principal of the elementary school, Gary was invaluable as a liaison between the church and the elementary school's faculty. It was a good arrangement since many of the parents from our church were also active members of the elementary school's PTA and maintained a good working relationship with their children's public school teachers.

As the church's membership grew and its financial base increased, it became apparent that the congregation had reached the point where it could support a full-time minister. A parsonage was purchased within the Fairwood Community and a fine young pastor, Rev. Larry Speicher, was appointed as my successor. I continued to pastor the Kennydale UMC and remained close friends with Gary and Madeline Patrick, and Dan dated their daughter Colleen and occasionally met with the Fairwood Youth group. I am grateful for Gary's friendship and for his partnership in establishing the Fairwood Community United Methodist Church.

Jack Lockledge, EdD

CHAPTER 7

JACK LOCKLEDGE

JACK LOCKLEDGE, EdD, like many of the other men in this book, was not only an outstanding parishioner, but he became a highly esteemed, trusted and close friend. That friendship has lasted far beyond the time I was his pastor at the **First United Methodist Church, Canton, Pennsylvania**, and it led to an unanticipated serendipity for both of us later on in another parish setting, about which the reader will learn more in a later chapter.

*   *   *

Because of Mary Elizabeth's terminal illness I requested from my home Conference a *supernumerary leave of absence* from active pastoral appointment. From July of 1970 through the following spring I continued to work with Jim Kirkman in our Investment Builders, Inc. development project at Squire Estates in Olympia, Washington. As the summer passed and fall approached, Mary Elizabeth became weaker and finally after a four-year battle against cancer, she went to be with the Lord on December 22, 1970. After Mary died I requested an appoint to a pastorate in my home Conference and was appointed by Bishop Herman Kaebnick to serve a two-point charge as pastor of the First United Methodist Church in Canton, Pennsylvania and the Ward United Methodist Church located in the nearby rural parish of Ward, Pennsylvania.

I had no idea where Canton was or what I would find when I arrived, but I was looking forward to being back in pastoral ministry. What I found was a small town with a population of about two thousand persons nestled in a valley tucked among the Allegheny Mountains in the southwest corner of Bradford County. Canton is located about half way between Williamsport, Pennsylvania, which was about thirty miles to the south of Canton, and Elmira, New York, which is an equal distance to the north of Canton. There was no hospital or even a medical clinic in the town, so residents traveled to Elmira, Williamsport and Wellsboro, to the west or to the town of Sayre, to the northeast. The town was originally founded by a group of hardy Yankee farmers who moved southward from Connecticut to the Canton Valley where they settled and farmed the land along the small creek that runs eastward through the valley until it eventually connects with the eastern branch of the Susquehanna River.

The town had a respectable shopping district and an excellent public school system, and a number of light industries provided steady employment for the local work force. The nearby Minnequa hot-springs resort on the northern edge of town became a famous health spa frequented by the wealthy who traveled from the New York and Philadelphia areas via special trains to bathe in the medicinal waters of the Minnequa hot-springs. Canton became a favorite winter home for many entertainers from the stage and for the famous Ringling Bros. and Barnum & Bailey circus performers. The famous author, composer and clergyman Phillips Brooks, Episcopal Bishop of Massachusetts, who wrote the Christmas carol *O Little Town of Bethlehem,* built a grand house at Minnequa Springs as did many other notable persons of the late 19th century. In fact, the residents of Canton erected a significant number of handsome churches representing all of the major Protestant and the Catholic denominations, and from their pulpits several renowned clergymen preached eloquent sermons. At one time both the American Baptists', the Methodists' and the Presbyterians' men's Sunday School classes each boasted over a hundred regular members. Reportedly cigars and pipes were allowed during class time in the Presbyterian Men's Bible Class, but the teetotalling Methodists were stricter about bringing either alcohol or tobacco into their church buildings.

The Methodists built a fairly large frame church structure on the corner of East Union and Center Streets. Twin entrances to the church were located in a large corner tower, and the Church, like all of the others in town, was replete with stained glass windows and an excellent pipe organ, and like all the other Protestant church buildings, the sanctuary chancel held a choir loft located behind the central pulpit. Only the Roman Catholic Church had an open chancel with a central high altar, and the American Baptist Church and the Disciples of Christ Church buildings both had baptismal pools (tanks) built into the center of the back chancel walls, while the others had carved baptismal fonts. The Methodist Church, which was constructed of wood rather than masonry materials, over the years had accumulated dry-rot and termites in its basement walls, but the Methodists took great pride in their church and made costly repairs to keep their building in the best possible condition. The Methodist parsonage was located two houses to the east of the church on Union Street and sat next to the old Elementary School building with its small playground across the street. Like the church, the parsonage had been built in the late 1800s and showed the wear and tear of use by numerous parsons' families.

The membership of the First United Methodist Church of Canton was around three hundred twenty-five persons. Among its members were many of the prominent citizens of the town including the mayor, Donald Thomas, who was also the Editor of the local Canton Newspaper; Torrence Keeler who was the Superintendent of the Canton Area School System; Tillman Williammee who was a former Superintendent of the Canton public schools; John Hyde, Jr, who was the Principal of the Canton area Jr.-Sr. High School; Dr. Jack Lockledge who was the principal of the Canton area Elementary School; Dr. Jake Young who was a doctor of optometry; Albert Wrisley who was the former Elementary School Principal; and several other local businessmen, bankers and a dozen or more school teachers.

*   *   *

At the end of June, 1971, I had flown back east from Seattle and borrowed my parent's automobile to drive to Canton for my first Sunday in the pulpit, which was during the Fourth of July holiday weekend. I found the empty parsonage to be a rather bare and lonely place. There was no bed other than a mattress lying on the floor of one of the upstairs bedrooms, and although the women of the church had cleaned the parsonage in preparation for my arrival, I had little inclination to hang around the town by myself over the holiday. So after church I drove the two hundred and fifty miles south to spend the Fourth with my father, Rev. Glenn David Jones, Sr. and my mother, Evelyn Marianna Hallin Jones, who lived in York, Pennsylvania.

On the way to York, I stopped at the Laurel Hills Cemetery in Columbia, Pennsylvania, and visited Mary Elizabeth's grave. I sat on the grass by her grave and wept 'till I had no more tears to cry. My heart ached with loneliness and grief, and not knowing how I could fill the empty hole in my heart that Mary's death had left, I prayed to the Lord for his comfort and guidance. For me dating any women in my new parish was unthinkable. I knew that if I dated more than one woman I would very soon be tagged with being a Casanova, and if I selected one woman whom I might date regularly it would very soon become an expectation that I would marry that person. It seemed that I was damned if I did and damned if I didn't. Going back to Columbia resurrected a host of nostalgia and a plethora of memories and emotions that only added to my sense of loneliness and sadness.

I spent the Fourth of July with my parents and we visited my younger brother Everett's family who were living in Lancaster, Pennsylvania. The following day my parents sensed that I was restless and at a loss with time on my hands, so they suggested that I drive south to Frederick, Maryland to visit my youngest sister Lois Jones Oster and her family. I wondered what I would do when I arrived in Frederick, and then I remembered that after Mary died, Lois had tried to play cupid by writing to me about a pretty young blond single woman in her congregation in Frederick. It occurred to me that perhaps I might meet this young lady. I phoned Lois and said that if she could arrange a blind date with the blond, I would drive to Frederick to visit her (meaning both Lois and the blond). Lois phoned back assuring me that she had arranged the blind date, and thus it was that on July 5th, I met for the first time Barbara Ann Hillman who is a Swedish American originally from my mother's hometown of Jamestown, New York. After a brief courtship, Barbara and I were married that summer in the Chapel of my father's home church, Calvary United Methodist Church in Frederick, Maryland. For the past nearly four decades Barbara has been a faithful companion and a superb partner in the ministry.

*   *   *

The first Sunday morning after Barbara and I were married was her first time attending a worship service in our new parish. There was a baptism that morning—the baby was the first grandchild of the town's mayor and newspaper editor Donald Thomas. I had begun the baptismal litany and was proceeding per the printed text in fine fashion sailing right along until I came to the place in the service where I was supposed to actually sprinkle the baby with holy water. I looked to my right-hand side where the baptismal font ordinarily stood. It had been there the day before when I took Barbara over to see the sanctuary of the First United Methodist Church. But now, all of a sudden, there was no font . . . it had mysteriously disappeared as if into thin air and unthinkingly I had not missed it until that critical moment. I was stunned and didn't have the presence of mind to know what to do! I just stood there holding the infant in my arms. I was dumbfounded.

Great beads of perspiration immediately bursted out on my forehead from my sudden panic and stunned embarrassment. I was already past the point of no return and not having the equanimity to ask the congregation if anyone knew where the Baptismal Font might be, I plummeted right on and swiping my hand across my dripping forehead, I baptized that blessed infant with the very sweat of my brow! I guess everyone else was just as stunned as I was and wondered how this new minister would solve the obvious dilemma. No one laughed but instead the sanctuary became quiet as a morgue while I concluded the litany, handed the baby back to the arms of its mother, shook hands with the father and grandparents, pronounced a pastoral blessing and they returned to their pews and I to the chancel where I sat momentarily emotionally exhausted and thoroughly mortified.

After the service several of the members offered to me their apologies and explained that the sexton had removed the Baptismal Font and placed it in the Sacristy, not realizing that there was going to be a baptism the following morning.

It was my colossal blunder that I did not phone the sexton to alert him about the scheduled baptism, and that blunder was compounded when I failed to double-check to make certain that there was still water in the font when I entered the church on that Sunday morning. Of course, if the Methodists had adopted the Biblically correct mode of baptism by immersion as our Baptist friends do, I suppose we would not have had that problem—serves 'em right! And shame on me for not knowing where to find a pond.

The congregation buzzed with questions and misgivings about this absent minded fellow whom the Bishop had appointed to be their new pastor; and Barbara was appalled and wondered "Dear God, what have I done marrying this man?"

It was my good fortune that the people in that church were too surprised for words and must have thought they would stick around out of sheer curiosity to see what other zany things I might do.

In spite of that colossal fiasco, God was merciful to me . . . and to the congregation . . . and we enjoyed a significantly successful time together over the next three years. The First Presbyterian Church, no doubt having heard of the antics of the Methodist's pulpit clown, nevertheless struck a bargain between the two congregations and agreed to "share this minister" between their congregations. Hence, I had full clergy orders as a *bona fide* ordained elder in both the Methodist and Presbyterian denominations simultaneously and we formed the Canton Ecumenical Parish which grew to a combined constituency of over nine hundred souls and became the strongest religious enterprise in southeast Bradford County. But that's another story. No, it's a whole series of stories for some other time. You can read part of that story in the next chapter of this book.

*   *   *

Jack Lockledge, his wife Ann, and their three elementary school aged boys lived on Minnequa Ave., just two houses south of the playground. Our youngest son, Mark Bradley, soon became a close friend of the Lockledge youngsters; and we grew very quickly to enjoy the friendship of the Lockledges who became our closest parishioners both spatially and socially. Jack was the new Principal of the Canton Elementary School and his wife Ann was also a school teacher.

The Superintendent of the Canton School District, Mr. Torrence Keeler and his family, who were also members of the Methodist Church, lived across the street from the Lockledges, and Mr. John Hyde who was the Principal of the Canton area High School and his wife Marcella, who was also a school teacher, lived on North Center Street just a couple houses south of the Methodist Church. There were a significant number of other school teachers in the Methodist congregation, and since I had taught school in Seattle, it was easy for me to relate to this fine group of educators, and it was an honor for me that both Jack Lockledge and John Hyde invited me to serve as a substitute teacher in their respective schools. In fact, at the suggestion of one of these teachers, Mr. Donald Ayers, who was head of the high school English department, he and Principal Hyde instituted an English course on *The Holy Bible as Literature*, and I was hired as a part-time teacher for that special course.[1] Don Ayers' wife Larene was also a teacher and both of them taught Sunday Classes, and a number of Larene's relatives were also active in the Methodist Church.

Jack Lockledge was an active member of the Canton Rotary as were several members of both the Methodist and Presbyterian Churches, and he and Ann also had a membership in The Wheel, which was a private social club about sixteen miles south of Canton. The Wheel was a restaurant and "watering hole" where most of the socially prominent citizens of Canton and the surrounding area gathered for dining, dancing and social events. Jack sang in the church choir and both he and Ann taught Sunday School classes. They also socialized with the members of the adult Bible Study class, which was presided over by the former Elementary School Principal, Albert Wrisley. It was through Jack and a couple of other good and loyal parishioners that I was kept informed about some of the derogatory and undermining lobbying against the cooperative ministry with the Presbyterians that, under Wrisley's prompting and encouragement, was fostered within that particular Sunday School class. Jack also shared with me some of the political dynamics that made his job more difficult because of a position that the local School Board had created to make a place for Wrisley when the Public School Board replaced him with Jack Lockledge as the new Principal.

Jack had been brought to Canton because of his outstanding record as an educator and school administrator, and it was under Jack's leadership that the School Board approved the building of a brand new elementary school whose design incorporated the "open school" design and concept of team teaching. There were no walls in the new elementary school except those surrounding the kindergarten area and the administrative offices. All of the teaching/learning areas were open, without any walls or partitions separating them. Teachers planned and taught "units" of subject materials that could be presented in small "conversation pit" areas recessed into the floor, and teaching materials were shared by several classes with students rotating around the building to various learning stations much as is done in high school or college settings. It was a fascinating and stimulating experience for me to substitute on several occasions in that kind of a learning environment. At that time neither Jack nor I had any idea that fifteen years later Jack would become the Principal of our St. Andrew's United Methodist Parochial School in Annapolis, Maryland.

I had kept in contact with Jack over the intervening years, and during Lent in 1986 I picked up the phone on an impulse and called Jack to wish him a happy Easter. He asked me what I was doing and I told him about the pre-school and elementary parochial school which we had founded as part of the Christian Education and community outreach program of the St. Andrew's United Methodist Church in Annapolis, Maryland, and about the handsome new church complex we were developing on a fifteen-acre campus in the Maryland State Capital. We had started the school with only two little pre-school girls who were the first to enroll in our summer child-care "camp" the previous year. During that summer the enrollment grew to 19 and when the new school year began that September, nearly 50 children had been enrolled in kindergarten through sixth grade. By spring the enrollment had continued to grow passing the one hundred fifty mark, and it looked like the school had the potential of starting the following fall with an enrollment between two hundred fifty and three hundred. I had been the first Headmaster of the new school and had personally written the school's application for accreditation by the Maryland State Department of Education.

I invited Jack to be our guest over the Easter holiday weekend, to visit our new facilities, to meet the faculty and staff of our St. Andrew's Parochial School, and to meet with members of the congregation's Parish Staff Relations Committee, the Christian Education Committee and the Parochial School's Board of Directors. We negotiated a contract with Jack for him to serve as the Principal of the School beginning in the fall of 1987. While in Canton Jack had completed his Doctor of Education degree and had acquired a reputation as an outstanding Elementary School Principal and one of the creative and innovative pioneers in the development of the "open space" pedagogy which had been initiated, tested and refined in the model school he had administered in Canton.

Jack's experience and expertise were invaluable in helping our new school achieve full academic accreditation not only with the Maryland Department of Education but also with the Mid-Atlantic Public School Accrediting Association. That was a coveted achievement which many of the older prestigious private and parochial elementary schools had not obtained. An excerpt from the school's website reports the following achievements:

> St. Andrew's United Methodist Day School opened on May 6, 1985 as a child development center and was also licensed as a summer camp under the *Maryland Department of Health*

and Mental Hygiene. In response to interest from parents and the congregation's dedication to providing a quality education in a Christian environment, the church expanded the educational program to include a preschool, kindergarten, and elementary school. The school met all standards set forth by the **Maryland State Department of Education** and received full accreditation on June 30, 1988. In the fall of 1996, the school expanded to include a middle school. The school received its accreditation from the **Association of Independent Maryland Schools**, *AIMS*, in June of 1997.

Our second accreditation was awarded by **AIMS** in June, 2007. St. Andrew's is one of a select few independent Maryland schools that has also received accreditation by the international organization, **Middle States Commission on Elementary Schools**. In recognition of the school's environmental program, the **Maryland Association of Environmental and Outdoor Education, MAEOE**, awarded St. Andrew's their Green School award in May, 2008.[2]

The school grew so fast that within the third year four large trailers were leased for portable classrooms, a playground was developed and the parking area was blacktopped through a generous gift of one of the parish families. The core curriculum included a religious education segment utilizing the Lutheran parochial school religious studies, and in addition to the basic study courses that paralleled the public schools of Anne Arundel County, the curriculum was enriched by offering ballet, arts and crafts, computer science, the foreign languages of Spanish, French and German, and music appreciation which was taught by the church's organist-choir director, Mrs. Dorothy Preisser.

Dr. Lockledge began aggressively to expand the school's library and textbook acquisitions and to institute some of the policies and practices that had proven so successful in the model "open space" school where he had been the Principal in Canton, Pennsylvania. The school's excellent reputation grew, and soon the local St. Mary's Roman Catholic parochial school and some of the neighboring private schools began referring their enrollment overflow to St. Andrew's parochial school. A good collegiality with the Annapolis community has been fostered by the St. Andrew's Church and its school.

Over the past two decades the St. Andrew's parochial school has continued to grow and to enlarge its faculty, to expand and enrich its curricula, to develop an enviable sports program and to erect several new school buildings on the church/school campus. Today the enrollment of the St. Andrew's parochial school is between four hundred to five hundred students. The combined assets of the church and its school have increased to surpass the $5,000,000 mark, and the congregation has been able to complete the interior of the Sanctuary building, expand its evangelism and missions programs, increase its membership to over five hundred sixty-five active parishioners and it continues growing with a promising future ahead as it moves forward into this 21st Century. Dr. Jack Lockledge also set a noble example as a Christian layman taking his place within our congregation and faithfully, as he had done in Canton, he sang in the Chancel Choir and participated enthusiastically in the parish activities.

In the summer of 1989 I accepted the position as the Director of Pastoral Care and Counseling at the Charlestown Community in Baltimore, Maryland and served as the "organizing pastor" of the Charlestown United Protestant Church, but Dr. Lockledge remained as the Principal and the key administrator of the St. Andrew's Parochial School in Annapolis until a few years later when he retired for the second time and moved to Florida. Over the years we continue to correspond and occasionally to phone one another, but I shall always count Jack among those special parishioners without whose loyal support we never would have been able to achieve the goals we were able to reach in our ministry as workers together with Christ.

NOTES:

[1] In today's secular anti-Christian world such a course would be challenged by the negative political activism and anti-religious litigation of the ACLU and other far-left secularists who are hell-bent on forcing an unconstitutional exclusion of all religious life from the public arena. Such a cordial and supportive affirmation of the place of religion in our American life and culture as existed in the Canton School District at that time is almost unheard of in American public schools nowadays.

[2] Visit the St. Andrew's UM Day School's website at: **http://www.standrewsum.org/ Home.html** and visit the St. Andrew's United Methodist Church's website at: *http:// www.standrewsum.org.*

Orlo G. McCoy, MD

CHAPTER 8

ORLO G. McCOY

ORLO G. MCCOY, MD, was a member of the **First Presbyterian Church, Canton, Pennsylvania.** He maintained his offices in his home on North Center Street in the next block north of the Presbyterian Church. Dr. McCoy became not only our family physician, but he also became my most trusted confidant and consultant regarding the politics of the Canton community and the two congregations that I served as Senior Pastor.

The Presbyterian and Methodist Churches were situated on Union Street just one-half block from each other. The Presbyterians had constructed a beautiful stone building with a handsome tower and spire that was patterned after a Presbyterian Church in Scotland. The men of that congregation used horse-drawn wagons to bring tons of native rock down off the surrounding mountains and built a beautiful and substantial structure which followed the lines of classical church architecture found in the United Kingdom. Like the other mainline churches in town, the Presbyterian Church edifice was graced by beautiful stained glass windows and a splendid pipe organ, and the choir was seated in a loft behind the high central pulpit. The rear wall of the nave was constructed of large folding doors that opened upon a large hall surrounded by Sunday School rooms. There was a formal reception room with a fireplace across from the main tower entrance, and from the Narthex a stairway led to the Pastor's Study and a small parish office. More Sunday School rooms were arranged around the fairly large Parish Hall and church kitchen in the undercroft below the Nave. A manse (parson's residence) was located just north of the church.

The membership of the Presbyterian congregation paralleled that of the Methodist Church with around three hundred twenty-five members, among whom were two physicians, Dr. Elwood Slingerland and Dr. Orlo McCoy. Other members were Dr. Dorothy Dan Bullock who was President of the National Federation of Women's Associations and an ambassador to the United Nations UNESCO, Dr. Russell Stetler who was a former Superintendent of Canton Schools, a pharmacist Bill Most, a mortician Dean Morse, the town postmaster James Taylor, a number of businessmen including a couple of millionaires who owned and operated two of the factories in the area, and several public school teachers.

Dr. Stetler was a staunch Presbyterian, and when he had the opportunity to select a teacher from among several candidates for public school faculty positions, usually the preferential nod was given the one who showed an interest in the Presbyterian Church. Dr. Stetler was followed by a new Superintendent, Mr. Till Williamee, who was the son of a circuit riding Methodist minister and, as could be expected, the number of Methodists among the local school faculties grew to rival the number of Presbyterians. There was a keen competition and rivalry among the churches which was typical of the sectarianism that marked the era prior to the emergence of the ecumenical movement during the last half of the past century with the formation of the World Council of Churches, the Council of Churches in the USA, the Churches of Christ Uniting (COCU), and local Councils of Churches and ministerial associations across the country.

Because of the conservative Scot background of Presbyterianism, and because of their astute attention to the matters of Christian stewardship and careful management of their tithes and offerings, the Presbyterian Session (Board of Ruling Elders) could see the handwriting on the wall when some of their wealthiest members moved to Florida and their membership and financial resources began to shrink, while at the same time the costs of providing a parsonage and a minister's stipend continued to climb ever upward. When the Session learned that their minister was planning to accept the call to another congregation, the Session agreed to request informal discussions with their Methodist neighbors about the possibility of having their two churches "share" a minister. Presumably such an arrangement would reduce the related costs required for a minister's salary, housing expenses, medical insurance, pension retirement, travel allowance, continuing education allowance, secretarial help & office expenses incurred by each congregation as established by their respective denominations. Because of the long-standing rivalry between the two congregations, the Methodists were extremely reluctant to accept any arrangement that might give an edge to the Presbyterians. However, since "ecumenism" was the politically correct focus to which each denomination had given lip service, the Methodists yielded and agreed to a temporary "trial" accommodation to see how such a "shared minister" might work out.

Nevertheless, secretly, several of the Methodist's key congregational leaders had determined that they would do everything they could to "torpedo" such an arrangement within the first few months.

The arrangement that was agreed upon provided that the minister and his family would reside in the Methodist parsonage but the pastor would have his study in the Presbyterian Church and the Presbyterians could rent out their manse to help provide for their part of the minister's salary. I was granted full ordained "teaching elder" clergy orders in the Presbytery of Lackawanna, Synod of Pennsylvania, Presbyterian Church in the United States of America (PCUSA), and on the first Sunday in October during an "ecumenical" service I was duly installed as the pastor of the First Presbyterian Church.

The arrangement permitted the Presbyterians to accrue sufficient funds to redecorate the Sanctuary and Parish Hall and to remodel the church kitchen in the undercroft. When the work was accomplished the refurbished church truly shined and I was delighted that my office was located in that building which was about half-way between our parsonage residence and the downtown shopping district. For me it was an ideal situation. I had been keenly interested in engaging in an "ecumenical" ministry back when we were exploring the possibility of developing the Lake Boren Ecumenical Parish on the east side of Lake Washington across from Seattle, Washington. Now I was going to have the opportunity to engage in an ecumenical ministry in my home conference. It would be different from the older typical "union church" federations, "yoked parishes," or one of the earlier forms of interdenominational cooperative ministries—this would be a prototype of a truly *"ecumenical* parish" which united the resources and activities of congregations from one or more denominations while preserving the theological integrity and ecclesiastical affiliations of each church.

Dr. McCoy became a very integral part of the development of the *Canton Ecumenical Parish.* With his keen insights into human nature and his knowledge of both the town and church politics, as well as his clear understanding of the theological distinctives and contributions of each ecclesiastical entity, he provided a very effective liaison to me, to the Presbyterian Session and congregation, and to his friends and patients who were members of the other churches in town. Because of his professional knowledge, wisdom and personal integrity, he was trusted and respected by the townspeople of Canton. Although he is not specifically mentioned in the saga which follows, his personal influence and imprimatur helped make this venture a success.

*   *   *

One day while I was exploring and rummaging around in the undercroft of the Presbyterian Church I noticed that an area of the floor was covered over by sheets of plywood. When I asked the Sexton, Charles Tarbox, about the loose sheets of plywood, he explained that beneath them was an old bowling lane! When he uncovered the hardwood lane for me I asked him if it would be a lot of trouble and expense to refurbish the old bowling lane. He assured me that a little elbow grease and some cleaning materials were all that was needed. Even the old bowling balls and ten-pins were in usable condition. It was then that the spark of an idea was ignited in my cranium and the birth of the Canton Ecumenical Parish Youth Center was begun.

It was a serious, embarrassing and often a heart-rending problem for the community that there were an inordinately high number of illegitimate un-wed pregnancies among some of the students of the local high school. Other than the theatre, there was no place in the community where the teenagers of the community could gather, so after high school football and basketball games, the common thing was for those with cars to head up into the hills around the town and to congregate in off-the-road hideaways where they would get drunk and make babies—two very bad and destructive behavior patterns. It occurred to me that if we could convert the basement of the Presbyterian Church into a Youth Center where the teens of the community could gather after school to study and socialize on weeknights and after ball games on the weekends, perhaps we could make a difference in the lives of the youth of the community.

The Presbyterians had rented out the classrooms and auditorium space in the undercroft of their church for use by the Canton public elementary school during the interim period while their new elementary school was being constructed. After the new school was opened, only a handful of children used the undercroft for one hour on Sunday mornings and the rest of the time the undercroft just sat empty gathering dust and clutter. When I presented the idea of remodeling the undercroft and utilizing it as a Parish and Community Youth Center, a couple of the Sunday School teachers protested asking what would become of their Sunday School Classes. I suggested that we broach the matter to the United Methodists and request that they permit the Presbyterian Church to unite its Sunday School Classes with those which met in the United Methodist Educational building at the end of the block and that the Presbyterian Sunday School teachers "team teach" with the Methodist Sunday School teachers. Since several of the Sunday School teachers from both churches taught side-by-side in the new open-space elementary school, it was an obvious solution that would be advantageous to both congregations and to the community, so the Methodists quickly accepted the proposal.

I invited the youth and their adult sponsors from both congregations to meet together to discuss and plan the remodeling of the Presbyterian basement undercroft and to design a program of appropriate activities that would be open to all of the youth of the community.

Youth and adults from both churches gathered together over the next couple of weeks to refurbish the old bowling alley, remodel the church kitchen, and create a "coffee house" with checkered tablecloths and candles atop upended surplus electric cable spools acquired from the local power company. There was a little stage in the undercroft beneath the chancel area of the sanctuary above, which could serve as a place for musical groups and performers to play for Saturday evening sock-hops and square dances, and for the performance of stage plays. When the Canton Ecumenical Parish Youth Center opened, it was a thriving success. The kids managed their own food concession providing soft drinks, pizzas, soup and spaghetti suppers, finger foods and potato chips, and they soon had a burgeoning business. It was not unusual for over three hundred young people to gather at the Youth Center after ball games. Some kids would even drop in for a couple of hours on their way home from school on weekdays to bowl or play table games or have a Coke or Pepsi and chips, as they chatted, read or studied together

When some of the other churches in town became worried that they might not be able to compete with the newly formed Canton Ecumenical Parish and its growing youth program, I assured my clergy colleagues in the local ministerium that it was not our intent to proselytize their members, and I invited them to join me as consultants to the new ecumenical ministries and to appoint one youth and a youth counselor from their respective congregations to serve on our Canton Ecumenical Youth Council. That gesture diffused the typical rivalries that so often thwart a concerted and united Christian witness in the cities and communities of our nation. With the establishing of that relationship among the churches, a new spirit of mutual trust and ecumenical cooperation was fostered and each of the churches began to experience a renewed spirit of interest and vitality.

Neither the Methodist nor the Presbyterian congregations by themselves could sustain a full choir nor afford to hire a choir director, so in each church the organists did double-duty, also serving as choir directors. It occurred to me that if the two choirs were to join together, they would have a full-voiced choir and they might be able to afford a part-time choir director, provided that the united choirs would sing at both worship services. The local high school music teacher, Mrs. Beverly Madigan, was hired as the new parish choir director. Beverly was an enthusiastic and capable musician, and under her able leadership it was not long before the congregations asked her to direct a youth choir, then a children's choir, and finally a "cherub choir" for pre-school children.

Mrs. Madigan brought to the youth choir youngsters who sang in the high school choirs, and the youth choir performed Christian musicals like *Joseph and the Amazing Technicolor Dreamcoat,* which was performed in both of the parish churches and also in churches of the neighboring towns of Troy and Blossburg, Pennsylvania. On Sunday mornings the adult choir and children's choir would sing in one service and the youth choir and the cherub choir would sing at the other church. Because a number of families had children who sang in the youth choir as well as the children's choir or the cherub choir, the parents wanted to hear each of their children sing so they would attend both worship services! As a result the attendance at both services swelled and the excitement and enthusiasm for public worship grew as word spread throughout the community about what was happening in the newly formed Canton Ecumenical Parish.

The Presbyterian Sunday morning worship service was at 8:30 AM, the united Ecumenical Parish Sunday School met at 9:45 AM, and the Methodist worship service was at 11:00 AM. Every three months the congregations would reverse their worship times so that both congregations took their turn worshipping at the early and traditional hours. On Palm Sunday and on many other occasions when the weather was good, the combined robed choirs would march arm-in-arm the one-half block distance between their respective church buildings. It was a Sunday morning parade that caught the attention of the community.

*   *   *

With the aid of federal funding through HUD and by the initiative and commitment of one of our Presbyterian laymen, Elwin Loomis, a new 30-unit apartment building for senior citizens was constructed near the center of town. But like many elderly persons, the senior residents remained for the most part "holed up" in their apartments or homes and seldom if ever gathered together as a group. They simply had no place to go. It came as a natural sequel to the establishment of the Ecumenical Parish Youth Center that the senior citizens of the community should also enjoy a place where they too could gather for fellowship and entertainment.

An open invitation was extended from the pulpits of both congregations to all senior citizens to gather in the Presbyterian Church Parlor to explore together the possibility of forming a Canton Senior Citizens Association. Only six persons including myself met at that first gathering. Those who attended were discouraged and exclaimed: "See, nobody is interested in us senior citizens—not even those who are themselves elderly persons." I tried to encourage them by remarking that, "Maybe it was the weather and maybe we didn't advertise our meeting well enough; let's give it another try."

Two weeks later we met again and this time only three more persons gathered with us. "How are we ever going to get the senior citizens to come together in this town?" they asked.

"Well, everybody has to eat," I suggested; "Let's send out invitations to all the senior citizens to attend a "Potluck Dinner that will be especially "for Senior Citizens only" to be held in the Ecumenical Parish Youth Center in the Presbyterian Church undercroft.

We published an open invitation to Senior Citizens in the local newspaper, and we requested that the other pastors announce the event in their Sunday morning worship services and in their church's bulletins and newsletter. We set the occasion for Valentine's Day and, in spite of the winter weather, about sixty-five people showed up, each carrying a dish to add to the smorgasbord buffet. We had planned a short program of entertainment which was presented from the little stage in the Center, and to our delight everyone seemed to have a wonderful time—perhaps even to their own surprise! It was unanimously decided to hold another potluck dinner the following month, and the next time the attendance increased. Although the group was sponsored by our Canton Ecumenical Parish, the Senior Citizens Association, as with the youth group, was thrown open to all of the senior residents in Canton and the surrounding countryside without regard to their church affiliation, and over time the group grew to over one hundred fifty people. Again, as with the youth, the pastors of the other churches were invited to participate as co-sponsors of this new senior activity.

*   *   *

One of our neighbors who lived across the street from the Methodist parsonage was a member of the Episcopal Congregation whose small but well designed little church building was located back-to-back in the same block as the United Methodist Church. The Episcopal congregation had shrunk to only four active members, and since it was so removed at the far western boundary of the Diocese of Scranton, the Bishop decided to close the church and listed it for sale on the open real estate market. Our neighbor came to me heartbroken over the demise of his beloved Episcopal Church and lamented that he had heard a rumor that one renegade churchman wanted to purchase the church and use it as a vantage point from which to take potshots at our Ecumenical Parish; and that he also knew that other potential buyers had expressed an interested in buying the church building and converting it into secular uses as either a small sewing factory, or worse yet, as a tavern! He begged me to intervene somehow.

When I telephoned the Episcopal Bishop in Scranton and expressed an interest in acquiring the church building and converting it into a Community Center under the auspices of our Canton Ecumenical Parish, the Bishop informed me that it was listed for sale at $40,000. I stated that the building was in need of repairs and that we would have to invest several thousands of dollars to upgrade the church's kitchen to meet current building and safety

codes, and that it most likely would soon need a new roof. I also explained that
our financial resources were limited. He asked me what I thought we could
afford. When I suggested that $4,000 would be a stretch for our fledgling
Ecumenical Parish Youth and Senior Citizens Association, to my happy
surprise he agreed and invited me to submit an earnest money agreement for
that amount to the local realtor who was handling the listing. I had no idea
where we might acquire even the $4,000, but nevertheless I filed an earnest
money agreement and a note for $400 (*due and payable upon the exercise of
the purchase option tendered herewith*—a device I had previously utilized in
acquiring a purchase contract for the building site of the Fairwood Community
United Methodist Church, Renton. Washington). When news traveled by the
grape-vine that I had placed a valid earnest money agreement on the Episcopal
Church but that I didn't have a nickel with which to actually purchase the
property, some of our detractors in the United Methodist clique that opposed
the Ecumenical Parish quipped that I had just demonstrated what a fool I was,
that my unilateral effort would fall flat, and I would be disgraced. To my happy
surprise and to the amazement and dismay of our detractors, the Manager of
the local electric power company who was a member of the Disciples of Christ
Church, knocked on our parsonage door and offered to donate the entire $4,000
in memory of his recently deceased father! I thanked him for his generous offer
and suggested to him that I would like to give the members of the community
an opportunity to contribute toward the purchase of our new Ecumenical Parish
Community Center. He agreed and promised that if there were any shortfall
of funds necessary to acquire and remodel the church building, he would be
glad personally to cover the required amount.

The Episcopal Bishop made a trip from Scranton to Canton and conducted
a "deconsecration" service and turned the keys and the contents of the building
of the old church over to our parish. We salvaged some of the sacramental items
like the *pre duex* prayer bench, the paraments, etc. and transferred them to
the Presbyterian Church (I still have in my study the antique wooden candle
holders from the altar of that old Episcopal Church.) Adults and youth from
the community worked together to transform the old church into a suitable
Community Center. The former sanctuary made an excellent auditorium; the
former parish hall had served as a small gymnasium and was excellent for
recreational activities; and the basement kitchen located under the former
chancel area was remodeled to meet the health and safety requirements of
the local building code.

* * *

Canton was predominantly a conservative Republican community which
had traditionally refused to accept grants of any kind from the Democratic

administrations of Franklin Delano Roosevelt and his Democratic presidential successors in Washington, DC or from the local Democratic County Commissioners. Out of pride and a stubborn Yankee bull-headedness, the community fathers had rejected an earlier offer of federal funds to repair and expand its sewer lines and other infrastructures and, as a consequence, had forfeited several millions of dollars in funds that included part of their own federal and state tax monies. When I determined to apply to the County Commissioners for a grant to establish a Meals-on-Wheels program and a Congregate Meals program for the senior citizens and the medically home-bound residents of the Canton Community, the clique of detractors again made fun of our efforts and predicted that our attempt to gain any funding from the Democrat Commissioners would prove futile. To their amazement, the County Commissioners visited our new Ecumenical Parish Community Center and after inspecting the premises, they made an initial grant of $7,000 to underwrite the initiation of the Meals-on-Wheels proposal I had submitted. Volunteers from the community, under the inspirational leadership of Mrs. Wilma Morgan, wife of the town Chief of Police and the President of the Senior Citizens Association, staffed the Community Center's kitchen where the Meals-on-Wheels dinners were prepared and a fleet of other volunteers used their own cars to deliver the meals to appreciative recipients.

During the summer of 2006 my wife and I stopped in Canton on our way from our home in Fort Wayne, Indiana to visit my brother's family in Lancaster, Pennsylvania. We were happy to find the Canton Community Center open and were delighted to see the improvements to the building and the expansion of the community programs that had been made over the years. Now the Center's programs also include the operation of a "community pantry" and a "used clothing outlet" serving Canton and the surrounding area. When the manager of the Center learned that I was the founder of the Canton Ecumenical Parish and its Community Center, a reporter from the local newspaper was called and a photographer soon arrived to take my photograph. One of the parishioners clipped and mailed to me a copy of the news story about my visit that appeared in the local newspaper a few days later. It was a great joy and satisfaction to me to learn that our efforts three decades earlier had borne fruit that still continues to carry forward a ministry to that community in Christ's Name.

*   *   *

One day, quite unexpectedly, I began to experience severe chest pains, and thinking that perhaps I was having a heart attack, Barbara called Dr. McCoy, who came quickly making a house call at the parsonage. (Some doctors in small towns still made house calls in the early 1970s.) Upon examining me, he diagnosed my pain as being a severe attack of pleurisy. He realized that the inflammation of my chest wall and the pain were symptomatic of the strain and stress which had accumulated as a result of the mounting pressure from the opposition generated by a clique of detractors within the Methodist Church and by the sheer workload that increased with the growth of the parish. Doc McCoy was candid and firm in warning me that if I did not somehow find a way to handle the growing load of pastoral responsibility and manage to deal with the small but influential cadre of dissidents within the Methodist congregation, the mounting stress could in all probability lead to a heart attack or some other debilitating physical problems.

The opposition to the Ecumenical Parish centered around Albert Wrisley and his Methodist Adult Sunday School Class, and that dissension was fomented by Dick Franklin who was the manager of a local milk processing plant and the Chairman of the Administrative Council. Aware of the growing success and obvious enthusiasm and support from the Canton community for the Canton Ecumenical Parish and its multi-faceted outreach ministries, the clandestine "old guard" within the Methodist congregation was determined not to be obsolesced by a possible merger of their congregation with the Presbyterians. They rightly reasoned that the Presbyterian Church was for many apparent reasons the superior and more economical to maintain of the two buildings, and in the event of a merger their termite infested and deteriorating building would not likely be the structure of choice. In an attempt to dig their heels in and to further entrench their hold on their beloved frame building, the trustees violated the corporate and canon law (*Book of Discipline*) of the Methodist denomination and proceeded with an unauthorized expenditure of over $30,000 to replace the furnace in the church's basement. They believed that such an investment would certainly justify their claim of the suitability of their building and would discourage the other members of the congregation from considering a merger with the Presbyterians under the Canton Ecumenical Parish umbrella. However, time would prove them wrong and eventually the two congregations merged. In time, the old clapboard church building was sold to a Mennonite congregation whose workmen made a considerable investment of time and money to insulate and upgrade the wooden frame structure.

*　　*　　*

Fortunately, in the providence of God, while we were remodeling and redecorating the Presbyterian Church I had the fortuitous opportunity to meet the Rev. Badon Brown, brother of the interior designer who was in charge of the redecorating/painting of the Presbyterian Church's sanctuary. I learned that Rev. Brown had been the Senior Pastor of the Highland Park Baptist Church in Detroit, Michigan which was one of the emerging mega-churches with over two thousand members, a parochial kindergarten through 12th grade school, an hour-long live radio broadcast every Sunday evening, a large professional staff, and a congregation that included some of the influential industrialists associated with the automobile industry of Detroit. When I learned who Badon was and that he was at the time serving only part-time as interim pastor of a small rural Baptist Church near his boyhood home about ten miles from Canton, I managed to persuade him to serve as the Associate Minister of our Canton Ecumenical Parish, at least on a part-time basis. He and his wife Marion accepted the primary responsibility for the development of a special ministry to the young married couples and their families within our parish. As with the Ecumenical Parish's ministries to the youth and senior citizens of the parish, this outreach ministry rapidly grew and was thrown open to the young and middle-age parents of the community. Like our other parish ministries, this program attracted couples and families from some of the other churches and from the community at large. Badon's ministry was for me a real God-send. Later on, when I was serving the St. Andrew's United Methodist Church in Annapolis, Badon and his wife who were then living in New Jersey once again became part of our professional staff and accepted pastoral responsibility for the same age-group to whom he had so successfully ministered in Canton. Eventually Badon accepted the pastorate of a Baptist Church close to the Lakehurst Naval Air Station made famous by the Hindenburg zeppelin disaster. Badon continued to pastor that congregation until his retirement and relocation to Aiken, South Carolina.

*   *   *

Doc McCoy realized that part of the strain of my pastoral workload was directly related to the distance, time and cost associated with making pastoral calls upon parishioners who were hospitalized. Since there was no hospital in Canton or any of the closer small towns, Doc's patients were sent to one of the hospitals of their choosing either in Williamsport, Pennsylvania, twenty-five miles to the south; to Sayre, Pennsylvania, forty-five miles to the northeast; to Wellsboro, Pennsylvania, thirty-five miles to the west; or to Elmira, New York, thirty miles to the north; and some patients traveled to the Geisinger Cancer Center or the State Hospital in Danville, Pennsylvania which was about seventy miles south of Canton. Trips to these widely separated hospitals required at least a half-day's time and even when I planned to make a wide loop to visit parishioners in more than one hospital in a single day, it required a great deal of time and was costly as well. On Sunday mornings or at odd hours I would receive word that some parishioner was in one of the hospitals, and it followed as a matter of course that I was expected by some persons to immediately drop everything and make a quick emergency trip to the designated hospital to check up on the welfare of the particular parishioner. Doc overheard someone giving me the news (gossip) about so-and-so who was in such-and-such a hospital and urging me to get myself over to visit that parishioner pronto. Doc took me aside and said, "David, I get the same kind of information about my patients as you do about your parishioners, and do you know what I do?"

"What?" I asked.

"I tell the caller or the informer of such news that I sincerely regret that the patient is ill, and I will pray for them and wish them the very best in their recovery. But I don't immediately drop everything and go ambulance chasing! Unless the patient specifically telephones me or a member of their immediate family phones me about some life-threatening emergency, I will have them make an appointment to come to my office where I will examine them and prescribe an appropriate medication or medical procedure. If they need surgery I will refer them to one of the physicians or surgeons located in the town of the hospital of their choosing, and I will phone that doctor and turn the care of that patient over to the professional attention of that doctor or surgeon. I will only make hospitals visits if I am requested to do so by that physician or surgeon or if I am personally directly involved in their post-op follow-up care through their referral back to me by the other doctor." Then he cautioned me, "David, if you don't stop trying to visit every one of your parishioners who enters a hospital you are going to kill yourself trying. What you need to do is to request that if a parishioner knows in advance that they are going to a hospital for selective or required surgery, they should let you know well in advance and make an appointment either at your office in the church or at your mutual convenience to go to their home and administer to them the Sacrament of Holy Communion and pray with them; and then you need to turn them over to the care of the Great Physician and to the spiritual care of the chaplain on duty at the hospital in which they are to be entered." Doc McCoy was an enormous help to me by sharing that good counsel with me. I was then free to make hospital and house calls on a more productive basis.

Doc asked me an intriguing question one day: "David," he asked me, "do you know the difference between your job and mine?"

"No, what is the difference, Doc?" I replied.

"Well, we are both engaged in practicing the healing arts. I practice medicine and you practice theology. We refer to our respective professions as a *practice* precisely because neither medicine nor theology is an exact science. They both are a mixture of science, the art of human relations, faith and a mix of good luck and God's mercy. I am a "body-and-parts" mechanic, but instead of repairing automobiles I work on the human "bodies and parts" of my patients. You, on the other hand, have to deal with the illnesses of the mind, the soul and the spirit of your parishioners. When one of my patients does not respond to medical treatment and dies, we just call the undertaker. But when one of your parishioners does not respond the psycho-pneumatic treatment and the Scriptural remedies that you prescribe . . . they just go to hell!"

Of course I laughed at his diagnosis; but the more I have thought about it the more Doc's words have driven home to me the tremendous responsibility that is incumbent upon every clergyman for the welfare of his parishioners' everlasting and immortal spirits. And all the more earnestly I have prayed to God for the knowledge and wisdom and professional skill and integrity to fulfill to the very best of my ability my responsibility for the spiritual welfare of those entrusted to me for pastoral care and spiritual nurturing.

After we moved from Canton to a pastorate in Middletown, Pennsylvania, and later in Baltimore, Maryland, Dr. McCoy kept in contact with us. Whenever he would travel to the Harrisburg, Pennsylvania area to attend the annual meeting of the Pennsylvania Medical Association, he would phone me and extend his personal invitation for me to be his personal guest at the PMA conventions. After I earned my Doctor of Ministry degree from Drew University, whenever he would introduce me to his medical colleagues Doc McCoy would with a twinkle in his eye present me as Doctor C. David Jones from Middletown, Pennsylvania. When his colleagues would inquire regarding the nature of my particular medical specialization, Doc would quip, "Oh, Dr. Jones is in *family practice.*" Since family practice had become one of the fields of medical specialization, that designation worked quite well until on one occasion one of the physicians to whom Dr. McCoy introduced me said with a keen interest, "That's great, I'm in family practice also. Where did you train?" Doc just grinned and then he explained that I had trained at the Theological Seminary of Drew University in Madison, New Jersey and that I was formerly his pastor at the First Presbyterian Church in Canton, Pennsylvania, where he practiced medicine.

After me moved from Middletown, Pennsylvania to pastor churches in the Baltimore-Washington Conference of the United Methodist Church, Doc McCoy, his vivacious wife Loreen, and their teenage daughter Enola made a special trip all the way from Canton to our home on Rumsey Island in Joppatowne, Maryland. It was Doc's way of demonstrating his friendship and his interest in my career as a minister of the Gospel of Jesus Christ. Doc never wore his religion on his sleeve, but there was never any doubt in my mind about his deep and abiding religious convictions and his commitment to the Lord whom we both served. He truly was a good physician and a trusted and esteemed friend.

William Boyd

CHAPTER 9

WILLIAM BOYD

WILLIAM BOYD owned and operated a clothing store in the Main Street business district of downtown Canton, Pennsylvania. He was also Chairman of the Administrative Council of the **Ward United Methodist Church, in Ward, Pennsylvania**.

*   *   *

The Ward UMC is a small white frame one-room country church house located high atop a mountain ridge about two miles up a dirt road west of Canton, Pennsylvania. The church was founded and supported by the farming families scattered through the Ward area. They were hardy folks who had learned how to carve out a living from the fields they had cleared and planted with corn and whatever else would grow in that climate. They came to town occasionally to buy groceries and supplies for their small farms. Before the days of automobiles it was not an easy trip to make up and down the mountain roads with a horse and buggy, and travel was especially difficult even with a sleigh in the severe winters of the Pennsylvania Northern Tier country. It was easier for families living in this rugged rural area to build their own church rather than to make the trip to worship in one of the churches in town.

In earlier post-colonial days a pastor might be furnished with a parsonage and a small stipend, but he would be expected to earn part of his income by planting and harvesting his own vegetable garden, keeping a few chickens, maybe a pig and a cow and, of course, a sound horse which he could ride while making the rounds of regular visits to the farms of his parishioners. He might have some other handcraft or skills like a woodworking shop attached to the barn. He might also receive produce and a quarter or side of beef or pork in the fall when the farmers in his parish butchered. In exchange for the largess of his parishioners, he would be expected to help with the harvest as a spare farm hand at haying time and to pitch in at butchering time, etc. His wife would busy herself canning vegetables and fruit just like the farmers' wives of the parish. These small rural churches were the social center for the surrounding farm families, and Sunday afternoon picnics in the spring and summer months and an occasional potluck dinner in the fall and winter months were important events in the life of the parish.

Then when the one-room country school houses began to be consolidated into area wide elementary and high schools located in the larger towns, school busses managed to pick up school children from the rural areas and bring them into town every day of the week.

As automobiles and gas powered tractors became more common and transportation was easier, rather than to continue the back-breaking work required to earn a living by farming, many of the men from rural areas began to travel to the towns and cities to work in factories or wherever other employment could be found. More and more rural families frequented the nearby towns, and their children often chose to live and work in a town rather than to continue farming as their fathers had done. But the ties to the small rural churches were so strong that, although these rural families had no control over the local government and the county public school boards who closed their country schools and consolidated them into the larger school districts, these farming families were determined to keep their rural churches open. After the granges dwindled, the church remained the one last place that these rural families were unwilling to surrender. With a determination and tenacity they clung to their rural churches with a fierce pride and loyalty, and in many cases made significant financial sacrifices to keep them open.

Over the years the little church was kept in good repair, but the congregation was too small to support a full-time pastor. As was often the case, a small rural church would be associated with a larger church in the nearby town, as was the case with the Ward United Methodist Church. Many of these small congregations were served by circuit-riding parsons who traveled from town to town and from one church to another by horseback or by a horse-drawn buggy, and later in their "tin-lizzy" Model T Ford automobiles. Some widely scattered congregations might only have a parson visit them once a month and Holy Communion might be commemorated only once a quarter.

A circuit-riding parson might conduct a worship service in the morning in one church, ride his horse to the next church where he would conduct an afternoon church service, and then ride on to the next church where he would conduct an evening worship service for those rural parishes that were in closer proximity to each other. The Methodists referred to those clusters of churches that were served by a single parson as "multiple point charges." During my career I served three "two-point charges" (Kenneydale and Fairwood UMCs in Washington, Cowenton and Ebenezer UMCs in Maryland, and the Canton and Ward UMCs in Pennsylvania). When the First United Presbyterian Church joined with First UMC and the Ward UMC to form the Canton Ecumenical Parish, that combined parish became a *de facto* "three-point charge." A couple of other clergy colleagues of mine served five-point charges, and those were grueling appointments. Often these small churches ultimately proved to be thankless efforts in futility and in spite of the Herculean efforts made by their pastors and laity, and because of other extenuating circumstances related to a combination of dwindling memberships and finances that posed insurmountable odds, one by one many of those small rural churches have been closed.

*   *   *

At the time the Canton Ecumenical Parish was formed in the fall of 1971, I was conducting a weekly Sunday evening worship service at the Ward United Methodist Church. Quite often I would bring with me soloists or choral groups from the churches in town. For some of the town folks it was a joyful Sunday evening trip up the mountainside, and it was an encouragement to the Ward parishioners to have their church house filled for worship. However, when we invited the Ward parishioners to participate in some of the Ecumenical Parish activities in town, the Ward members were extremely reluctant to reciprocate and it became for the most part a one-way affair. It was understandable that the Ward parishioners would fear that if their children were to participate in the Canton Ecumenical Parish Youth group and attend the Ecumenical Parish's combined Christian Education Sunday School Classes with their public school friends, the Ward youth might develop a closer bonding with the town churches and choose to affiliate more closely with them than with their little rural congregation. It never seemed to have occurred to the Ward congregation that since they wanted the members of the in-town churches to worship with their congregation on Sunday evenings, the Ward members, out of courtesy if nothing else, ought to have shown their appreciation by attending Sunday morning worship at one of the congregations in town. That never happened. However, as the success of the Ecumenical Parish grew, the anxiety and fear of the Ward members that the Conference might close their church and merge their congregation into the Canton Ecumenical Parish seemed to mushroom and turned into a quiet animosity toward their pastor. They never openly expressed to me their fear or their hostility but in a cunning and devious manner they clandestinely registered their request with the District Superintendent that he appoint in my stead a local school teacher who had "the preacher's itch" and aspired to be a "lay-pastor." When I learned about the hostile attitudes of some of the Ward members and that the school teacher would assume the responsibility for that congregation beginning in July of 1972, I considered it a relief. I had enough on my hands as it was without being further burdened with a thankless responsibility for the Ward Congregation; but I remained friendly toward those people and continued to hunt deer around the Ward Church vicinity. (Bradford County has one of the biggest white-tail deer herds in Pennsylvania and my son Dan and I went bow and rifle hunting in the woods around the church and found not only deer sign but evidence that a large size black bear also lived in the woods close by.)

*   *   *

Bill Boyd and his wife had been very cordial toward my wife and me when we first arrived in Canton. Bill was a big help to me in introducing me to the Ward parishioners. The Boyds invited Barbara and me to be guests in their home for some good country cooking. Their neighbor Francis Segur, a dairy farmer who was one of the members of the Ward congregation, loaned me one of his snowmobiles and he and Bill introduced me to that winter sport.

When the annual "Canton Pioneer Days" festival that was sponsored by the local volunteer fire department cordoned off the first block of Main Street for the festival activities, it was Bill and his wife who found Barbara and me and insisted that we engage in the celebration by joining in the popular street dancing, so we took our places in a square dance group and got in the polka and rumba lines along with the other town folks. I had feared that some people might think that it was out of place for a clergyman and his wife to engage in open street-dancing, but the Boyds and other parishioners insisted that it was quite all right and that they hoped that we would enter into the life and community events of the town. After that we were often invited to be chaperones at the high school dances and enjoyed participating in other community events. I am grateful to Bill for his encouragement and for the support and assistance that he gave to me.

Many of the Ward Church parishioners were good, hard working and upright Christian people even though they were averse to closing their church and worshipping in town. I understood their deep emotional ties to their country church and didn't blame them for being loathe to disband and forsake the religious heritage that it represented to them. But what concerned me was that not only were these adult Christians missing out, but it was their children who were being forced to forfeit the spiritual nurture and fellowship that they should have been enjoying with their school-age friends in the town churches. The Ward Church had no Sunday School, no Vacation Bible School, no Women's Missionary Society, no Men's Fellowship—nothing but a Sunday evening service which was discontinued during the hard months of winter when travel on the mountain roads was often treacherous.

As a result of my challenge to parents of the Ward congregation who had children and teenagers that they get their children into Sunday School and the Youth Fellowship in the town churches, some of the parents decided that rather than close their church they would start their own little Sunday School and would conduct a Vacation Bible School during the summer. No doubt, that took a great deal of effort, like home schooling does, but it was a choice they made to justify in part the retention of their country church. I suppose that is to their credit, even though those kinds of ongoing programs are very difficult to sustain over a long haul. Nevertheless, their dedication and determination is to their credit and we laud them for whatever degree of faithfulness to Christ they had that motivated them to undertake the course they chose.

Bill's mother who was a lovely and gregarious Christian woman occasionally attended the Canton Senior Citizens monthly potluck dinners and was friends with many of the town's people. I continued to patronize Bill's store and hoped that we could retain a good relationship with him and the rest of the Ward congregation, but after the school teacher *wanna-be-preacher* took over the Ward church we saw very little of Bill except when we shopped in his store.

For Barbara and me it was one of those disappointing and sad things that sometimes come with the role of pastoral ministry. Some acquaintanceships, though relatively short in duration, develop into lifelong friendships as was the case with the bonds of friendship which I shared with most of the men about whom I have written in this book. Some acquaintanceships tragically end over issues that are inconsequential, much like some marriages that have lasted for many years end in separation and divorce. Other friendships though strong at the outset just drift apart and disintegrate. Because I appreciated Bill Boyd's friendship it was a real disappointment and sadness to me that our friendship was lost along the way, partly because of the provincial pride and sentimental ties of the Ward congregation to their little church building and all of the emotions and good memories they associated with their church during their earlier childhood and bygone days.

It does not have to be that way. Some congregations that have merged or moved to a new and larger building elsewhere have learned that, because of the value of their past legacy and heritage symbolized by a beloved country church, they can still keep the old church house and its adjoining cemetery where family and friends are buried. Instead of just abandoning or tearing down the old church, they conduct a special Sunday afternoon worship service during the summer and have a picnic lunch on the church grounds. In that way they celebrate and honor their earlier religious heritage and they manage to keep the old church property off the public tax rolls even though they have moved on as a congregation to some new site keeping pace with the times and advances of each new generation. That seems to me to be a better way.

Richard Alwine

CHAPTER 10
RICHARD ALWINE

RICHARD ALWINE is a successful owner and manager of a large dairy farm just a stone's throw from the Three Mile Island nuclear reactors along the Susquehanna River south of Middletown, Pennsylvania. The Alwine dairy farm which covers several hundred acres of tillable and pasture land has been owned and operated by the Alwine family for several generations and continues to be one of the model dairy operations in Dauphin County. As with many farming operations, it requires a rigorous regime of year round early rising and long days of hard work, feeding and milking one hundred fifty cows twice a day during the changing seasons of blistering heat under summer sun, through rain, sleet and snow in the fall and winter months and more rain through the spring. It is a never ending cycle which allows little time off and only sparse time for a short few days of vacation whenever the weather and a relief crew of farm hands can permit it.

In addition to his demanding duties as the owner and manager of the Alwine farm, Richard was the Chairman of the Administrative Council of the **Geyer United Methodist Church** which is a rural congregation located half way between **Middletown** and **Elizabethtown, Pennsylvania**. Richard Alwine also served his term of rotation as the Lay Leader of the Geyer Church, and taught a Sunday School class, and was a leading participant in all of the activities of the congregation.

The Geyer Church was founded by the Brethren in Christ denomination which was an offshoot of the Amish and Mennonite groups that migrated to the United States from Europe as part of the sixteenth century Protestant

Reformation. The Mennonites are a group of *Christian Anabaptist* denominations named after *Menno Simons* (1496-1561) who, through his writings, formalized the teachings of earlier Swiss founders. The teachings of the Mennonites were founded on both the ministry and mission of Jesus Christ, to which they adhered with great conviction despite severe persecution by the European states dominated by the Catholic Church. Rather than fight, the majority survived by fleeing to neighboring "states" where ruling families were tolerant of their radical belief in the necessity of the baptism by immersion of adult believers in Christ as their Savior and Sovereign. Over the years, Mennonites have become known as one of the historic *peace churches* which are committed to *nonviolence*, nonviolent resistance/reconciliation, and *pacifism*.[1]

The Brethren in Christ Church began sometime between 1775 and 1788, and the place of origin was near the present town of Marietta in Lancaster County, Pennsylvania.[2] For the most part, the founding mothers and fathers of this denomination had an *Anabaptist* background and were deeply affected by the revivals of the great awakening of the eighteenth century under the preaching of George Whitfield and John Wesley. The *Pietistic* movement was spread in America among the Moravians and German Baptists as well as among the colonial "Methodist" Anglicans. These revivals emphasized a personal, heartfelt conversion experience and a lifetime pursuit of sanctification and holiness living.[3]

The strong and close relationship between the Brethren in Christ and the Wesleyan revival is acknowledged in the following statement taken from their website: "We Brethren in Christ have also been deeply influenced by the teachings of the eighteenth-century British scholar and preacher, John Wesley. The Wesleyan movement in America—also known as the Holiness movement—emphasizes conversion as a conscious acceptance of God, the empowerment of the Holy Spirit, and daily growth in holiness. Brethren in Christ value the free gift of salvation in Christ Jesus and the transforming power of the Holy Spirit and we are unashamed in sharing the Good News of the Gospel with others." [4]

The Geyer Church is only about fifteen miles north along the Susquehanna River above Marietta, Pennsylvania, and it was these Brethren in Christ Christians who built a staunch rural parish at the Geyer country crossroads. It was because of their close association with the Wesleyan revival that the Geyer Congregation through a subsequent series of mergers would eventually affiliate first with the Church of the Brethren, then with the Evangelical United Brethren and eventually with the United Methodist Church and that they would carry with them their pietistic as well as their evangelical heritage. Some of the women in the Geyer UM Congregation still wore the little bonnets traditionally worn by Amish and Mennonite girls and women.

Closely associated with the Brethren in Christ is the United Brethren in Christ denomination.[5] In 1767 an inter-denominational renewal movement was sweeping through the colonies. Back then, Christians would gather in what they called "Great Meetings." These were lively affairs. During the middle of summer, after the spring crops had been planted and before it was time for the fall harvests, old fashioned "camp meetings" were held and several hundred people from all over the area might gather together and spend several days hearing a string of stirring speakers. The people would gather from the surrounding countryside, pitch tents and literally "camp" for a week or more to sing hymns and listen to fiery preachers warn of the punishment of sinners in hell and the reward of the righteous in heaven.

A farmer, Isaac Long, hosted a "Great Meeting" at his big barn in Lancaster, Pennsylvania. Martin Boehm, a Mennonite preacher, related his story of becoming a Christian and a minister. It deeply moved William Otterbein who was a German Reformed pastor. Otterbein rose from his seat, embraced Boehm, and said loudly enough for everyone to hear, "*Wir sind bruder.*" Back then German was spoken in their public worship services as well as in private homes. Otterbein's words declared, "We are brethren."

From this revival movement a new denomination was born, and it took its name from Otterbein's words: United Brethren in Christ.

For a period of time, two denominations used the name "Church of the United Brethren in Christ." In 1946, the other "United Brethren" church merged with the Evangelical Association to form the Evangelical United Brethren Church. Thereafter there was again only one Church of the United Brethren in Christ. The EUBs merged with the Methodist Church in 1968 to form the United Methodist Church.[6]

It was primarily because I wanted to continue graduate theological studies toward a doctoral degree that Bishop John Warman graciously appointed me to the Geyer Congregation in June of 1974. The following September I began meeting with a group of doctoral candidates who studied together in the Harrisburg, Pennsylvania area as one of the newly formed satellite extensions of Drew University's School of Theology. It was while serving the Geyer United Methodist Church that I completed studies for my Doctor of Ministry degree. Dr. James South who was the academic dean of the Pennsylvania State University—The Capital College, otherwise known as the *Harrisburg Campus*, was a great help to me by introducing me to the head of the Department of Computer Science at the Middletown campus. He helped me run a Chi-Square statistical analysis program on the sociological research which was an integral part of my doctoral dissertation, and for their assistance I will ever be grateful to those two men. Dr. South's wife Gail served as my secretary for a while.

The Geyer congregation was a relatively strong and vibrant rural congregation. In addition to several farming families, some of its members worked at the Three Mile Island nuclear plant; others worked at the nearby Hershey chocolate plant; Barbara worked in the Army Logistics Division at the New Cumberland Army Depot, and most of the other members were gainfully employed in the various industries and businesses around the Harrisburg area. The congregation outgrew the original frame structure building which, to the south of the church, was abutted by a large and historic cemetery. The congregation purchased six acres directly across Geyer Road from the old church. The old parsonage was torn down and a handsome new brick parsonage and a contemporary brick church were built. The architect who designed the new church apparently had no experience or training in the design and symbolism that is integral to traditional ecclesiastical architecture, and although the new church was solidly constructed and served the special needs of the congregation, it left a great deal to be desired as related to the aesthetics of its design. From the outside it appears as a big two-story windowless brick box. The only religious symbol to identify it as a church other than the signage on the corner of the church property is a disproportionately small thin spire that juts up from the roof line above a stucco panel displaying the Methodist cross and flame logo.

*　　　*　　　*

It is, however, much to the credit of the congregation and to neighboring friends in the surrounding community that the parishioners were deeply committed to meeting their church's budget, including the full share of their Conference apportionments (ecclesiastical taxation) and the ambitious goal of paying off the mortgage on the church and parsonage within a targeted fifteen-year period. To meet this significant goal, with the assistance and guidance of several of the members who were employed at the Hershey Company, the season of Lent was dedicated not to the traditional period of prayer and fasting, but it became the busiest time of the year for the congregation. In their effort to augment their regular tithes and offerings, the basement of the church was converted into a miniature candy factory that during Lent made literally thousands of delicious Easter Eggs! Over the years the congregation built a wide reputation for its seasonal Easter Eggs and annually earned $15,000 to $25,000 net from the sale of its Easter egg confections. By word-of-mouth advertising of its hand-delivered boxes of candy eggs, the Easter Egg project served not only as a great fund-raiser but it also served as a rallying point for fellowship and fun for everyone in the congregation and for their neighbors and friends as well.

I confess that I always had mixed feelings about this activity since it inadvertently undercut the traditional spiritual emphasis of Lent as a time of preparation for the celebration of Christ's vicarious suffering and death upon the cross. At times I felt that I was Willy Wonka pastoring the Geyer Chocolate Candy Factory instead of the Geyer United Methodist Church. Somehow rationalizing about the necessity and virtue of this collective effort (as being the equivalent of a sacrificial offering of their energies and resources to God) still left me with doubts about the efficacy of this endeavor as an acceptable substitute for a Lenten focus upon prayers of contrition and of meditation upon the supreme sacrifice that Christ offered to purchase our redemption through his suffering and death at Calvary. For me it was a conflicted enterprise, but one with which I found it difficult to argue inasmuch as expediency seemed to justify the timing of this united offering of labor, time and talent in Christ's Name and for the welfare of His church at Geyer. So against our personal reservations, Barbara and I jumped in and did our part in the Easter egg project, hoping that on Easter morning the power and joy of the resurrection would in and of itself exert its own impact and inspiration in the hearts of our parishioners. As tired out as they were from their concerted labors in the Easter Egg project throughout the Lenten season, on Easter Sunday morning the Sanctuary was filled with happy worshippers and I believe they genuinely rejoiced in the victory of Christ's resurrection.

* * *

There were other compensatory enterprises that were for me, and hopefully for the Geyer parishioners, special times of spiritual enrichment. Three events stood out among all of the other occasions in the normal life of a congregation. In each of these Richard Alwine played an important role as the Chairman of our Administrative Council. The first was a weekend emphasis on lay evangelism when we invited a group of around thirty dedicated lay persons from neighboring churches within the Central Pennsylvania Conference of the UMC to lead a concerted effort of renewal and evangelism. Arrangements were made in advance to house each of the visiting volunteer laypersons in the homes of our parishioners. In the typical manner of these kinds of weekend campaigns, we hosted a dinner on Friday evening where our visiting guests were introduced and gave their personal testimonies of God's grace at work in their own lives.

Saturday morning each host family provided breakfast for our visiting guests, and at 9:00 AM 'till noon we met in the parish hall where our visitors made a series of presentations about personal commitment and methods of personal witnessing and evangelism. The ladies of our church served lunch, and afterward we paired off and went two-by-two to visit "cold turkey" (without previously having made appointments) systematically knocking on doors, introducing ourselves as emissaries of the church, handing out information about the Geyer Church, inviting the householders to worship with our congregation, and offering to say a prayer if that was acceptable with the residents of the home. On the priority list of persons to be visited were inactive members and persons who worshipped occasionally with our congregation but who had not made a public declaration of their faith in Christ or yet joined our Church. Richard Alwine and my wife Barbara Ann were teamed together. (We tried to have teams composed of a man and a woman who were not married to each other, so a dominant spouse would not take over the conversation, and so those we visited would feel more comfortable talking to our visitation teams.) That afternoon several persons upon whom calls were made accepted our invitations, and later they made confessions of faith and joined our congregation. The weekend concluded with an inspiring Sunday morning worship service that proved to be a high point in the life of the congregation. Following that weekend a program of regular planned visitation was launched, and Richard and Barbara had such good success working together that they continued from then on to work together as one of our regular visitation teams.

The second special event that I vividly remember was a weekend when we invited the Reverend Peter John Marshall, son of the former U.S. Senate Chaplain Rev. Peter Marshall and his wife Catherine Marshall who wrote the best selling biography *A Man Called Peter* about her famous Scot clergyman husband. Barbara and I had stumbled upon Peter John Marshall's church on the north side of Cape Cod when we went on a belated honeymoon vacation and worshipped with Peter John Marshall and his congregation the Sunday morning we were on the Cape. Because Peter John Marshall was so well known and in demand as a preacher, we felt fortunate that he accepted our invitation, and our congregation committed itself to financially underwriting this special event. We paid his air fare from Boston to Harrisburg, met him at the Harrisburg airport and took him to the Hershey Hotel where we had reserved a room for him for the weekend he was with us. We ran ads in the local newspapers and solicited the co-sponsorship of the neighboring churches in both Middletown and Elizabethtown and the neighboring communities. The Middletown High School auditorium was rented for both Friday night and Saturday night meetings and choirs from the neighboring churches were scheduled to provide special music. That weekend we had the biggest snowfall of the season and one of the biggest snow storms on record. In spite of the inclement weather and the treacherous roads, a crowd of stout hearted Christians and a number of curiosity seekers turned out to hear the young Rev. Marshall preach, and he did not disappoint them but delivered inspiring sermon addresses even though the crowd was not anything like what we had anticipated and hoped for. Perhaps it was bad timing to schedule such a major area-wide event at that time of year; but after what could only be regarded as a well-intentioned but nonetheless dismal fiasco, that was the the last time that I ever proposed to our congregation that we undertake such a major event.

The third memorable event was during the American Bicentennial celebrations in the summer of 1976. I had received my doctorate that June and with that intense period of graduate studies behind me I was ready to enter into the national festivities and to take part in the Bicentennial celebrations in Dauphin County. Mrs. Donna Moore who was an excellent seamstress tailored a handsome colonial costume for me, and replete with white knee length stockings, a powdered wig, Oxford collar-tabs, and my John Wesley pulpit robe, I rode on horseback from our church to the County Fairgrounds close to our Geyer Church on the outskirts of Middletown.

*   *   *

Here also, Richard Alwine had a major part in making possible that colonial circuit-riding preacher's horseback appearance to preach the commemorative sermon on the Sunday afternoon of the July 4th weekend Bicentennial celebration:

Dr. Gingrich who was an uncle of Richard Alwine lived on his farm just down the road from the Church. Dr. Gingrich was an equestrian devotee and a member of one of the local riding clubs that sponsored fox hunts in the surrounding countryside. On several occasions I had seen the fox hunters in their jodhpurs, riding boots, red jackets and black velvet helmets, astride their magnificent equine jumpers as they leaped wooden fences and stone walls and galloped past our parsonage chasing the fox. How neat it would be, I thought to myself, if I could have a horse and ride with the hounds. I had been around horses as a boy visiting on my Uncle Clarence Hutley's farm and when working on my cousin Ellsworth Hale's farm, and I had ridden George Jendresen's cow pony Babe, but I had never had a horse of my own. But what would I do with a horse if I could find one, and how could I afford to purchase and keep a horse and also purchase the tack necessary to ride a horse?

As I looked around the parsonage yard, I realized that the church property covered six acres but that the church and parsonage covered less than half of the acreage and the rest was just standing empty and idle growing hay and wild flowers. That vacant acreage on the north side of the property would make an excellent pasture and a couple of horses would look good quietly grazing in the field. But where would I keep a horse? Then I remembered that when the old parsonage was torn down the old two-car frame garage was left standing next to the new parsonage. Little by little the old garage had become a dumping place for broken chairs and odds and ends of used equipment and an assortment of junk and trash—it was little more than a haven for mice and rats and the snakes that chased them. But an idea began to germinate in my mind as I thought about the possibilities that the empty pasture and the old garage could provide.

Before I dared say anything to Barbara or anyone else about what was going through my mind I decided to scout the riding stables in the surrounding area to see what if any kind of horses might be available. Upon inquiry I found a stable that was boarding a handsome chestnut colored Tennessee Walker gelding that was about four years old and saddle broken. The horse belonged to a young woman who was serving in the military in Germany, and the horse just stood there day after day confined to his stall with no one to really care for him and take him out to stretch his legs. Of course he was fed and watered and occasionally brushed and let out into a corral where he could walk around, but he really needed to be ridden and exercised; he needed human contact and attention. When I expressed an interest in acquiring the chestnut, the stable manager offered to saddle the horse and let me take him for a couple of circles around the indoor riding ring attached to the stables. The horse was fitted with an English saddle and I climbed on and at the first nudge the horse moved out at that incredibly smooth stride that is unique to the Tennessee Walker breed. When I asked if the horse's owner was interested in selling him and what the price might be, the stable manager said that the girl's father owned the black Tennessee Walker that was predominately a quarter horse strain in the stall next to the chestnut's stall, and that he worked in nearby Elizabethtown. I contacted the man, Mr. Shenefelt, and we set a time to meet at the stable. He told me that his daughter wasn't interested in selling her horse, but that he was looking for an alternate place to board both horses where the chestnut would receive more attention and be ridden more to keep the horse in shape and disciplined to the bit.

As we talked, the idea that was brewing in my mind began to take more concrete shape. I explained to Mr. Shenefelt that there was a possibility that I might be able to provide a two-stall stable and hay for both horses in exchange for the privilege of taking a sort of "temporary ownership" of the gelding whose name was *Apollo*. Shenefelt agreed! He would buy the grain and provide the English riding tack, and he also had western tack for his quarter horse named Pride. Shenefelt offered to help me convert the garage into a stable if I would supply the building material. But first I had to gain permission from the church's Board of Trustees for the remodeling of the garage into a stable and the use of the three-acre field as a pasture.

When I approached Richard Alwine with my idea about the horses, he immediately gave his consent and his support to my proposal. He offered to serve as my liaison with the Board of Trustees and, on top of that, he offered to bring his tractor, haying mower, and baler and to cut and bale the hay off the three acres. He even offered to store the baled hay in his big dairy barn! That had not even occurred to me before he volunteered to do so.

The next question was about how we were going to fence the pasture! I had noticed when driving by the Dauphin County building just north of the church along Geyer Road, that there was a big pile of rusting metal fence posts lying along the parking area beside the county's work shops. The stakes were used in the winter to hold up snow fences along the country roads and highways, but the pile had lain unused for a long time. When I inquired about what the county planned to do with the extra metal stakes, the manager said, "Parson, we have more than we need so if you need some for your pasture just help yourself." I could hardly believe how my dream of having a horse was taking shape. Shenefelt brought his pickup truck and helped me haul off the accumulated junk and trash that we emptied out of the old garage. He also volunteered to help remodel the garage into a stable, but the very first hour we started working was a disaster and I could see that Mr. Shenefelt was a willing worker but he just couldn't saw a straight line through a board or drive a nail straight without bending it or splitting the wood. Having had a good deal of experience in the construction trade working with church construction in Columbus, Kansas and at Buckley, Washington and then at Brighton Church in Seattle, and with Investment Builders, Inc. constructing apartment complexes with Jim Kirkman, I decided on the spot that I would do all of the carpenter work and let Shenefelt do the grunt work to help me.

The first thing we did was to build a wall between where the two cars had been parked, and covered the stud walls with plywood up to about six feet high all around the outside walls. Then we built "Dutch" double-doors, one over the other, for each stall and built a manger in a corner of each stall, fastening a water bucket beneath each of the mangers. Above the stalls I built a small haymow that would hold about 30 bales of hay (a truck load). I built saddle racks in the tack area on each side of the front part of the converted "stable," and beneath the tack we placed large size galvanized metal garbage cans which we used to store the feed grain for each horse. On each side I also built a shelf for grooming brushes and various ointments, salves, hoof polish, etc. The last thing we did was to dig out about a foot of the dirt in each stall and laid drain tile in the floor of each stall. We covered the tile with about a foot of pea gravel so the floor of the stalls would drain out into the paddock area abutting the side of our new stable. Each side of the stable had one of the double garage doors that opened outward, and in each door jam I screwed big eyebolts from which we fastened ropes to the horses' halters and used that area which opened out onto the black-top driveway as a grooming area.

Shenefelt helped me drive the stakes around the boundary of our pasture, and he bought the wire and fence post insulators and helped me install an electric fence battery-powered shock-charger and gate. Among the junk in the old garage we had found an old bathtub which we hauled out to our pasture, and we ran a hose from the church out to the pasture to fill the tub with water for the horses. After we had everything ready, I rode Apollo from the boarding stable over to his new home at the "Jones Stables" next to the Geyer Church

Parsonage. and later Shenefelt rode Pride over to join Apollo so the two horses had each other for company as stablemates. I purchased a pair of jodhpurs and riding boots and a helmet to go with my Harris Tweed riding jacket. It was fine to use the English tack and riding dress when I was just going for a leisurely ride around a cleared riding trail, but when I was riding cross-country on uneven terrain, I felt much more comfortable seated in a western saddle, so I bought a western saddle at a local tack store in Middletown, and had the best of both worlds. In my jodhpurs and English saddle I looked and felt like Squire Jones, and in my western jeans, cowboy boots and hat and seated in my western saddle I was the rough and ready cowboy from out West.

Tennessee Walkers come from a combination of thoroughbreds crossed with quarter horses. Apollo stood sixteen hands high and the thoroughbred breed was predominantly evident in his build and his stride and speed. Pride was shorter and stood only fifteen hands high and his predominant build was stocky and his initial fast burst of speed was typical of the quarter horse breed favored by many cowboys and rodeo hands, especially for roping and barrel racing. When we would stand the two horses side-by-side and count down "3-2-1-go" and then give each horse a swift kick in the ribs, Pride invariably beat Apollo out of the gate for the first fifty feet or so, but inevitably Apollo would get his long thoroughbred legs stretched out under him and he would soon overtake and outrun Pride every time. It was a given. Yet it was an interesting thing to note that when we were out trail-riding Apollo liked to take the lead and Pride seemed to prefer to follow him. Because the two horses had been stablemates for a long time they were well acquainted and got along quite well. Apollo was more high-strung which is typical of the thoroughbreds, and Pride was a strong and hardy animal typical of quarter horses, but you had to watch Pride—at least I did. Every once in a while he would buck or deliberately break his gait like George Jendresen's horse Babe used to do, and if I was not careful when I rode Pride he would look for a chance when he thought he could catch me off guard and buck me off. Apollo on the other hand seemed to bond with me as his master, but he was so high strung that when I would first take him out of the stable, saddle him and try to mount him he would tend to want to take off before I was really fully seated in the saddle, and I had to be careful mounting him lest he dart out from under me and leave me hanging in mid-air. I learned to pull his bridle to the left toward me and try to calm him down so he wouldn't dart off before I was fully in the saddle.

I suppose it was not good horsemanship on my part, but I knew that Apollo was so full of pent-up energy that he was just bursting with anticipation to stretch his legs out and run. I didn't have the heart to hold him back, so when I would first mount him I would head him down the lane and let him have his run for about a half mile, and after that he would settle down into that wonderful smooth gait that is the unique signature of his breed. He had an uncanny natural animal instinct and sixth sense. Whenever we would be riding in open fields or wooded areas, sometimes he would stop and snort and sniff the air and paw with his front hooves. This was his way of telling me that there was something unusual up ahead. I would carefully nudge him forward and invariably we would jump a deer, or a covey of quail, a pheasant, wood cock, a fox, a rabbit, or some other wildlife creature.

Both Dan and Debbie took to the horses with delight, but what surprised all of us was the way our youngest son Brad took to Pride. Brad had always been a rather quiet boy. He had been a Cub Scout and a Boy Scout and played Little League baseball, but he was never as rambunctious as his older brother and sister. There was something about the horses, however, and the way that Brad took to them and their response to him that we had not anticipated. Brad was a sophomore in the Lower Dauphin Senior High School in Hummelstown, Pennsylvania, which was a considerable distance from our home, so he rode the school bus. Every morning before he would board the school bus, he would stop by the stable and feed each horse a carrot or an apple or a sugar cube or some fresh grass. And the first stop he would make when he got off the school bus in the afternoon was to see how the horses were and to give them each another apple. Pride, who would try to unseat me if I was not careful, seemed to bond with Brad. We thought at first that Brad might be a little skittish around the horses, but he would mount Pride and ride off like John Wayne, much to our delight. Brad seemed to thrive and enjoy living in the country, and the horses became an important part of his daily routine.

On one occasion it was Brad who saved the life of Apollo. I was away studying at Drew University, so in my absence Brad volunteered to feed and water the horses. One afternoon when he returned home from school, he found Apollo lying down in his stall and his stomach seemed terribly bloated. Then Brad noticed that the door to Apollo's stall was open and the lid was off the 50-gallon can in which we kept Apollo's feed. Apparently that horse had figured out how to open the latch on his stall and he knew where his grain was kept: he had gorged himself and had drunk all of his water. Not being able to get outside, he had become bloated and would have died, had Brad not discovered him foundering. Brad called one of the old Pennsylvania Dutch farmers of our congregation, Mr. Tillman Reider, and somehow they managed to prod and pull Apollo to his feet. Horses cannot regurgitate, so the only thing to do was for Brad to walk Apollo around the paddock area next to the stable, and for several hours Brad kept walking that big gelding until finally he was able to pass the grain that almost did him in. It wasn't until several days later when I returned home from New Jersey that I learned that it was Brad to whom I owed a great big "Thank you" for his role in saving Apollo's life.

The Geyer Church property abutted the Middletown Country Club's eighteen hole premier golf course, which had originally been the U.S. Air Force Officers Club and Golf Course of the Olmsted Air Force Base that was located in Middletown, Pennsylvania prior to its closure in 1969. The pro at the Golf Club had grown up in the Geyer Church and his mother was an elderly but loyal member of our congregation. I had played the golf course with my brother-in-law Joe Pryor at the Middletown course and had met the pro. When I approached him about the possibility of marking out a riding trail around the periphery of the fairways, he consented when I promised him that we would not ride the horses anywhere near the fairways and that we would keep a lookout for the golfers and any errant golf balls headed in our direction. Having golfed a good bit, especially when I was pastoring in Washington State, I understood the rules and etiquette required for that sport by both private and public golf courses. The last thing I wanted to do was to violate any of those rules and thus forfeit the privilege of riding around the outside edges of the rough. It turned out to be an ideal place for riding, and the horses seemed to enjoy the open spaces as much as I did. When we finally moved to my next pastorate in the Baltimore Conference of the UMC, one of the things that I really missed was Apollo. He was truly a magnificent animal, and I became very much attached to him and felt that perhaps to some degree he had begun to regard me as his friend and master.

*   *   *

I am grateful to Richard Alwine for his leadership and godly example as a leader in our Geyer Congregation, and I am also grateful to him for his personal friendship and the big favor he gave to me when he opened the way for me to enjoy the pleasure of having Apollo and Pride during the remainder of my tenure at the Geyer Church. I suppose if I could have been able to afford the expense of boarding a horse at a stable in Maryland, I would have been very tempted to try to negotiate the purchase of Apollo or to have acquired another horse to take Apollo's place but our circumstances didn't permit that luxury.

When we vacationed in Pennsylvania a couple of years ago we stopped by the Alwine Farm and found Richard stripped bare above his waist working and sweating in one of his fields in which they were raking and baling hay. He was thinner and aging from the years of hard manual labor working in the fields and working with his dairy herd, and he had also suffered from the sadness of losing his wife Edie. But he still had the same bright smile and glow of a devout and godly Christian gentleman who was as keen as we had remembered him to be when thirty years earlier it had been my privilege to be his pastor. It was a joy to visit with him briefly before he had to get back to his tractor and the harvest in which he was engaged. We continue to correspond and exchange Christmas Cards and letters by which we keep up with the news of our families. Both Barbara and I thank the Lord for sending into our lives Richard Alwine and the other good Christian people in every pastorate whom we learned to love as our brothers and sisters in Christ.

NOTES:

[1] *Vide*, http://en.wikipedia.org/wiki/Mennonite

[2] The writer graduated from Columbia High School, Columbia, PA. Columbia is just 5 miles south of Marietta in Lancaster County, PA. Lancaster County is considered the very heart of the early Amish and Mennonite communities in colonial America.

[3] *Vide*, http://www.bic-church.org/about/history.asp

[4] Ibid.

[5] To learn more about the Brethren in Christ visit: http://en.wikipedia.org/wiki/Brethren_in_Christ

[6] *Vide*, http://www.ub.org/about/history.html

William Mercer

CHAPTER 11

WILLIAM MERCER

WILLIAM MERCER worked in the offices of the Chiquita Brands International, Inc. import/export shipping company which owned and operated a fleet of banana boats that traveled back and forth between Central American ports and the Port of Baltimore, Maryland. He was a confirmed bachelor, a tall, slim man who was a "straight arrow" and had an ethical and moral backbone of steel with as high a standard of conduct as any man I have ever known. At his job he was a hard-working manager who kept fastidious records and gave a full accounting for every shipment that came across the docks to his company's warehouses and that left for delivery to the food distribution wholesale companies that his firm supplied. Bill Mercer's personal integrity and his spiritual life and commitment to Jesus Christ were impeccable and his loyalty to me as his pastor was unwavering and immensely helpful to me as I made the adjustment coming from the Central Pennsylvania Conference to the Baltimore Conference of the United Methodist Church. He was the Lay Leader of the **Cowenton United Methodist Church, White Marsh, Maryland**, which is a suburban area immediately northeast of Baltimore.

The Cowenton Church had been established around the time of the American Revolution by a group of farmers who moved down the Susquehanna River from Lancaster and York Counties of Pennsylvania and settled in the White Marsh area at the head of the Gunpowder River which empties into Chesapeake Bay. Tall three-masted schooners and fishing boats used to tie up at the White Marsh dock to unload and load cargo during the colonial days when the river was still navigable. The more recent rapid development has caused the estuaries around the Bay to become filled with silt that has decreased the depth of the Bay and the rivers that feed it. During the American Revolution General George Washington marched his troops past the church along the Red Lion Road that ran between Baltimore and Philadelphia. Eventually, the old Philadelphia Highway that ran behind the church property was paralleled on the front side of the church site by the new US Interstate Route 40 which bore a constant stream of eighteen-wheelers and automobile traffic, creating a "road noise" that at times was almost deafening. Between the church and the old Philadelphia Highway the Baltimore & Ohio Railway had laid down twin railroad tracks along which ran both passenger and freight trains. Since there was no overpass or underpass for pedestrians or automobiles to use to get across the tracks, the locomotive engineers pulled on the whistles as the trains came barreling through the community and approached the railroad crossings. This caused the traffic to sometimes back up going both east and west through the country-crossroads business section that grew up around the Cowenton Church. To add to the noise of the trains and the traffic, the local volunteer fire station was just a few feet west of the train tracks, and every time there was a fire or some other emergency the firehouse sirens would scream out their blaring alarms throughout the surrounding area, but it was the parsonage residents who took the brunt of all the noise that was constantly generated.

It was in this noisy and bustling neo-suburban community that the Cowenton congregation decided to build a spacious new brick parsonage. The Cowenton Congregation had been placed on a two-point charge that linked it administratively with the Ebenezer United Methodist Church which is located two miles further east in Chase, Maryland at the mouth of the Gunpowder River where it empties into Chesapeake Bay. The two congregations had shared joint-ownership of a handsome stone parsonage that was situated halfway along Ebenezer Road between the two churches; but one of the members of the Cowenton congregation who owned a construction company offered to build a new parsonage on the vacant lot next to the Cowenton Church. The Ebenezer congregation, with considerable reluctance on its part, was maneuvered into going along with the arrangement. Much to the understandable dislike of the Ebenezer congregation the stone parsonage was sold and not only were the entire proceeds from the sale transferred to the financial underwriting of the parsonage next to the Cowenton Church, but to add salt to the wound the Ebenezer Congregation was required to make a monthly "rental" payment for its "share" of the parsonage costs!

There was little love lost between the congregations of the Ebenezer and the Cowenton Churches. The founders of the colonial Cowenton parish were Yankees who had moved down from Pennsylvania and during the American Civil War their loyalty was clearly and unapologetically given to the Union and the armies from the Northern States. The founders of the Ebenezer Congregation were southern plantation owners who had settled along the western shores of Chesapeake Bay north of Baltimore. During the Civil War these "Johnny Rebs" were surreptitiously aligned with the Confederacy of Southern States and, like other Southerners living in Maryland, they fought against their fellow Methodists who were Yankees. Those old Civil War animosities die hard and below the Mason-Dixon Line there are to this day those who hold strong feelings of loyalty to the old South and their Confederate ancestors. When we bought our own waterfront home on a cove at Rumsey Island near Joppatowne, Maryland about eleven miles north of White Marsh, some of the members of the Cowenton Church were upset because the minister would no longer be living in the parsonage next to *their* church. Apparently, it seemed to them that they had suddenly lost the "control" over their minister and the edge that they had over the Ebenezer Congregation by having the pastor live in *their* parsonage where they could keep a closer eye on him.

When we moved from Pennsylvania to Maryland we were grateful for the spaciousness of the Cowenton parsonage which included a study room for the pastor just off the front entrance. But not long after moving into the Cowenton parsonage, and even before we had fully unpacked all of our belongings, I immediately began a search for a home somewhere nearby that we could purchase as our own for investment purposes toward our eventual retirement. If we lived in our own house, I could deduct part of my stipend as a tax exempt "parsonage/housing allowance." One of the primary reasons for my desire to change my Conference affiliation was that in the previous year the Central Pennsylvania Conference had voted to require that all pastors must live in a church-owned parsonage; and if a minister owned his own home, he was required to vacate it and rent it out or let it sit empty while he moved into and lived in a church parsonage. That foolish and myopic resolution imposed upon every minister in that Conference the forfeiture of the right to live in his own home and to build up equity that over the years could accrue from that "housing allowance" tax exemption under IRS regulations.

That same year, however, the Baltimore Conference, through the wisdom and foresight of a number of its pastors who owned and lived in their own homes, adopted a resolution which was the exact opposite from that of the Central Pennsylvania Conference. The Baltimore Conference of the UMC affirmed the right under the federal law for every citizen including its clergy to own and live in their own home and to receive a fair and equitable housing allowance from the church(es) they served that would be equivalent to the monetary value of living in a church-owned "company house." That battle had been fought by John L. Lewis and the United Mine Workers Union when they lobbied to ensure the right of miners to live in their own homes instead of being forced by the mining companies to live in "company housing" and to be paid in "company script" so they would be forced to purchase their groceries, clothes and other household and personal items at the company-owned general stores. The Central Pennsylvania Conference of the UMC should have known better inasmuch as some of their churches were located in coal mining towns where there was strong feeling against the demeaning and financially punitive demands of being forced to live in a "company house."

When I had suggested that the Cowenton Board of Trustees rent the parsonage, and that a dentist had offered to rent the house for $450 a month (an excellent rental income at that time) and use it for his dental offices, utilizing the church's parking lot during the week days without tying it up on Sundays, the trustees regarded the proposal with favor. Since the Ebenezer UMC provided me with $250 a month as their church's part of the housing allowance stipulated by the Conference's newly adopted housing option for ministers, the Cowenton Church would benefited from a $200 monthly rental surplus which would be more than sufficient to pay the costs of maintenance and property taxes on the parsonage.

There was a fly in the ointment, however. We learned from our Cowenton laymen that the Superintendent of the Baltimore-Harford District, the Rev. Mr. Doug Cooney, had been dishonest with both the Cowenton church leaders and with me. Bill Mercer personally reported to me that Mr. Cooney had been "two-faced." When I met with Cooney and the officers of the Staff Personnel Relations Committee, the Board of Trustees and the Chairman of the Administrative Council, Superintendent Cooney had supported my right to purchase and live in my own home and the responsibility of the two churches to share equally in providing an equitable housing allowance for me. However, behind my back, when I was not around, he was quick to urge them to hold off and not rent the Cowenton Parsonage or to give me the housing allowance that was rightfully mine under the new parsonage regulations adopted by the Conference. He indicated that he would try to work it out somehow to make sure that I would be moved and that they would get a pastor who was willing to be subject to living in their parsonage—noise abuse from the highways, firehouse siren, railroad trains, etc. notwithstanding.

Bill Mercer came to me and expressed his great consternation, surprise and sadness over Cooney's blatant dishonesty and underhanded double-dealing. He stated that neither he nor the trustees knew what to do since Cooney had as much as ordered them not to accept the rental of their parsonage by the dentist who was waiting to occupy it and who gladly would have paid the higher rent on what for his purposes was an excellent location for a business/dentist's office (even if it was far less than ideal for use as a personal residence). When Bill Mercer told me about the dilemma into which Cooney had placed him and the other officers of the Cowenton Church, I gained a tremendous respect for Bill's high moral and personal integrity. He said that he and the other officers would pray that somehow the Lord would work it all out and that Barbara and I would not be hurt because of Cooney's despicable behavior and double-dealing.

*   *   *

Cooney had raised certain doubts in my mind about his sincerity and trustworthiness by his strange and pompous behavior on an earlier occasion. There had been some talk among a group of the Church's leaders about the advisability of exploring the possibilities of relocating somewhere other than in the noisy business strip flanking the US Interstate Highway 40 and the adjacent Ebenezer Road intersection. A prominent and wealthy woman parishioner, whose family owned and operated the local hardware and building supplies store a block from the Church parsonage and who was alert to the commercial and real estate development that was taking place, came to me with a report about the proposed large shopping center that was being planned by the Rouse Corporation (the company founded by James W. Rouse, the attorney and master developer who had developed the model community of Columbia, Maryland that is strategically located approximately half way between Baltimore and Washington, DC).

Mrs. Jane Bickel was an astute and very knowledge lay person and a successful business person in her own right. It was rumored that she was a millionairess, but you would never guess it because she was a modest woman who did not let her good fortune go to her head but lived a quiet and ordinary life and dressed in a manner that did not reveal her true wealth. Because of her knowledge of what was planned and being implemented in the surrounding area, she realized that the burgeoning commercial development and large new residential developments being constructed would radically alter the nature of what had in the past been a small rural saltwater port community on the north end of Chesapeake Bay. She could see the handwriting on the wall and suggested that it would be in the best interests of the Cowenton Church and the Conference if a feasibility study were to be made regarding the securing of the best possible location for the relocation and construction of a new Cowenton Church campus. She had obtained from the Rouse Company copies of their land plats and development plans and offered to discuss them with the District Superintendent and members of the District Church Building and Location Committee.

I related Jane Bickel's suggestion to Doug Cooney and invited him and the District Committee to meet in our parsonage at Cowenton with Mrs. Bickel to review the immediate and long-range plans being developed by the Rouse Company and their investment associates, so that the Conference might be afforded an opportunity to get in on the ground floor rather than to wait until land costs for a suitable church building site skyrocketed beyond the reach and financial resources necessary to carry forward such a relocation program for the church. On the day that we met with Cooney and the District B&L Committee, we laid the large blueprints out on the dining room table; but in a grandstand gesture, Cooney spread the blueprints out on the living room floor and, ham actor that he was, he got down on the floor on his hands and knees and poured over the blueprints as if he were Napoleon planning the battle of Waterloo! He ooh'd and aah'd and harrumphed and scowled over the blueprints as if he were going to personally draw up some humongous battle plan and mount a white charger to lead us all upward and onward into the fray. After posturing as if he were agonizing and envisioning some grand scheme to stake a claim for the Baltimore Conference to some strategic site in the center of this acreage of marsh and swamp lands and sand pits that would eventually be drained and converted into shopping malls and housing developments, he rolled up the blueprints, handed them back to Mrs. Bickel and that was the last we ever heard anything from Superintendent Cooney about the possible relocation of the Cowenton Church . . . and today the church still sits on the same spot past which George Washington marched his colonial troops more than two centuries ago! So much for General Cooney.

It came as no surprise to me when I learned that the real motive behind Cooney's bizarre and dishonest behavior was his sheer jealousy because Barbara and I had purchased a waterfront home but he was stuck in a district parsonage. What compounded Cooney's envy was his own stupidity: he admitted to me that he and his wife had borrowed against their life insurance policies to raise the money for a down payment on a building site on the side of a hill in the Pocono Mountains of Pennsylvania which he had seen advertised in a Philadelphia newspaper. Thinking that it would be a wise thing to buy the property looking ahead toward the day when he would retire, he had purchased the parcel of property site-unseen! Later on when Cooney and his wife went to see for themselves what they had purchased as the sight for their future retirement home, Cooney discovered that he had been sold a "pig in a poke": there was no legal right-of-way or road by which he could ever gain access or egress to or from his landlocked piece of the steep hillside. In his gullible naivety he had failed to personally investigate the bogus real estate company or to inspect the property before he signed on the dotted line and submitted his check for the down payment. There was no legal way that he could get out of the contract, so instead of just walking away from a bad deal he had kept on paying the monthly mortgage payments on a useless piece of mountainside upon which he would never be able to build. In his disgust and self-loathing and his envy of our waterfront home, Cooney had betrayed himself and the trust that had been placed in him as a superintendent by the good people of the Cowenton Church. After that I lost all respect for Doug Cooney and avoided him whenever possible.

*   *   *

About 10 o'clock the Saturday morning before Christmas, Doug Cooney phoned me and said "I want to see you in my office in Bel Air, Maryland at three o'clock this afternoon," and he abruptly hung up on me! I had no idea what his problem was but knowing his deviousness, I had an unhappy apprehension that whatever he was up to most likely would not be good. When I arrived at his office that afternoon, without any explanation he declared that I was through as the pastor of the White Marsh charge, and that it was decided and a "done deal" that I would go to one of the smallest and most difficult churches in Annapolis. No discussion—no negotiation—end of conversation.

*   *   *

Cooney seemed to take a personal delight in his abrupt and bullying mannerism as he exercised the power of his office as a district superintendent, and it appeared to me that he found some vengeful satisfaction in having accomplished his goal of getting rid of me and removing me from *his* district. What he didn't realize was that he had just done for me a tremendous favor—I was rid of him!

God in His goodness turned Cooney's malice and mischief against me into what eventually proved to be a favor of His divine providential guidance and grace. Bishop James K. Mathews appointed me pastor of the Edwards Chapel United Methodist Church in Annapolis, Maryland, and charged me with the responsibility of leading that congregation in a relocation and building program in which I would become engaged for the next decade. That's another fascinating story of God's marvelous providence and goodness.

*   *   *

It was a considerable consolation to me that Bill Mercer and the Cowenton parishioners had not initiated nor been party to Cooney's deceitfulness and chicanery; and when the Cowenton and Ebenezer parishioners learned that Barbara and I would be able to continue to live in our own Rumsey Island home, they were actually happy for us. Because the parsonage of the Edwards Chapel Church had been deemed no longer suitable as a residence, the fact that we owned our own home was actually one of the considerations that led to my appointment to the Annapolis church. It was a plus factor for both the Edwards Chapel Congregation and for my family that we could continue to live in our home: I would receive an equitable housing and travel allowance, and I could commute back and forth to Annapolis while serving that parish. For us and for the Edwards Chapel Congregation (and for the Conference) it was a win-win situation. That's a story for another chapter.

Once again God was faithful and demonstrated that he can truly work good out of seeming evil for those who are called according to His purpose (Romans 8:38).

Bill Mercer, who is now in his eighties, continues to remain a faithful and active member of the Cowenton United Methodist Church. Throughout the passing years he has provided spiritual inspiration and administrative expertise to the Cowenton congregation. His personal integrity and loyalty to each of the ministers who have served that church is an example of the kind of Christian character and dedication that is exemplary and is essential to the success of every congregation. May his tribe increase!

Earl Bolling

CHAPTER 12

EARL BOLLING

EARL BOLLING was a handsome southern gentleman, a red-blooded American who served in the military, and who was an outdoorsman and a member of a black-powder, muzzle-loading, long rifle gun club with a definite attachment to his ancestral roots associated with the southern Confederacy. Earl was proud of his allegiance to the "Old Glory" national flag of the United States and the colorful state flag of Maryland, but he just might stand the Rebel Flag beside the others as a salute to his Southern heritage. Earl was a fine and noble Christian who served with distinction as the Chairman of the Administrative Board of the **Ebenezer United Methodist Church, Chase, Maryland.**

Earl was an avid fisherman and lived close to the Gunpowder River. When Barbara and I bought our home on Rumsey Island, the Ebenezer Congregation was now more than delighted to pay the monthly housing allowance directly to their minister rather than to have to pay it as a rental fee to the Cowenton Congregation for its parsonage. They would rather have their portion of our housing allowance accrue equity for their pastor rather than to have it accrue equity for the other church without any equal equity accrual for the Ebenezer parish. Earl Bolling was a staunch supporter of this new arrangement and encouraged us; he was genuinely happy for Barbara and me that we now had the same privilege of being homeowners that everyone else was free to enjoy. When we first arrived in White Marsh, Earl and his wife Lois graciously entertained us in their home and befriended us from the very outset.

*   *   *

The Ebenezer Church was founded by colonial plantation families and other colonists who settled on farms surrounding the larger plantations that formed the waterfront community of Chase, Maryland. On the east side of this historic church is a large and well-maintained historic cemetery that dates back to colonial days, and on the southwest side of the chapel a two-story Christian Education building was constructed following World War II.

It was the Methodist missionary Joseph Pilmore who organized the first Anglican Methodist Society on June 22, 1772, at the "Dutch" church (now Old Otterbein), in the city of Baltimore, with the unordained layman Francis Asbury becoming "pastor" in 1773.

The circuit riding pioneer Methodist preacher "Bishop" Francis Asbury and his colleague and fellow attorney Thomas Coke had been sent from England by John Wesley to oversee the Anglican "Methodist" Class Meetings and Societies that were developing in the colonies. Asbury preached from the pulpit of the Ebenezer Church in 1786 just two years after he had convened the dubious "Christmas Conference" at the Lovely Lane Chapel in Baltimore. Neither Coke nor Asbury, who were English attorneys, had any formal theological training. Coke was a short heavyset John Bull kind of fellow, but Asbury was a tall, handsome, imposing figure who had a way with the ladies. He and Coke had collaborated to cleverly arrange a specially called meeting. They deliberately scheduled it during the height of the 1784 Christmas holidays season at a time when they knew that the more educated and astute clergymen in the larger cities of Philadelphia, New York, Boston and the other major cities and towns along the Atlantic seaboard would not be able to attend. Asbury knew that because of their pastoral responsibilities to their own larger parishes during the Christmas holy day celebrations the more informed and capable clergy would be precluded from attending.

The group that Asbury and Coke managed to collect together in Baltimore was composed primarily of women and a few young semi-literate circuit-riding preachers, "most of them mere striplings in age and experience" whom Asbury and Coke could easily manipulate. Asbury and Coke cunningly maneuvered to have themselves elected as "Deacons" on one day, ordained "Elders/Priests" on the next day, and on the following day managed to have themselves confirmed by their gullible followers as the "General Superintendents" and eventually as the "Bishops" of the denomination which they founded at that conference as The Methodist Episcopal Church in America. Outraged particularly by Asbury's conduct and his fawning manipulation of the women whom he charmed and persuaded to vote for him and his English colleague Coke, a group of older pastors and men led by an angry Irishman James O'Kelly and his associates eventually withdrew. Later, when the Reverend John Wesley learned of the impertinent presumption and manipulation by Asbury who claimed the high office of a Bishop (an "overseer" of the church), he was understandably deeply disconcerted and angered. He grieved that the American Methodists had broken away from the Anglican Church to form their own American religious sect under the adopted name of the Methodist Episcopal Church. It was just three years later, in 1787 that another group of American Anglicans formed the Protestant Episcopal Church and broke formal ties with the English Crown, although to this day they remain a part of the worldwide Anglican Communion and its House of Bishops under the questionable political aegis of the Archbishop of Canterbury.

Ultimately a wave of nearly thirty thousand others, who were angered over Asbury's cunning manipulations and his autocratic use of the episcopacy, left the Methodist Episcopal Church, formed the Methodist Protestant Church and eventually founded their own theological seminary in Westminster, Maryland. Years later, after the Methodist Protestant Church was merged into what eventually became the United Methodist Church, Westminster Seminary was moved to the campus of American University in Washington, DC where it was renamed Wesley Theological Seminary. Bishop John Warman, who was ordained in the Methodist Protestant Church and eventually became the Bishop of the Central Pennsylvania Conference (formerly the EUB Susquehanna Conference) of the United Methodist Church, wrote a revealing if not condemnatory exposé of Asbury's role in the Christmas Conference entitled "The Dark Side of the Christmas Conference" which was published in the United Methodist publication *The Circuit Rider.*[1]

*   *   *

On the first Sunday morning that I arrived at the Ebenezer Church, the chapel was filled with parishioners and friends who were interested to see what the new preacher would be like. The church was buzzing with the sound of chatter and gossip and speculation about the new pastor. As the crowd of gathering worshippers grew, so did the noise level. When the organist began the prelude the sound level of voices increased, and when the organist increased the pressure on the sound pedal of the organ the noise of clattering voices grew proportionately. When I stood in the pulpit for the first time I just stood there and looked out at the congregation waiting, and waiting, and waiting . . . until the noise subsided and finally you could hear a pin drop. "Good morning, friends" I began, and we proceeded with the worship service following the traditional liturgy used for over two hundred years by that historic congregation.

The following Sunday and the Sunday after that parishioners entering the Chapel were greeted by the mounting crescendo and clatter of human voices visiting with one another to catch up on the gossip that had accumulated over the previous week. This was not the kind of an environment conducive to preparation for worship to which I was accustomed. In the church that my father pastored in Columbia, Pennsylvania painted in gold letters across the chancel wall were the words "Seek ye the Lord while He may be found, call ye upon Him while He is near," and in the Sunday bulletin were printed the words, "When you enter the Sanctuary, please remain silent unless you are talking to God in prayer." As children we were trained to respect the house of God and to show reverence by being silent in church. In another church the words from the Psalm were imprinted on a plaque on the wall, "Enter his gates with thanksgiving and into His courts with praise." This is God's house. He is to be approached with awe and reverence and the respect due to a King.

I spoke with Earl Bolling about the noise and irreverence in the chapel prior to the worship services and suggested that perhaps we could institute a "Coffee Hour" where coffee, cocoa, tea, soft drinks and donuts would be made available in the Christian Education building adjacent to the Chapel. Earl thought it was a stellar idea and he and Lois offered to buy the coffee and donuts. I announced from the pulpit the next Sunday morning that beginning the following Sunday and thereafter everyone was invited to the Christian Education building for coffee and donuts and a time of fellowship where we could visit with our friends and neighbors, but when we entered the Sanctuary of the Chapel all conversation was to cease and we would focus our attention upon prayer and meditation in preparation for the beginning of the worship services. The idea of free hot coffee and donuts was a big hit, and the organist and most of the parishioners welcomed the reminder that we ought to be reverent when we enter God's house; but as might be expected there were a few old die-hards whose pride in their piety was wounded and out of sheer stubbornness they refused to visit with their neighbors during coffee hour in the Christian Education Building.

In spite of the one or two disjointed souls (who seemed to carry a perpetual chip on their shoulder and perhaps a grudge toward God over some imagined wrong they had suffered at His hand or by His failure to intervene in some sickness or the death of a loved one, or some other perceived slight by a fellow-parishioner or a pastor) the rest of the congregation entered with a new found joy into fostering Christian fellowship during the coffee hour. And it was soon apparent that there was a new awareness that when we entered the Chapel we were setting foot on *holy ground*: we were coming to meet with Almighty God, to sing His praises, to offer to Him our prayers of adoration, thanksgiving, intercession and petition, to hear what He had to say to us through the reading and preaching of His Holy Word, to commune at the Lord's Table, and to offer our tithes and gifts and ourselves to Him in gratitude for His love and His mercies toward us.

*   *   *

I preached identical sermons at both the Cowenton Church and the Ebenezer Chapel; we sang the same hymns, read the same scriptures, and followed the same litany for the celebration of the Holy Eucharist . . . but something different was happening in the Ebenezer congregation that was not evident at Cowenton. Partly because of the enthusiasm of Earl Bolling and others in the Ebenezer congregation, new faces began to appear in the pews, several parents brought their babies and small children to be baptized, and a number of teenagers and adults also requested the sacrament of Holy Baptism. In the short seven-month period that I served the White Marsh Charge it was my privilege and joy to baptize twenty-eight persons and to receive a number of teenagers and adults into the membership of the Ebenezer Church. During the Morning Prayer time I invited worshippers to come to the communion rail and kneel to pray and when at the close of each service I gave an invitation—an old fashioned Methodist "altar call," several persons came forward and made a public confession of faith. A renewed spiritual awareness and a growing commitment to evangelism and missions began to emerge. The Youth Fellowship group under the enthusiastic leadership of their adult sponsors became active and participated in the worship and life of the church. In October the Ebenezer youth planned and produced a "Biblical" Halloween haunted house in which they depicted with live characters scenes like the three Hebrews in Nebuchadnezzar's fiery furnace, Daniel in the Lion's den, the deliverance of the demoniac of Gadara, Saul and the witch of Endor, etc. It was such a hit with people in the community that the "Biblical" All Hallows Eve haunted house became an annual project of the Youth Group at the Ebenezer Church.

As spiritual renewal gave rise to enthusiasm and new found joy in their Christian faith, so also the commitment to tithing and good stewardship began to result in increased offerings and a growing balance in the church's treasury and budget. By the time I was appointed to another pastorate, in Annapolis, Maryland, the Ebenezer Church realized that their congregation had grown and their offerings had increased to the point where they were ready and able to have their own full-time pastor. That spring the Board of Trustees built a lovely new parsonage on the property next to their church. A retired minister served as interim pastor until the new parsonage was completed and that spring their first full-time pastor and his family moved into the new parsonage. From that time forward the Ebenezer congregation has continued to enjoy the benefits of being a strong and self-sustaining single-station church. With the coming of an Amtrak rail line running through the community connecting Chase, Maryland with Philadelphia and points north and with Baltimore and Washington, DC and points southward, the Chase community has continued to grow and the Ebenezer Church has also continued to grow and to faithfully bear witness to God's love and grace and to have a positive impact upon their community.

Throughout my brief tenure at the Ebenezer United Methodist Church, Earl Bolling was an enthusiastic supporter, advisor and advocate of the institution of our "Coffee Hour" fellowship time, he encouraged the spiritual direction which we endeavored to bring to the congregation, he was a supporter of our desire to live in our own home, and he was an outstanding "public relations" advocate. His big smile, cordial spirit and southern gentlemanly manner made him an ideal "greeter" to welcome newcomers to the church. It was a real pleasure for me to enjoy Earl's partnership and friendship and to share the joy of seeing the Ebenezer congregation grow into a single-station church.

NOTES:

1   John B. Warman, "The Christmas Conference, The Dark Side," *Circuit Rider*. Nashville, TN, The United Methodist Publishing House, Vol. 8, No. 3, March, 1984, pp. 6, 7.

Harvey Gable

CHAPTER 13

HARVEY GABLE

HARVEY GABLE worked for Baltimore Gas & Electric Company, starting out first as a lineman and eventually working his way up in the company to a position of management. He and his wife Mildred owned a lovely brick waterfront home in Annapolis, Maryland that stood on a high bank overlooking the South River. Harvey and his good and long-time friend Ed Tucker, were good fishing buddies and spent many happy hours together fishing in the waters around Annapolis. Harvey was the Lay Leader of the **Edwards Chapel United Methodist Church of Annapolis**, and he was the Sunday School teacher of the Adult Bible Class. He and his wife faithfully tithed and generously supported the congregation and later its new church building program.

Harvey was a man strong in body, mind and spirit. He was a handsome man about six feet tall whose stature evidenced that in his younger years he had been strong and well able to handle the strenuous work of a lineman. When I met Harvey he was in his sixties, with gray wavy hair, and when he was not inside the church you would usually find him with his favorite pipe filling the air with the aroma of a sweet cherry tobacco. He was a quiet sort of fellow, with a twinkle in his eye and a bit of a smile curling the corners of his mouth. He was a man you could always count on, one of those quiet saints who are rock solid in their faith and commitment to Christ, "pillars" in the church. It was his trustworthiness and his dependability and faithfulness that were so appreciated by his fellow parishioners and upon which I came to rely. I had a great respect for his good sound judgment and his honest candor and wisdom and the soft-spoken unruffled manner in which he could bring order and common sense to bear upon issues where others might tend to speak before thinking or to jump to unfounded conclusions or to fly off the handle and get all fershimmered. Harvey was steady as a rock, unwavering and unflappable, firm in his convictions but not noisy or bullying about anything, yet he was able to keep a cool head in conflicted situations and to maintain his mental, emotional and spiritual equilibrium. His was a settling and reassuring influence that helped keep our congregation and some of its younger and impetuous church officers on an even keel. I am grateful to him for his friendship, his solid faith in Christ, his level-headedness and the able leadership that he gave to our congregation.

*   *   *

The Edward's Chapel United Methodist Church which later became the St. Andrew's United Methodist Church of Annapolis, Maryland, is a congregation whose life and history is deeply rooted in its antecedent beginnings that can be traced back to the colonial days prior to the American Revolution

In 1734 the renowned English evangelist, George Whitfield, came to Annapolis and preached in "the Athens of America" as Annapolis was then known. Whitfield was a contemporary of John Wesley and one of the founders of the "Great Awakening," as the spiritual revival of which Methodism was a part has been called. Whitfield described the town as a place where "pomps and vanities eat out the vitals of religions." It was a place of wickedness, sophistication and politics.

Francis Asbury wrote in his journal, on November 25, 1773, that he "Had occasion to go to Annapolis, and found some desire to preach there. But perceiving the spirit and practice of the people, I declined."

In Annapolis, Asbury found a spiritual friend in Catherine Small, a Scottish woman who opened for him her house in which to preach, and they started a small class meeting of women. There has been some suggestion that Asbury, who was a tall and handsome bachelor, may have been perceived as something of a "lady's man." Later that year Asbury reported that there were one hundred twenty-nine *Methodist* Anglicans in Annapolis and adjacent areas.

One of the first members of the Anglican Methodist Class Meetings was John Chalmers, a silversmith. It was Chalmers, who in 1784 offered the Annapolis Anglican Methodists a lot (on the present grounds of the United States Naval Academy), on which to build a church. Catherine Small solicited contributions among "the higher classes of citizens" and collected the money for the building.

During the years that followed, the original congregation of Annapolitan Methodists had grown and been given a variety of names, and built churches on a number of sites. In 1931, the original congregation later adopted the name

Calvary Methodist Church and eventually constructed its present building on Rowe Boulevard. In the Narthex of that church is the pew in which the French mercenary General Gilbert Lafayette once sat as he worshipped with the Anglican Methodists when he was in Annapolis during the American Revolution.

*   *   *

A small rural congregation was begun by a group of Methodist farmers and country folk who began meeting in the old rural schoolhouse in the Camp Parole area of Anne Arundel County.[1] The old one-room country school was located along a dirt road at what is now the site of the present facilities of Nationwide Insurance Company on Riva Road. Started in 1894 as a Sunday School, primarily for the children of the rural families who lived on nearby farms, these devout Methodist Episcopalians soon added worship services. One year later, on March 19, 1895 the group was duly organized as a church, and that year they began the construction of a new church building.

Ground for the building of the original one-room frame church house was donated by George W. Cole at the country crossroads corner of Riva Road and Defense Highway, which at that time was located about half-way between the old Parole Railway Station and the Three Mile Oak landmark. The original church building was constructed by W. Brewer Garner for the sum of $756. The cornerstone was laid on September 12, 1895.

In 1898, the Reverend John Edwards, pastor of the Methodist Episcopal (Calvary) congregation, served a circuit of five churches. The Reverend Mr. Edwards was a tinsmith by trade from Cornwall, England, who was inspired by a genuine zeal for evangelism and for the planting of new congregations. Because he followed in the tradition of the old circuit-riding parsons, Edwards was referred to by many who knew him as the "Francis Asbury of his time." Among those churches on his "circuit" was a small rural congregation located about three miles from the Maryland State House, out West Street along the road leading toward the nation's capital city Washington, DC. The congregation was identified by the name of its first pastor, the Reverend John R. Edwards, and came to be known as the "Edwards Chapel."

Additional land was subsequently given and purchased for the establishment of a church cemetery. This country church was located in a picturesque pastoral setting with historic significance. Abutting the church property were fields where horses and cattle grazed. It was also adjacent to the old race track where George Washington and Thomas Jefferson and others among our nation's founding fathers used to race their horses when they would visit Annapolis during the sessions of the First Continental Congress, which met in the Maryland State House.

Back in the nineteenth century, when a five-mile ride in an open wagon or horse drawn buggy on a cold rainy or snowy winter day or in the blazing heat of a hot summer afternoon was a long trip to the churches in town, this historic country church played an important role in the religious and social life of the neighboring countryside. From the pulpit of that old country church house, in the tradition of early Methodism, old fashioned circuit riding parsons faithfully preached the Gospel of God's love and called sinners to repentance, salvation and holy living. Dedicated Sunday School teachers taught the Holy Scriptures to children and young people. Many noble persons from the prominent families in the area found Jesus Christ as their Savior through the ministries carried on by this rural congregation.

*　　*　　*

With the passing of time came growth to the area and in the church. Following World War II, in 1947 the congregation added an educational wing to the rear of the original building, and fifteen feet were added to the front of the church to include a bell tower and a foyer entrance. The entire structure was brick-veneered and the old pot-bellied wood stove was replaced by an oil burning forced-air central heating plant. The remodeling and expansion program was completed at a cost of about $3,000.

On October 12, 1952, through a gift of $5,000 from Frederick Essex, the congregation was enabled to burn the mortgage on its building. In 1953 the Fellowship Hall was rebuilt, and a handsome modern brick parsonage was added in 1955.

Edwards Chapel was one of the five congregations that were originally on the circuit of its first pastor and remained part of a multiple-point charge until 1954 when it became a single-station parish. Although at that time it was still a "country" parish, the congregation experienced a rapid growth spurt in the 1950s, and with its growing membership some of the parishioners began to consider the necessity of building a new church.

During the 1960s the area around the church underwent a dramatic demographic change. The colonial City of Annapolis is located at the point of a peninsula jutting out into Chesapeake Bay on the east and bound by the Severn River on the north and the West River on the southwest. The historic waterfront community had no way to grow except to the west toward Washington, DC. The Parole area surrounding the Edwards Chapel site underwent a radical shift as the rural farms and residences were displaced by the development of commercial properties. A developer from the Philadelphia area bought up the farmland abutting the church property and began construction of the first major shopping mall in the Annapolis area. With the construction of the Parole Shopping Center came the building of additional offices and other commercial businesses. The area immediately surrounding the church became the geographical center of the newly emerging commercial hub of Annapolis. It became undeniably more apparent that the church needed to relocate in order to have a more vital growth and religious life, indeed, even to survive.

*   *   *

When Bishop James K. Mathews and his cabinet began their search for a minister to fill the vacant pulpit of the Edwards Chapel Church, Superintendent Doug Cooney saw an opportunity to get rid of Dr. C. David Jones from *his* district and Cooney recommended that Jones be considered for the appointment to Edwards Chapel. Bishop Mathews and some of the other members of the cabinet were familiar with my pastoral record and were aware that I had led two congregations in major building programs and had been the "organizing" pastor of another congregation, so it seemed to be a good place to appoint me. The worst that could happen would be that the congregation would not survive, and the best case scenario would be for the new minister to provide the pastoral leadership necessary to bring success to the faltering dreams for the congregation to relocate and build a new church.

It seemed almost from the very beginning that this appointment was not going to be an easy one for the new pastor. During the first two months in my new parish there was a slip-up on the part of the Annapolis District Superintendent Rev. Richard Clifford regarding my stipend and benefits package. That created a difficult problem for me, but with the able assistance of Harvey Gable and others leaders in the congregation, that matter was resolved and eventually led to the development of a strong bond of friendship and mutual support between the Rev. Dr. Richard Clifford and me. Rev. Clifford became our staunchest supporter and champion. When the Edwards Chapel Building program came under duress from a new bishop who had his own political agenda and authority concerns, it was Richard Clifford who had come to our defense both inside and outside of the Cabinet, so once again God worked good out of a bad situation. Not long afterward I was appointed the Resident Director of Drew University's satellite Doctor of Ministry degree program in the State of Maryland, and we experienced an unexpected role-reversal when Richard Clifford entered Drew's doctoral studies program. I made every possible effort to assist him in earning his degree, which was not an easy task for him because of the demands made upon him as a District Superintendent. I was delighted when later he joined the Academy of Parish Clergy and served on its Board of Directors during the same period when I was the Dean of the Academy's College of Fellows.

*   *   *

My transfer from White Marsh, Maryland to Annapolis caught Barbara by surprise and upset her terribly. We had just moved into our new home on Rumsey Island in Joppatowne, Maryland at the end of October in 1957. Less than two months later, the District Superintendent had announced abruptly that I had been appointed to a small church in Annapolis. Our youngest son, Brad, had just entered his junior year in the Joppatowne High School and it did not seem right that he should have to be jerked out of that school after only one semester there and thrust into another school somewhere else. Also, Barbara had an excellent position at one of the largest law firms, Weinberg & Green Attorneys at Law, in downtown Baltimore and was not ready to give up her new job. We needed her income to help us meet our financial commitments and living expenses. Even after she learned that the Bishop had agreed (actually supported for expediency's sake) that we would continue to live in our new home, for over two months Barbara could not bring herself to face adjusting to another congregation, especially after the unhappy encounter we had with Mr. Cooney. Our oldest son Dan and our daughter Debbie, on the other hand, were excited about my relocation to Annapolis. Dan, like his father, is an avid sailor and had purchased a twenty-four foot Buccaneer sailing sloop which he moored at our bulkhead on Rumsey Island. Dan and Debbie knew that Annapolis is the yachting capital of America and the home of the U.S. Naval Academy, and they were excited about our becoming part of that great maritime community. So for the first several weekends it was Dan and Debbie, both of whom were working in Philadelphia, who would catch an Amtrak train from Philly to the Edgewater station just above Joppatowne where we would meet them. They would go sailing or yachting with us on the weekend. I had a sleek hardtop twenty-four foot Sea Ray cruiser moored at our bulkhead on Rumsey Island and enjoyed very much cruising that small yacht on Chesapeake Bay. Dan and Debbie attended church with me in Annapolis and they were entranced by the city and all the maritime life around the waterfront. They also enjoyed having Sunday dinner with us at one of the famous seafood restaurants located around the downtown dock area. By their good reports about Annapolis and with their encouragement eventually Barbara's curiosity got the best of her and she began to make the commute to Annapolis with me on Sunday mornings. But it was not until Tom Smith, Sr., who was a personal friend of the Naval Academy's football coach, offered us tickets to a Navy football game that Barbara fell in love with Annapolis and the Naval Academy Middies. When the Academy brigades marched onto the field and the flag was raised and the crowd in the stadium lustily sang our National Anthem, all of a sudden Barbara's eyes filled with tears of patriotism and a sudden realization of how truly fortunate we were that God in His providence had guided my path and made it possible for us to be in the one place in America where I would truly feel the most "at home"—with a name like *Davy Jones*, nowhere else could possibly be better!

* * *

Over the next ten years we devoted our lives and our energies to the relocation of the Edwards Chapel Congregation and the building of the new church which Bishop Mathews had charge me and entrusted me to do. There were a whole series of tasks that had to be accomplished, and to make matters more difficult in 1984 we found ourselves in the middle of one of the worst financial crises our nation had faced, all of which made the tasks more challenging, but each step forward and each victory became even more sweet in the end.

Under the leadership of my predecessor, Dr. Dan Henderson, the congregation had purchased a three and one-half acre parcel of land upon which they had hoped to build a new church further west on Riva Road toward the South River, but that site soon proved to be inadequate. The following is a listing of some of the hurdles we had to jump:

1. We had to find an architect and have blueprints developed for the site and buildings. Christian Builders, Inc. from Nashville, Tennessee was selected and proved to be a superb choice. A two-story "L" shaped design with a stately central bell-tower and spire at the conjunction of the Sanctuary wing and the Christian Education wing incorporated a neo-colonial motif that was in keeping with the colonial architecture which gives to Annapolis and to Williamsburg, Virginia their special charm.

2. When it was discovered that the proposed three-acre building site which the congregation had purchased was not sufficiently large enough to accommodate the expanded off-street parking that would be required to permit the construction of a larger main sanctuary building in the future, an extended series of attempts to purchase additional acreage was met with frustration caused by an unstable and unscrupulous seller who thought to gouge the church, causing the congregation finally to abandon the site and to despair about moving forward with the project.

3. It was determined to sell the unusable acreage and to seek another site. Eventually the Riva Road acreage was sold at a barely break-even price, but we were glad to get that white elephant off our hands, even if it meant going back to the drawing boards at square one.

4. Before the old church site on the corner of West Avenue and Riva Road could be sold, it was necessary to exhume and relocate the bodies buried in eighteen graves that have been marked off in a second

cemetery plot that abutted the parsonage yard, which was laid out by the trustees when the original cemetery became filled. That involved a very expensive investment and a struggle with some of the members whose relatives were buried in those graves. Eventually arrangements were made with one of the Annapolis cemeteries and permission was finally received from the Anne Arundel County Courts to permit the exhuming and reinterment of the graves at a cost *ten times* that of the mere $50 originally paid for the grave sites. I shall always be grateful to our Administrative Council Chairman, Bob Gaither, who in his quiet, compassionate manner was able to make those difficult negotiations.

5. Through another series of providential circumstances a buyer was eventually found for the old church site. The Sogecliffe Corporation of Paris, France purchased the old church for $550,000. The buyers obtained a zoning variance to erect a water stand-pipe required for the building of a French-style motel on the church site at the busy intersection where West Street crossed under U.S Interstate Highway 50 which runs between Washington, DC and the Maryland eastern shore.

6. A choice fifteen-acre parcel of land that fronts on State Highway 2 just south of the up-scale Gingerville residential subdivision was purchased for $265,000. That purchase was made possible by the generous gift of $65,000 that the sellers returned to the church as a donation. On a Sunday afternoon in the spring of 1982 Bishop Fred Wertz officiated at the ground breaking ceremonies for the new church. The die was finally cast, but the unanticipated struggles that lay ahead were just about to begin.

7. It occurred to me that the new building site would accommodate a design which would reposition above ground the basement parish hall that had originally been designed to be beneath the sanctuary and the Christian education wing which had been placed beneath the Administrative/office wing of the original blueprints. We could salvage the original blueprints by lengthening the sanctuary and parish hall and by placing those structures across from each other. We could locate the administrative offices at the front of the site and the Christian education on the opposite back side of the site with the four buildings surrounding covered brick cloisters and a colonial style courtyard and central fountain in the open area between the four structures. The tower would stand at the inside corner of the courtyard at the conjunction of the Sanctuary building and the Administrative building. There would be a large parking space in back of the

Christian Education building. When I showed my revised blueprint overlays to our architect, Mr. Moneypenney, he did a masterful job of making the adjustments that gave to the congregation a beautiful and functional church complex behind which additional buildings would be constructed as the new church's parochial school grew and expanded.

8. Once the old church properties were sold and the new church property was purchased, in preparation for filing the deed to the new property, a special church meeting was convened and a new name for the congregation was chosen to provide a new identity for the church. We were surprised when upon investigation we discovered that, other than a small chapel in the undercroft of the Naval Academy Chapel, there was within the boundaries of the Annapolis Community no church with the name of the Patron Saint of all Mariners, so when I proposed that the new church be given the name of St. Andrew, the name of the first of the Apostles was chosen. We had a local artist design a unique logo for the new church depicting a *St. Andrew's barge* (fishing boat) with the St. Andrew's flag (one of the flags adopted by Scotland) incorporated into the sail of the barge. The logo was purposely engraved into the granite cornerstone of the church so some later minister or generation could not, in a whimsical effort to be novel, forget the church's roots and its Christian heritage as epitomized by the Apostle St. Andrew.

9. In the meantime, the congregation needed desperately to find an interim location where it could continue to worship and carry on its parish life while the new church was being built. The congregation petitioned its parent congregation, Calvary United Methodist Church on Rowe Boulevard, for permission to rent its Sanctuary in which to hold an early 9 o'clock worship service on Sunday mornings. We proposed that the Edwards Chapel Sunday School might merge with the Calvary Sunday School, and the Edwards Chapel Sunday School teachers could assist by "team teaching" and serving as substitute teachers. At first we were assured that would be fine, but the wife of Calvary UMC's pastor was on the church's payroll as its Director of Christian Education and she did not want our Sunday School children and our teachers invading her turf; so to our shock and dismay, on the Monday just prior to our last Sunday in the old church, we received a phone call from the minister of Calvary UMC, Vernon Thompson, informing us that the invitation was being withdrawn and we would just have to fend for ourselves the best we way we could!

10. I made a frantic phone call to Dr. Ed Ankeny, pastor of the Eastport United Methodist Church in Annapolis. The Eastport Congregation was one of the five churches which together with First/Calvary UMC and Edwards Chapel and two Negro UMC congregations were part of the five-point charge pastored by the circuit riding parson Rev. John Edwards in the late 1890s. Dr. Ankeny had been one of the Drew University doctoral candidates with whom I had worked in the Annapolis satellite study group, and later he would become a District Superintendent. When I explained to him the predicament in which the Edward's Chapel congregation was placed by the unexpected and un-Christlike behavior of the Calvary UMC and its pastor, he and the members of the Eastport UMC opened their hearts and doors and welcomed us with open arms. Their trustees made the church library available to me as a pastor's office and relocated their collection of books elsewhere, allowing me to paint and redecorate my new office and furnish it to meet my own needs and taste. Although they did not ask us for any rent, our congregation insisted upon paying a token rent as an expression of our appreciation. On special holy days like Christmas, Lent and Easter, Pentecost and other special high days of the Christian year, our congregations worshipped together and our choir joined with the Eastport Church Choir in presenting cantatas and other special sacred music. Our children and teachers were welcomed to join in the Eastport Sunday School and for about eighteen months we were the beneficiaries of their hospitality and largess.

11. On the last Sunday afternoon in 1982 the last worship service was held in the old Edward's Chapel and a deconsecration ritual was invoked. The chapel was filled to capacity and there were tears of sadness mingled with joy as nostalgic and happy memories of bygone days were relived. I wore my colonial costume and white wig in honor of the faithful circuit riding parsons who had served the Edwards Chapel congregation and others like it during the days of the early colonies and of the new nation whose first capital was in the Maryland State Capitol building on the hill above the harbor. It was the end of an earlier era, and for us the beginning of a new adventure in faith.

12. The following week the men of the church removed all of the stained glass windows, the tower bell that had been salvaged from a World War II Liberty Ship, the pulpit, the Communion table, the pews, the organ and all of the other furnishings. Everything taken from the old church was stored in a big commercial trailer loaned to the Church

by Orville Lee and Dorothy Bowen, and the keys to the property were turned over to the new owners, thus ending the saga of the Edwards Chapel Church.

Harvey Gable was among the faithful bridge builders without whose faithfulness, cooperation, leadership and support this transition from the old church to the new would not have been possible.

NOTES:

[1] The area around the old Edwards Chapel Methodist Episcopal Church was dubbed "Parole" because during the Civil War the pasture land close by the church had been commandeered by the Union Army and made into a prison camp where captured Confederate soldiers were kept under military guard. It was the practice to permit the Southern gentlemen who were officers to leave the prison encampment of tents on "parole" and ride horseback or hike under their own recognizance into the nearby waterfront port town of Annapolis where they could visit the bars and other places of entertainment. These officers were sometimes accompanied by Union Army officers who acted not so much as guards as fellow officers and comrades. Because of the strict code of military honor it was expected that an officer and a gentleman would keep his word and not attempt to escape either by water or some other circuitous route. Those who attempted or tried to escape were usually quickly recaptured and returned to the military prison at "Camp Parole" in disgrace, which to some was a fate worse than death itself. The name "Parole" stuck and the area which has become the new city-center and commercial area of Annapolis is often still referred to by its Civil War name of "Parole."

Mark Brown, DBA

CHAPTER 14

MARK BROWN

MARK BROWN, DBA, was a Green Beret in the US Army Special Forces, and knows what it means to command, to give orders and to obey orders. Mark was an outstanding soldier and is an exceptional Christian who reminds me of the Centurion of Capernaum.

Although he is not a big man physically, he is extremely strong and in superb physical condition. Even before becoming a Special Ops soldier he held the black belt in martial arts and was capable of lethal bare hand-to-hand combat. He was not the kind of man to mess with—not the kind of man you would want to challenge to a physical fight. He is a no-nonsense, straight arrow, a valiant and noble individual. He is a great comrade to have covering your back, and your worst nightmare if you are his enemy. He is relentless and unflinching and is totally committed to carrying out his appointed mission.

One day a big man with a big loud mouth came into Mark's business office in Washington, DC, and confronted Mark in a manner intended to intimidate and threaten him. Mark is about my height, maybe a tad shorter, and the big loudmouth man was obviously used to bullying people. When Mark just looked at the bully with steel eyes, the man became infuriated and came around the desk to physically assault Mark. That was a big mistake. Mark quickly "cleaned his clock!" The big fellow wound up with a broken nose, a couple of cracked ribs and a fractured arm. The big man took Mark to court but when the judge saw Mark standing next to this big six-foot plus, barrel-chested fellow, the judge asked the plaintiff, "How could this little fellow do to a big man like you what you claim he did?" What the judge and the man did not know was that he had tangled with a veritable wolverine—a Green Beret Special Ops soldier, who could just as easily have taken the man's life.

Mark Brown is a man with a strong and vital faith in God. When he was in training to qualify for commissioning as a Green Beret, Mark was the oldest man in his outfit. He was competing with young boys just out of high school and college, men who were ten to fifteen years younger than he was and who were in their prime physical condition, most of whom were taller and larger than he was. The training was strenuous, pushing the trainees to the maximum limits of their human endurance and strength. Mark determined that anything the drill sergeants and the other men in his platoon could do, he would do better. If he were required to do fifty pushups he would do one hundred, etc. When the day for the final qualifying tests came, each man was required to run one hundred yards in fifteen seconds carrying a full military field pack and rifle. Anyone who failed to meet that stringent test in physical stamina and endurance would be disqualified and denied entrance into the coveted Green Beret Special Services Division. When Mark's turn came to run the final qualifying dash, about halfway through this grueling test he felt as if his legs were turning to rubber and that they would collapse beneath him. In desperation Mark shouted out to the top of his voice, "GOD"! Panting and near exhaustion, it was all he could muster. It was a prayer to God for help in his time of trial. One more time he shouted to the top of his lungs, "GOD," and Mark testifies that it was as if instantly someone had picked him up and he felt as if he were floating through the air. He finished the course in what for him was a record time with seconds to spare! Mark's life has truly been one of faith and obedience to God and of dedication to his family, to his church and to his country.

Before becoming a Green Beret, Mark had studied business law and accounting and had earned his MBA from the University of Maryland. After earning his CPA license, he became an FBI agent, working out of the FBI office in Washington, DC. Later, he opened his own business as an insurance broker.

Because of his sterling character, his professional skills, and his genuine Christian consecration, the **St. Andrew's United Methodist Church of Annapolis, Maryland,** elected Mark to the Trustee Board and to the Building Committee. Because of his expertise as a CPA and a businessman, he was elected to the Finance Committee and eventually to the office of Church Treasurer. It was critical that a person of Mark's character be elected to this position, especially during the construction of the new multi-million dollar church building project in which we were engaged.

*　　*　　*

I vividly recall the first time I met Mark Brown. It was a hot humid Sunday morning in the summer of 1979. Following the morning service Tom Smith, Sr. and I were talking together as we stood in the parking lot of the old Edwards Chapel church. I was still wearing a white alb and a red clergy stole. Most of the parishioners had already left when a big black automobile wheeled into the parking lot and a young man in a three-piece blue suit jumped out of the car and was followed by three small boys dressed in suits identical to their father's. The father strode toward me with a brisk step, the three youngsters falling in line behind him. He marched up to us, and addressing me, he demanded:

"Are you the minister of this church?"

"Yes, I'm the Pastor."

"What kind of church is this? Is this a church that preaches the whole Gospel of Christ?"

I recognized immediately that this young fellow was a no-nonsense man who demanded a straightforward answer, and the most important thing to him was that the *whole* Gospel be faithfully preached by a minister of Jesus Christ. I invited him to come with me into my office in the educational annex at the back of the church building. First, I assured him that I believe in and preach the *whole* Gospel of salvation by faith in the atoning sacrifice of Jesus Christ upon the Cross of Calvary and in the power of His resurrection. Then, having satisfied his inquiry about that essential fact, I handed to him a copy of the brochure we had just printed outlining our plans and hopes for the building of a new church.

"Fine, we will come and hear you preach next Sunday, and maybe then we will join your church."

He had made it clear that he was a United Methodist and that he had just come from visiting a United Methodist Church where a female minister had delivered a sermon that he enormously disliked. He was looking for a church where he and his family could worship and hear the Word of God faithfully preached from the pulpit. It was obvious that with this young man there was no confusing *black and white* with equivocal *gray* areas that merely muddied the waters. With him you had better let your "yea" be "yea" and your "nay" be "nay." And no gobbledygook, either!

The next Sunday morning during the singing of the opening hymn the front door in the old tower entrance of Edwards Chapel opened and in walked Mark Brown in his blue serge three-piece suit, followed by his wife, and trailing along behind them were their three little boys, carbon copies of their proud dad. They marched right up to the very front pew and took their places in front of the pulpit on the left-hand side of the church. I do not remember what Biblical text I preached about that Sunday morning, but whatever I said I must have passed muster, because the next Sunday the family returned, and again the Sunday after that. Shortly thereafter the Mark Brown family joined our congregation and came to play a gargantuan role in the leadership and stewardship affairs of our church.

*   *   *

When the telephone on my study desk rang one July morning in the summer of 1980, I had no inkling that it marked the beginning of another profound lesson I was to experience about the meaning of Christian consecration, faithful obedience, stewardship and Christian discipleship. When I picked up the phone, the voice at the other end of the line was Mark Brown's. In his usual abrupt no-nonsense manner, Mark blurted out, "Dr. Jones, I'm working on a business deal. Please pray about it with me, and if it works out I will make a contribution to the church." (Plunk . . . the line went dead). Mark had hung up just as abruptly as he had called . . . no explanations, no elaborations, no details—just a simple request—"Pastor, please pray!"

I didn't have the slightest notion what it was all about, and I realized that it was really none of my business—I didn't need to know. God knew!

I must confess that it was a rather weak and perfunctory prayer that I offered: "Dear Lord, I don't know what it is that Mark is working on, but if it is your will, please bless him." And forthwith, I dismissed it from my mind.

A month or so went by and again the phone rang, and again it was Mark Brown calling. "Dr. Jones, you remember that deal I asked you to pray about? Well, keep praying, because I am working real hard on it and if it comes together I will make a contribution to the church." (Plunk . . . again the line went dead). I didn't realize it at the time, but his phone call was really an act of faith on Mark's part. So again, I mouthed some simple prayer, and I must admit, it was rather perfunctory like the one I had prayed the first time he called: "Lord, whatever it is, if it is your will and it pleases you, please bless Mark Brown." And I let it go at that, and turned my attention to other things, forgetting all about it.

Time passed, and then one day, out of the blue, the phone rang again, and when I answered, once again it was Mark. Only this time there was a recognizable excitement in his voice: "Dr. Jones, you know that business deal that I asked you to pray about—well, it's getting real hot, so pray real hard, and if it all works out I will make a contribution to the church." And again, just as abruptly as the first two times, there was a *Plunk* . . . and as before, the line went dead. No explanations, nothing. Just an obvious sense of urgency and excited expectation, and a sincere pleading that, as his pastor, I would offer intercessory prayers on Mark's behalf.

This time Mark got my attention. I still didn't know what it was all about, and there was no way that I could pray with any specific knowledge of what was involved. But I knew that God knew. That was enough. Although I was still oblivious as to what was entailed in Mark's urgent request for prayer, once again I offered a prayer. This time, however, it was with a heightened curiosity and with a deepened hope that whatever it was, God would grant an affirmative answer to Mark Brown's earnest entreaty.

Time went by and since nothing more was said to me by Mark about his requests for prayer, I assumed that whatever it was, it didn't pan out. Again I dismissed the whole thing from my mind.

The weeks went by, and everything seemed to be stalemated and in limbo for Mark and Suzanne. The Halloween, Thanksgiving and Christmas holidays seemed to come in rapid succession as the days flew by. We had a white Christmas that year with fresh fallen snow blanketing the ground on Christmas Eve. I was in my study at the church, when just a few minutes before the traditional 11 o'clock Candlelight Communion service, there came again on my study door the sound of a knock, knock, knock. I called out, "Come in." The door opened and in walked Mark and Suzanne Brown and their three small boys. With a solemn look on his face, as if this were serious business, Mark handed a large envelope to me.

"What's this?" I asked.

"This is our Christmas present to Jesus," Mark declared with a voice and a bearing that indicated that it was an act of reverent devotion to the Lord Jesus Christ. "Go ahead; you can open it if you want to," Mark said.

Curious about what might be inside, I opened the envelope and took out three engraved pieces of paper which, upon closer examination, proved to be three stock certificates!

Surprised and baffled, I asked again, "What are these?"

Then Mark explained the mystery to me: "Dr. Jones, do you remember when I phoned you last summer and asked you to pray about a business deal I was working on?"

"Yes."

"Well, I was bidding on a big insurance contract for a large union with national headquarters in the District of Columbia. The bidding competition on that contract was really keen and tough. I'm just a young man, with a small office, and only a few years of experience in this insurance business; and I was competing against some very large insurance brokerage houses, and seasoned veterans in the industry with strong connections, lobbyists, and all that goes along with this kind of contract bidding. At first I didn't think I had a chance, but I felt prompted to have a go at it and I entered the competition. It seemed like a real long shot, and we didn't have a lot of money. We had our house on the market for sale, but couldn't seem to land a buyer. We signed a contract on a new home in College Heights, closer to my office, and I believed that was where we were supposed to move, but we really didn't have the money to close the deal on that purchase. And we wanted to get settled in the new house before our new baby arrives. But nothing seemed to happen.

"Then one day I was sitting at my desk in my office when something strange happened that I really can't explain. I was wide awake, my eyes were open and I was fully conscious when I saw something just as clearly as if I were looking at it on a movie screen. There in front of me were the words, 'Buy these three stocks,' and the names of the stocks were clearly spelled out for me. I thought, that's strange, I don't have the money to buy the new house; we are operating on a shoe-string; Suzanne is going to have a baby and we are going to have hospital and doctor bills and all the expenses that go with bringing a child into the world; and here You are asking me to buy these three stocks. Lord, I don't know how I will pay for these stocks. I don't even know how we are going to survive financially. Now, you want me to buy these three stocks—for St. Andrew's new church! We have been faithfully paying our tithes, Lord, and now you want me to buy these stocks!

"OK, Lord, if you say so, I'll do it!"

Somehow, Mark Brown knew that it was the Master who was speaking to him, who had come to him right there in his office, as he sat as his desk with his eyes wide open, and in his right mind! (Although I suspect that if we had been Mark Brown most of us would probably have questioned that latter assertion and would have wondered if we were just hallucinating. But being the no-nonsense person that he is, with Mark there was no questioning Almighty God and His marvelous and inscrutable ways.)

Mark did not say, "All right, Lord, you know how hard I have been working on this big insurance contract bid. You want me to buy these stocks! OK, first you give me this big deal, and then I will buy these stocks."

That is what most of us would have done—to bargain with God. Lord, if you do this for me first, then I will consent to do this for you. As if our giving ought to be some kind of exchange of our money to buy God's favors; but that is not how it works. *Consecration* and *Stewardship* are *acts of faith*—not "horse-trading" with God!

Mark Brown wrote down the names of the three stocks that had been shown to him; then he picked up the phone and dialed his stock broker: "I want to buy $4,000 worth of three different stocks: just put it on my account." Mark named the three stocks and it was a done deal, though Mark had no idea how he was going to pay for them. But it was enough for Mark that the Lord had given him a clear directive. As strange as it may seem to us, to Mark it was an undeniable and compelling order from his Commander-in-Chief—Jesus Christ.

Mark Brown is like the Centurion of Capernaum, who came to Jesus and asked the Master to heal his servant. When Jesus offered to travel with this Roman Soldier back to his home, the Centurion exclaimed:

> *"Lord, I am not worthy that thou shouldest come under my roof:*
> *but speak the word only, and my servant shall be healed. [Just say*
> *the word . . . and your command will be done]. I am a man under*

authority, having soldiers under me: and I say to this man, 'Go,' and
he goes; and to another, 'Come' and he comes; and to my servant,
'Do this,' and he does it." When Jesus heard it, he marveled, and
said, to them that followed, 'Truly, I say to you, I have not found so
great faith, no, not in Israel' . . . . And Jesus said to the centurion,
'Go thy way; and as thou hast believed, so be it done unto thee.' And
his servant was healed in the selfsame hour."—Mt. 8:5-13 KJV.

Both the Centurion and Mark Brown understood that Jesus is Lord, and
that He is sovereign, and His commandments are law, and we are to obey.
His commands are not grievous but are given to us for our well-being and the
welfare of our souls. When Jesus gives a command, and directs us to obey, it is
not debatable or negotiable or contestable—it is His to command, and it is ours
to obey. That is *consecration:* it is doing what God asks and expects us to do,
without arguing about it or debating it or attempting to bargain or to negotiate
or to change God's mind about it. Just do it—as an act of obedient faith. Trust
Him, like the centurion, and like thousands of Old Testament saints and New
Testament Christians have done and in so doing have proved God to be reliable,
trustworthy and true. And that is what Mark did, he trusted God!

"What shall I do with these three stock certificates?" I asked Mark and
Suzanne.

"On the first business day after Christmas, you take these three stocks to
the bank and cash them in; whatever they are worth, use the money in whatever
way you deem best, Pastor. We trust you to use it wisely."

That next Monday I took to the bank the three stock certificates, each of
which Mark had purchased for $4,000. I was astounded when the bank officer
handed me a check for $26,000 and some odd dollars and cents. I thought
there must have been a mistake. The banker assured me that there had been
no mistake; so I deposited the money in the St. Andrew's UMC Building
Fund account and designated that money toward the erection of the Brown
Memorial Tower, which today stands at the northeast corner of the courtyard
cloisters where the St. Andrew's UMC of Annapolis' Sanctuary building and
the Administration building converge.

Later I asked Mark how he had managed to pay for the stocks when he
didn't have the money at the time, and how it was that these three stocks
were worth over $26,000 when I cashed them in. Mark told me that since he
didn't have the liquidity to purchase the stocks, he decided that God, with
whom all things are possible, would supply the money. He had talked it over
with Suzanne, and they had agreed that if they could borrow money to buy
a car, and borrow money to buy a house, and borrow money to buy whatever
else they needed, they could surely borrow $12,000 to buy the stocks that
Mark had been directed, through that miraculous visitation/vision from the
Lord, to purchase. Mark explained to me that before he called his broker, he

prayed, and said, "Lord, you know that I don't have the money to buy these stocks, but your command is mine to do, and not to ask how or why. I will borrow the money and I will pay it back through part of the tithes from my future earnings. And, God, if I'm just plain crazy, and the stocks fall flat and tank, and I lose the whole $12,000, I will make it up to you—since it will be your tithe money; I will pay it back from my other earnings since it will be the tithes that belong to you. Lord, I won't be gambling with your tithe money, but I will just be using it as a kind of collateral, which I will pay back to you, one way or the other."

Now, remember, that at that point in time, Mark had no assurance that he would win the big union insurance contract—to service hundreds of insurance policies. All he knew was that God had said, "Go" and "do this—buy these stocks."

What happened during the six months that passed between the time Mark saw his vision directing him to buy those three particular stocks and that following Christmas Eve, is an incredible series of events. One of the stocks was issued by a bank in Virginia; another was issued by a manufacturing company in the Midwest; and as I recall the other was issued by some emerging company related to the computer industry in Silicon Valley. One of the stocks split four-for-one, and immediately thereafter dropped in the stock market, but rebounded and took off like a rocket, doubling in six months time; and the amazing thing is that both of the other two stocks also doubled over that same six-month period!

Mark said to me, "Dr. Jones, I can't explain what happened or how or why it happened—I just know that God told me what to do, and I did it. I don't know anything about the intricacies of the stock market, and there is no way that I could have picked three stocks that would all have doubled at the same time within the same six-month period. When I told my friends and associates what happened, nobody believed me; and when we ran the logarithms to calculate the odds of anybody randomly picking three winners that would all have the equivalent of a 200% annual gain in such a short period of time, the numerical number of those odds were incredible. Dr. Jones, it was no accident. I didn't do it by any genius of my own, but God surely guided me; and fortunately I obeyed His command."

Like the Centurion of Capernaum, Special Forces Green Beret Mark Brown knows what it means to give and to obey orders. In the military, under combat conditions it is often a matter of life and death. Mark chose to obey the Lord, and his obedience was vindicated (by 200%) many times over!

It was not until after Mark had purchased the stocks which he had seen in his vision that (to the utter astonishment of everyone in the Washington, DC area and elsewhere within the insurance industry who knew about the contract bidding) he had actually won that enviable insurance account!

* * *

In the spring of 1983 work began on the church's construction site at 4 Wallace Manor Road just off Highway 2 on the southwest side of Annapolis. The general contractor Christian Builders, Inc., assigned to our project a highly skilled construction foreman Farrell Jarrett, and his charming wife Shirley who served as our on-site construction office manager and bookkeeper.

Having had experience in church construction myself, I was able to work directly with Farrell in making critical on-site decisions regarding the various phases and details of the construction project. Working together over the course of the project we found ways to save the church an estimated $350,000 in cost reductions as follows:

1. The first of these savings was related to the excavation of the holding pond and the construction site areas. The U. S. Army Corps of Engineers, which controls water and hydraulic issues related to construction projects in the Chesapeake Bay area, had determined that before a single spade of earth could be moved for the construction of the buildings, a one and a half acre holding pond had to be installed on the northeast corner of the property. It would have to be of sufficient design and construction to handle the requirements of a projected 100-year flood plain drainage system. Farrell negotiated with a local company to make an even exchange of the topsoil from the excavation of the holding pond and the construction site, for the compacted earth materials that would be used as the base fill material to support the foundations and concrete slabs upon which the four buildings and tower would stand.

   Building permits were issued for the initial site development on a phase-by-phase basis. The roadways were laid out and the building perimeters surveyed and staked off. Then the huge earth-moving equipment was brought onto the site and bulldozing began. Literally thousands of yards of earth were excavated and hauled away in exchange for equal truckloads of the compact fill that was required for the site. During the excavations the workmen found extremely large scallop shells that were five inches or more in diameter giving evidence that in past eons the land had been part of the Atlantic Ocean floor. The only cost to the church for this exchange of thousands of tons of earth was the drayage (gas, oil and truck drivers) for the fleet of 30-ton dump trucks that moved the enormous tonnage of earth transferred to and from the site. By the time the 100-year flood holding pond was finally completed, over $80,000 had already been expended on blueprints and the initial site development.

2. Another hurdle was posed when the County Building and Zoning Board commissioners at first refused to approve the eighty-five foot tall bell tower and spire. Its height exceeded the limits imposed by the Annapolis Historical Association whose mission was to preserve the colonial ambiance of the down-town historic area around the State Court House and the inner harbor area. Eventually a variance was granted and the required permits were issued and the project moved forward.

3. Because of all the construction going on in the Washington, DC-Baltimore-Annapolis triangle, it was difficult to find competent and efficient workmen, and the construction unions made it difficult to meet construction schedules because of their feather-bedding rules that inflated costs. Farrell Jarrett was a seasoned builder and had a knack for hiring good workmen and weeding out the deadbeats, and he was creative in innovating unique methods to get the job done. When it became difficult to find good workers, Farrell contracted with a five-man masonry crew he knew from Kentucky. To help us stay within budget he set up a "bunkhouse" in a large truck trailer we borrowed from Orville Lee Bowen; he installed cots, a make-shift kitchen with a hotplate, a shower which he rigged over a storm drain, and portable toilets providing a "camp" for the masons. Those men were one of the hardest working and finest teams of craftsmen to be found anywhere. Their goal was to lay not just the normal union quota of three hundred bricks a day but to exceed that by having each of the three masons lay up one thousand bricks a day by. The two helpers who carted bricks and mortar to the masons managed to keep up with the three Kentucky masons and also with Farrell and his son Jimmy Jarrett who were master brick masons as well as master carpenters. When the masons missed a joint pattern on the front side of the Parish Hall, without complaining they dismantled nearly a thousand bricks and reset the wall according to the architect's blueprints. By their hard work and excellent craftsmanship those men saved the church at least fifty percent of the cost that local union masons would have charged, and they did such a good job and were such good sports about bunking in their makeshift quarters that we gladly paid them the bonus that Farrell had suggested to us.

4. By July the Administration Building and the Parish Hall were under roof. Our small congregation was so excited about their beautiful new church that one Sunday afternoon, after our worship service in our borrowed chapel at the Eastport UMC, a picnic was held in the newly constructed but yet unfinished Parish Hall. Sheets of plywood were set on top of stacked cement blocks and used for tables, and 2x12

boards that were set on top of cement blocks and used for seats. The picnic was a grand success. It was on that occasion that the church received the gift of a carillon for its bell tower.

After the picnic in the unfinished Parish Hall that Sunday afternoon, Mark and I were standing in the doorway of the Christian Education Building looking across the courtyard toward the bell tower which the masons had so far laid up to a height of about eighteen feet. I just happened to make a passing remark that some day there would be a carillon in the tower. When Mark heard me mention a carillon, he asked me, "Dr. Jones, do you think there really ought to be a carillon in the tower?" I responded off the cuff, "Sure, every church ought to have a carillon." I thought that perhaps someday in the far distant future, someone might bequeath a carillon as a memorial gift to the church.

Mark thought about it for a few moments, and said, "Dr. Jones, you've got it—you order the best state-of-the-art electronic carillon there is, and Suzanne and I will pay for it."

Then, several minutes later, as an afterthought, Mark asked, "By the way, Pastor, how much do you think the carillon will cost?" In his usual trusting manner, Mark had just instinctively known in his heart that if God wanted him to give a carillon for the bell tower, the Lord would enable him to earn the funds to pay for it, and that was all there was to it!

I was quite stunned, because I knew that in addition to their regular tithes and the Christmas gifts of those amazing stocks, Mark and Suzanne Brown were constantly giving for one special offering or another. That was typical of Mark and of the Centurion and of others like them whom we have known who, if God calls upon them to do something, they will be quick to respond, "Yes, Lord." "And, oh, by the way, Lord, how much do you think it will cost? And, Lord, if it pleases you, you might let us in on how You are going to help us accomplish this thing that is to come to pass!"

Well, it just so happened that the very week before that Sunday, I had been going over the catalogues from Shalamacher and Verdin and some of the other carillon manufacturers. I had wanted to make certain when the brick masons laid up the tower structure the electricians would at the same time install the necessary conduit and the contractor would install the necessary steel to accommodate such a carillon. I had studied the building specifications and the technical data on the various carillons, so I told Mark that the price of a good state-of-the-art electronic carillon system with all the bells and whistles would be somewhere in the neighborhood of $12,000 or more. (It would cost three times that amount today.)

"Well, Dr. Jones, I think our church should have the very best. You order whatever kind of carillon you think is the best and we will pay for it." And that is how the carillon bells came to ring from the bell tower when the St. Andrew's UMC of Annapolis was dedicated that following Christmas!

5. Construction continued toward the completion of the Sanctuary superstructure. Although the work was not yet finished on all four of the buildings surrounding the courtyard, the Administration Building and the Parish Hall had been completed and we were able to obtain occupancy on those two buildings. On the first Sunday of October, 1984, we held our first worship service in the Parish Hall which we used as a multi-purpose facility until the interior of the Sanctuary could be completed. Following that morning service the cornerstone was laid into the northeast corner of the Sanctuary building. For us it was truly *a new beginning*.

6. Several of our parishioners were members of the Parole Rotary Club, and we were fortunate that two fellow Rotarians who were the Presidents of two of the local banks agreed to jointly lend the Church sufficient funds to complete the entire superstructures of all four buildings so that structural integrity could be ensured by a contiguous construction of footings, foundations and the masonry walls of all four buildings at one time. A few months later one of the banks loaned our church an additional $50,000 with which to complete the interior of the Christian Education building.

7. On St. Andrew's Sunday, at the beginning of Advent on December 2, 1984, a Service of Consecration was held for the new church. That winter the interior of the Christian Education Building was completed and in May of that spring the St. Andrew's Child Day Care Center was opened. A young college student was hired as the Day Care Center Director and under a Maryland State Summer Day Camp license the Church's parochial school program was initiated. Beginning with two little pre-school age girls the enrollment for the Summer Day Camp grew to 19. We hired a consultant who owned and operated a daycare facility nearby and with her counsel and encouragement I wrote the six-hundred page protocol and license application which permitted us to open a Christian parochial school in the fall. We began with about one hundred twenty-five kindergarten through Sixth grade students. In the fall of 1985, the enrollment had grown to 259 students. To keep up with the growth spurt, four trailers which we used as satellite classrooms, were rented and positioned on the west and south sides of the Parish Hall. I served as the first Headmaster, and additional faculty and staff personnel were added to keep pace

with the increasing enrollment. In the fall of 1986 we were fortunate to add Dr. Jack Lockledge as the parochial school's first full-time principal. Dr. Lockledge gave unstintingly of his talent and time to help develop the curriculum, the school's library, the academic program, extra-curricular activities and to give oversight and assistance to the growing faculty and staff.

8. Mark Brown was determined that nobody was going to mess around or obstruct the mission of his church if he could help it. One of the neighbors whose property abutted the power company's thirty foot right-of-way along the north side of our church's property became unhappy with the noise and dust that was created during the construction period. Out of anger and in defiance of our protests, this neighbor deliberately constructed a large storage shed under the power and phone lines on the church's side of the property line. The man's recalcitrant belligerence and defiance of our protests irked Mark so he decided to do something about it.

We were also having trouble with the local Anne Arundel County Fire Marshal who refused to grant the church a temporary occupancy permit for use of the completed Administration Building. The problem centered around the installation of a reinforced plate glass window between the church secretary/receptionist's office and the main foyer entrance in the Administration Building. The local Fire Marshal, in a pompous show of his authority and his game of one-upmanship which was related to the running "turf battles" between the various county and city agencies, was insisting that our contractors remove the plate glass window and replace it with a laminated chicken-wire window pane which would have looked ridiculous and out of place in that building. We knew that the Fire Marshal had approved the same kind of fire-rated plate glass windows in all of the stores and businesses in the local shopping malls and stores in Annapolis, but he was just showing off his authority in this challenge as a counter to the authority of the Annapolis Building Department.

Mark Brown decided to *kill two birds with one stone.* Mark had contacted a Fire Marshal from Washington, DC to come out to our church site and meet with the local Fire Marshal to iron out the problems being created by the local Fire Marshal's obstinacy. What Mark did not tell me was that the man from Washington, DC, was really a Mafia godfather who had been made an honorary Fire Marshal by the Washington political machine. Mark knew that the godfather would make our troublesome neighbor and the arrogant local Fire Marshal an offer they wouldn't want to refuse. The local Fire Marshal must have been tipped off as to the identity of Mark's man from the District of Columbia, because he never showed up to keep his appointment with us. Mark was embarrassed and outraged and finally confided to me, "Nobody stands up the godfather!"

The DC Fire Marshal assured me that he would take care of the local Fire Marshal and invited me to get into the back seat of his big black chauffeur driven limousine and instructed me to show him where the neighbor lived who had encroached over our property line. When we drove past where the illegal shed had been placed, the godfather said, "Not to worry, Father. I will have my attorney send your neighbor a letter advising him of his infraction of the *law* and notifying him that if he does not have his shed removed from your property within ten days I will just send a bulldozer out here to clear the right-of-way for the power company!"

Nobody was going to mess around with Mark's church and his pastor.

9.   Though at first for purely political reasons, pressure was placed upon the Church by the new bishop, Joe Yeakel, to dissolve and abandon its parochial school, we remained steadfast to our commitment to provide *"A quality education in a Christian environment,"* and over the past two decades the St. Andrews Christian Elementary and Intermediate School has become a model private school with an outstanding reputation in the Annapolis area. The St. Andrew's Church, with a membership of around six hundred parishioners and its Parochial School which has between four hundred to five hundred students in Kindergarten through Eighth grades, is valued at over $5,000,000 today.[1]

*   *   *

That is not the end of the Mark Brown story. Later on Mark and Suzanne had two daughters and another son, giving them six children, all of whom are actively serving the Lord. Mark Jr., like his father, became an officer in the Army Special Forces and is currently on active duty as a helicopter pilot in Iraq. Please pray for J.R. Brown and for all of our military personnel who are serving in harm's way both at home and abroad. Eventually, Mark felt the call of God upon his life to enter the ministry. He and Suzanne sold their home in a fashionable Washington, DC, suburban area, and moved their family to Virginia where Mark completed studies for a Master of Divinity Degree at Liberty University. He pastored a church and eventually completed doctoral studies, earning the Doctor of Business Administration (DBA) degree in International Finance. While completing his doctoral degree, he served on the faculty of a nearby Christian university, training seminarians in the principles of sound church management and stewardship. The Lord has continued to bless and prosper Mark and his family. Mark and Suzanne moved from Virginia to Chattanooga, Tennessee, where he now serves as the Vice President of Finance/CFO and Head of the Business School at Tennessee Temple University.

Green Beret Mark Brown is a living example and testimony of how God will bless and honor those who honor Him and put Him first in their lives. Dr. Mark Brown symbolizes for us what it means today to be one of God's and one of David's "Mighty Warriors!"[2]

NOTES:

[1] The reader may find out more about the church at its website *http://www.standrewsum. org* and about its school at its website at *school@standrewsum.org*

[2] It is not possible here to name everyone, but many others have also made significant contributions to help make the St. Andrew's United Methodist Congregation what it is today.

Rudolph Wilson

CHAPTER 15
RUDY WILSON

RUDOLPH WILSON, better known by his friends and associates as Rudy, worked at the world headquarters of the McCormick Company, founded in 1889 in Baltimore, MD. Rudy had started as a young man working for the company that specialized in the processing and marketing of spices from around the globe. He became a manager in the shipping department of the McCormick corporate headquarters located on the waterfront of Baltimore's Inner Harbor. Everyone who knew Rudy respected and liked him. He was the kind of man you just couldn't help liking. Rudy was also a life-long devout Christian and a staunch member of the Episcopal Church. He became a close friend and was like my right arm, a man upon whom I could depend. He was candid, trustworthy, and a loyal and most helpful vestryman in our newly formed **Charlestown United Protestant Church** in Baltimore.

*　　*　　*

In 1983 John Erickson, a developer from Florida, purchased the one hundred fifteen-acre campus and buildings of the former St. Charles Minor Seminary that had been owned and operated by the Roman Catholic religious order of St. Sulpice, a religious teaching order founded in France. With the founding of Maryland under the Roman Catholic Lord Baltimore, the port city of Baltimore, Maryland became home to the "mother" diocese of American Catholicism and it was the Sulpician priests who built and established St. Mary's Roman Catholic Major Seminary and its nearby St. Charles Minor

Seminary. At the height of its existence as a preparatory college for candidates to the priesthood, there were as many as five hundred pre-seminarians enrolled at the St. Charles campus; however, following Vatican II there were dramatic changes that impacted both seminaries and it became more and more difficult to attract young American men to the priesthood. Eventually during the 1970s the St. Charles Seminary was closed. When John Erickson, who had himself studied for the Catholic priesthood under the Jesuits at Georgetown University in Washington, DC, learned that the beautiful campus with its magnificent basilica and dormitory buildings was sitting vacant, it occurred to him that the campus would be an ideal place to establish a model retirement community for senior citizens.

Erickson, who had married a staunch Presbyterian woman, dreamed about the possibilities and developed a vision of what would eventually become the Charlestown Retirement Community in the Catonsville area of Baltimore. It was a truly enormous undertaking over which John Erickson prayed and for which he asked God for His providential guidance and blessing. Three years later, in 1986 Erickson opened the doors to Charlestown, and among the very first residents was **Rudy Wilson**. The beginning of the Charlestown Retirement Community is a saga of faith, entrepreneurial vision, innovative creativity, and a tremendous amount of hard work which eventually resulted in the development of the Charlestown campus. It was the premier model flagship Community for the Erickson Retirement Communities, Inc., a conglomerate that has grown to include twenty-one retirement communities, built on the Charlestown model, that are now home to over twenty-one thousand senior citizens and twelve thousand employees.[1]

In the spring of 1988, at a time when the Charlestown community was still in its early development stages, I was offered a "call" and a contract by John Erickson to serve as the Director of Pastoral Care and Counseling at this new community for senior citizens, which I agreed to accept. Within the first two weeks after I began my duties as part of the Charlestown administrative staff, I made several discoveries that were to alter the way I proceeded to relate to the residents and to the management as well.

First, I discovered that two veteran priests, both of whom were exceptionally devout and competent men and both of whom were sixteen years my senior, were serving the Roman Catholic residents within the Charlestown Community. Fr. Charles Dillon, a Suplician priest, had been the President of the St. Charles Minor Seminary when it had been at its zenith in the fifties and sixties until the time of its closing. Upon comparing notes with him I later learned that I had met Fr. Dillon twenty-five years earlier when I had been the invited guest of the Sulpician fathers at the St. Edward Roman Catholic Seminary in Kenmore, Washington. While I was serving the Brighton Assemblies of God Church in Seattle, Washington, I had enrolled at Seattle University where I completed a Bachelor of Education degree, and among my classmates were two young Sulpician priests who were professors at the St. Edward Seminary. They were intrigued when they discovered that I was the first Protestant clergyman to ever enroll and earn a degree from Seattle University which is a Jesuit educational institution. We became good friends and it was through these two young priests that Fr. Dillon, who was the chaplain at St. Edward seminary, had learned about me. Fr. Dillon who became an esteemed friend and my "chief confessor" while I was at Charlestown revealed to me that he had an uncle who was a Lutheran minister. Fr. Charles Dillon, like Fr. James B. McGoldrick and other Roman Catholic priests whom I came to know and consider as true "brothers in Christ and colleagues of the cloth," helped me understand and experience the true meaning of ecumenism and our "oneness" in Jesus Christ our Lord.

The other priest at Charlestown was Fr. Basil Stockmeyer who was a monk in the Passionist Holy Order. He was a good and godly man who also became an esteemed friend, though I'm not certain that he fully accepted having a younger Protestant clergyman as the Director of our Department of Pastoral Care and Counseling.

The Reverend Fathers Dillon and Stockmeyer and their fellow priests from the Sulpician retirement home next door to the Charlestown campus conducted two daily Masses throughout the week and a high Mass every Sunday morning in the magnificent basilica which the Sulpicians continue to own and manage. It had originally been expected that because Charlestown had been developed on the campus of a former Roman Catholic seminary, the predominant religion of the residents would be Roman Catholic, but to the surprise of many that did not prove to be the case. Eventually the number of Protestant residents outnumbered the Catholic residents by a very large majority. Through the encouragement of Frs. Dillon and Stockmeyer it was not long before the Catholic residents expressed their desire to the Bishop that they be recognized as a full-fledged parish in their own right. The basilica was accessible to the Charlestown residents through two hallways that connected the church with the former dormitory and the rest of the Charlestown community via covered walkways. Residents did not have to go outside of the buildings to travel from one part of the campus to the other, which is a highly valued plus factor to senior citizens who are loath to go out into inclement winter weather or into the heat and humidity of the hot summer months.

With the Protestant residents it was another story. John Erickson had envisioned that the Protestant residents would return every Sunday to their respective denominational churches scattered throughout the greater Baltimore area, and that they would thereby encourage their senior friends to join them as residents in Charleston. Because of that, Erickson was afraid of offending any of the local Protestant clergy by permitting a Protestant congregation to form at

Charlestown. Part of my duty was to visit the Protestant residents, especially to make pastoral calls upon residents who were confined to the intermediate care and intensive care nursing wings. Erickson, however, expected me to invite the neighboring pastors to be pulpit guests for the Sunday Morning Protestant Worship Service held at 9 AM in the basilica. The Sulpician fathers were most gracious in welcoming the Protestants to use their basilica and granted me the privilege of eventually moving into a newly renovated office area in the basilica's undercroft and gave me full access to the sacristy, use of the vestments and altar ware (chalice, etc.) for use in our Protestant services.

The basilica is truly a masterpiece of classic church architecture and is unique in its design and beauty. It was a gift to the St. Charles Seminary from the wealthy parents of the seminary's first president. The benefactors owned a large fleet of cargo ships and operated a very successful export/import business from the Baltimore harbor. They had hired a master ecclesiastical architect who designed the basilica after the classic churches found in Rome. The chapel is lined with perfectly matched slabs of the famous white and blue-gray marble imported from the quarries of Carrara, Italy. The high chancel dome and the chancel walls and floor are covered with inlaid gold-leaf tile mosaics. A large marble high altar inlaid with precious gems sits against the back wall of the chancel. A magnificent Casavant Frères pipe organ is located in the balcony and there is a beautiful prayer chapel in the transcept on the front left side of the Nave. Marble statuary and beautifully carved Stations of the Cross adorn the chancel and the nave. The only other building in America that might be considered a second approximating the basilica is the national Library of Congress in Washington, DC which is also constructed with Cararra marble; however, that building cannot match the beauty of the *Our Lady of the Angels* basilica.

When Charlestown had first opened, there were between six to a dozen Protestants who gathered in the sacristy instead of in the basilica. They felt too few in number to warrant meeting and "rattling around" in the nave of the church where their voices would echo as if they were in a cavern. By the time I came to Charlestown, there were approximately five hundred residents, but most of the Protestants attended Sunday worship services elsewhere or simply stayed in their apartments and did not worship anywhere.

The first Sunday morning I conducted the Protestant worship service in the basilica I was in for two surprises. The first came as an unexpected disappointment when only around thirty persons came to worship. The rest of the Protestant residents had followed Erickson's suggestion that they attend one of the local Protestant churches in the area. The second surprise came as a warning and a threat. I was unapologetically and soundly rebuked because I had not recognized the acoustical problems of speaking in the basilica. Because the walls, ceiling and floor were made of hard-surfaced marble and tile mosaics, unless a preacher spoke with careful enunciation and did not run his words together, the sound of his voice would reverberate off the walls and create a bedlam of unintelligible noise which was only compounded by the public address system. If a speaker dropped his voice to achieve some dramatic affect, those who had hearing problems and wore hearing aids would either experience the amplification of the jumbled noise or they couldn't hear anything at all. The handful of parishioners, led by **Rudy Wilson**, gave me due notice that they would forgive my garbled sermon that one time only; and out of courtesy they would give me a second chance the following Sunday; however, if I did not correct my speaking so that they could understand what I was saying, they vowed not to return to another worship service conducted by me. I had been given fair warning. So the following week I watched for times when no one was in the church and I stood behind the pulpit in the chancel and practiced preaching, being careful to speak slowly and not run my words together. I prayed with desperation that God would help me adjust to the special demands and needs of my new congregation and asked the Lord to grant to me an utterance that could be both articulate and intelligible. I must have passed muster the following Sunday morning because, following the service, my examiners assured me that they were able to understand what I had said and that they would return the following Sunday and thereafter as long as I spoke the Gospel forthrightly and clearly.

It was obvious from the very outset that Rudy Wilson was the unofficial spokesman for the small group of Protestant residents that formed a nucleus around which a congregation might be built. Within the first month these residents made it clear to me that what they desired was not a "Chaplain", as if they were patients in one of the local hospitals; neither did they want a chain of different "visiting firemen" who would preach on Sunday mornings but who would not or could not (because of their pastoral responsibilities to their own respective congregations) provide the kind of "pastoral care" that they wanted and for which they felt a need. This feeling was especially keen among those residents who could no longer drive their own cars or who were afraid to venture out in icy winter weather or in the blazing heat of summer. What they wanted and needed was a minister—a *pastor* of their own!

It was important for me to make certain that what I was hearing from them truly represented their deep feelings and heart-felt needs for both a *pastor* and a Protestant *church* of their own. They felt that they were being discriminated against by the Charlestown management who recognized the authority of the Roman Catholic Bishop over the Catholic parishioners and his willingness for them to be constituted as a full-fledged parish in their own right; but the Charlestown management wanted to deny the Protestant residents the right to form their own *self-governing congregation* and to have a minister to whom they could look as their own *pastor*. I requested Rudy Wilson to give me his good counsel. He affirmed that my appraisal and understanding of a large segment of the Protestant residents' sentiments was accurate, and that he was anxious to do anything he could to help in the formation of a Protestant congregation at Charlestown.

Rudy Wilson knew everyone at Charlestown. He was one of those gregarious fellows who easily made friends with everybody, and he was one of the self-appointed individuals who went out of his way to make certain that newcomers to Charlestown were made to feel welcome and at *home*. I asked Rudy to recommend persons whom he knew would represent a wide cross-section of the Protestant residents from all of the major denominations. With Rudy's able assistance and his personal persuasion, we recruited an *ad hoc* committee of twelve men and women whose religious backgrounds included Episcopalians, Presbyterians, Congregationalists, United Methodists, Baptists, and Lutherans. After Rudy introduced everyone, I explained that the purpose of our meeting was to explore with them the possibility of forming a **Charlestown United Protestant Church** to give the Protestant residents a more equitable parity with that of the Catholic residents. There existed at that time a marked disparity between the ambiguous religious relationships of the Protestant Christians at Charlestown and the religious relationships of the Roman Catholic residents whose parish membership was clearly delineated by Roman Catholic polity, which automatically affiliated them with the neighboring Our Lady of Victory Parish. The Protestant residents were left in a religious limbo without a church entity at Charlestown into which they might have their church membership transferred or with which they might become members upon confession of faith.

The members who came together to form our *ad hoc* committee came from the three different major forms of ecclesiastical structures and religious polity: they were almost equally divided between episcopal, congregational, and presbyterial forms of church polity, and few of them understood any form of church polity other than their own. My first task was to provide them with a clear explanation of the differences and similarities of these three polities. Using a blackboard I slowly and carefully diagrammed and explained that under the episcopal polities followed by Roman Catholics, Anglicans/Episcopalians and Methodists, authority and institutional power resided in the bishops who in some cases acted in a dictatorial manner that came from the top down. In congregational polities followed by Congregationalists, Baptists, Disciples of Christ, and most independent Protestant churches, the ultimate power and authority was vested in the lay members of the individual congregation and was passed in a democratic way from the bottom upward to their elected trustees and deacons and then to the ministers and their respective judicatories. In the presbyterial polity there is a blending and balancing of power between the clergy and the laity through a three-way negotiation that involves (1) individual clergy, (2) the local congregation and (3) the presbytery which is a part of the larger synod and its national judicatory.

Having once defined those polity distinctions, and having explained the various advantages and disadvantages of each of the three forms of church polity/government, we began together to select those characteristics which seemed to best meet the unique requirements of a truly ecumenical church and parish. Everyone agreed unanimously that it would never do to single out and choose any one denomination over all others, or to affiliate with any one denomination, but that the Charleston United Protestant (CUP) Church would by its very ecumenical nature need to be congregational in its polity, and that certain polity nomenclature might lend itself better than others for the purposes of the proposed CUP Church. Although the *ad hoc* committee selected a "congregational" polity, in a deliberate effort to attract a wider ecumenical membership it was decided in an eclectic manner that instead of referring to the congregation's governing board as a *Board of Deacons* (Baptist) or as a *Session* (Presbyterian), partially in deference to Rudy Wilson and the other Episcopalians, to adopt the name "*Vestry*" to designate the nine-person governing committee composed of three classes of three members each. One new class of Vestry persons would be elected each year for a three-year term of office and no one could succeed himself, thus avoiding the development of a self-perpetuating clique. If a unicameral organization were adopted, the Vestry would also serve as the Board of Trustees, and as the CUP congregation grew, a bicameral structure could be adopted allowing for a separate Board of Trustees. With these criteria in mind, a provisional Constitution and Bylaws were drafted and submitted to the Charlestown administration for their review and input, and were subsequently adopted at a specially called organizational meeting held in October of 1988.

My own Bishop, Joseph Yeakel, and a neighboring United Methodist Pastor, Carroll Yingling, objected to the formation of the Charlestown United Protestant *Church* on the Biblically unsupportable assumptions that (1) the CUP ought not to be referred to as a full-fledged *church* since it had no ecclesiastical denominational affiliation and (2) that I had no authority to organize such an independent congregation. I wrote a theological position paper challenging Yeakel's false assumptions, and pointed out that other *bona fide* churches (e.g., many Baptist churches and other independent congregations) are constituted as autonomous churches that are not subordinate to any denominational hierarchy. I reminded John Erickson, Charlestown's founder and CEO, that under the First Amendment of the U.S. Constitution the citizens who reside at Charlestown have every civil right to organize themselves as they had done, and that they had incorporated into their Constitution and Bylaw provisions whereby the CUP would in fact have ecclesiastical affiliation and membership in the local Baltimore Council of Churches and thereby would be linked to the National and World Councils of Churches as well.

Recognizing that the Reverends Yeakel and Yingling might prod Mr. Erickson into bringing pressure upon the newly formed church and its pastors, I contacted the offices of the Consultation on Church Union (COCU) in Princeton, New Jersey, and through them learned about the International Council of Community Churches (ICCC) whose offices were located in the Chicago, Illinois area. The Reverend Dr. J. Ralph Shotwell, Interim General Secretary of COCU was also the Executive Director of the ICCC. He visited the Charlestown Campus and I introduced "Bishop" Shotwell to Mr. Erickson. Shotwell explained to John Erickson that the ICCC is not a denomination but is a *council* of independent congregational churches and that ICCC is in full ecclesiastical affiliation as a member of both the National Council of Churches in the USA and is a member of the World Council of Churches on whose Boards of Directors the Reverend Shotwell held a judicatorial membership. When Yeakel attempted to challenge Dr. Shotwell and the legitimacy of the ICCC as a *council* of independent congregational churches, Shotwell spoke to the President of the United Methodist Council of Bishops and Yeakel was forthwith stopped from further interfering in the CUP's internal affairs. Both Yeakel and John Erickson realized that by its membership in the ICCC the CUP congregation had every right under the U.S. Constitution to proclaim its standing as a legitimate *"Church"* in good standing within the major recognized national and international ecumenical bodies.

Yeakel had protested that only a bishop had a right to organize and institute a Church, but I reminded him that while it is true that only a Methodist Bishop is empowered to authorize the formation of a Methodist church, the CUP had no desire whatsoever to become a United Methodist congregation or to be governed by any bishop, and that what I had done was permitted under my contract and the terms of my ABLC appointment (*appointment beyond a local church*) standing. Yeakel was furious over the turn of events, especially since in his first assignment as a bishop in Central New York State he had a similar encounter with an independent congregation that had for several years been served by Methodist clergymen but which refused to be intimidated and manipulated by his high-handed methods and instead affiliated with the ICCC and broke off its relationship with the Methodist denomination under Yeakel's watch. For the Charlestown Protestants and for me, ours was a *coup de maitre*, a masterstroke of churchmanship.

When I first came to Charlestown in 1988 there were only around five residents, but throughout the next three years during which the Charlestown United Protestant Church was organized the community experienced a rapid expansion and grew to over fifteen hundred residents and has since more than doubled that number. The CUP congregation began with only three members who were publicly received as quasi-*members* by my predecessor the Rev. Dr. John Dixon in anticipation of the formation of the then unborn Protestant Congregation. The CUP Church thrived and grew as over two hundred persons joined the membership of the new congregation. Attendance at the Sunday worship services had begun in 1983 with less than a dozen in attendance. By 1988, the attendance averaged between thirty to fifty for Sunday morning worship but by 1991 the attendance to the CUP Sunday worship services and other special services began to rival that of the Roman Catholic congregation. As the two congregations approached a numerical and ecclesiastical parity a genuine spirit of true ecumenism had also begun to develop and to grow stronger between the two congregations. The two congregations united together in sponsoring a monthly prayer breakfast held in the Terrace Room Restaurant on the campus. On other special occasions like Thanksgiving, during Advent and Christmas, Veteran's Sunday and the 4th of July celebrations, the clergy and parishioners of the two congregations co-sponsored united services of worship in the Chapel.

*   *   *

Then, on Palm Sunday in 1989 something unheard of prior to that time took everyone by utter surprise: as Director of Pastoral Care and Counseling at Charlestown I often attended and participated in the Mass and was quite often invited to read one of the Scripture lessons from the lectionary. The Reverend Fr. Gerald L. Brown, who was the Sulpician Provincial from 1985 to 1997, had received me most cordially when I first came to Charlestown. On this special Sunday I attended the Catholic Mass to bring greetings on behalf of the CUP Congregation and to publicly welcome to our clergy staff a new Sulpician priest who was replacing Fr. Stockmeyer. I was seated in the chancel with the officiating priests, but I had never before participated in the celebration of the Eucharist nor had I ever received the Sacrament with the rest of the worshippers. As the Sulpician priest who was the primary officiant at the celebration of the Holy Eucharist proceeded with the litany of the holy Communion, he abruptly stopped, turned toward me and surprised me and shocked the congregation by motioning and saying to me, "Dr. Jones, please come here and join me and the other priests in celebrating the Holy Eucharist." Then he turned toward the stunned worshippers and asked them, "How can I not invite our Brother David to join us at the Holy Altar to celebrate with us the great sacrifice for our salvation by our Lord Jesus Christ who himself prayed that all of us who are his disciples might become *one* in Him?" The inviting of a Protestant minister to celebrate the Roman Catholic Mass was unprecedented in the Baltimore diocese, but Pope John the Twenty-Third at the Vatican Council II had opened the door for such special occasions and had given authority to cardinals, bishops, provincials and the superiors of the various Catholic holy orders to invite Eastern Orthodox and Protestant clergy to co-celebrate the Eucharist during events that were of particular ecumenical and historic significance. That was the first of a succession of such occasions when the Sulpician Provincials and Roman Catholic priests invited me to participate and co-celebrate the Mass and Holy Eucharist with them. On Worldwide Communion Sunday, the first Sunday in October, 1990, the Catholic and Protestant congregations at Charlestown united in an ecumenical celebration of Holy Communion and Fr. Frank Sweeny who was then serving as the parish priest for the Roman Catholic Church at Charlestown and I co-celebrated the Eucharist at the same altar in the basilica.

The traditional liturgy for the celebration of Holy Communion that was used by John Wesley was taken directly from the Anglican liturgy and Prayer Book and is almost an exact parallel of the ancient Roman Catholic Mass. The Catholic liturgy incorporates all of the universally common lectionary lessons for the day, but apart from the words in one of the prayers in the Catholic Mass which may be addressed to Mary the mother of Jesus, I found nothing within the Litany of the Roman Catholic Mass with which I could not in my heart agree. Protestant Christians revere Mary and are grateful for the role she played in bearing the infant Jesus and nurturing him throughout his childhood and adolescent years and we honor her for her example of righteousness in the early apostolic church. Protestants, however, do not pray to the departed saints nor consider them as intercessors or mediators of divine grace. Protestants hold Jesus to be the one and only mediator between God and man. Protestants regard Mary as being the mother of Jesus and his humanity but reject the notion that Mary or any other human being should ever be considered the "mother of God" for He is eternal and without beginning, having always been self-existent without any progenitors apart from Himself. Like other Protestants I could not in good conscience pray what is referred to as the "Hail Mary":

> *"Hail, Mary, full of grace, the Lord is with thee: blessed art thou among women, and blessed is the fruit of thy womb, Jesus. Holy Mary, **mother of God**, pray for us sinners now and at the hour of our death. Amen."*

Apart from that "Hail Mary" prayer and the notion held by some Roman Catholics that the consecrated bread and wine when it is consecrated by the priest during the Mass becomes the literal flesh and blood of Christ, our basic understanding of the meaning of the Holy Eucharist is parallel. Some Protestants consider the notion of transubstantiation and the parallel notion of consubstantiation held by Lutherans and Episcopalians to infer cannibalism and regard it as repugnant. Many Roman Catholics do not regard the host and the wine to magically become literal flesh and blood as if a consecrated wafer could somehow be used in an operating room surgical procedure as human flesh or the consecrated wine could be used to provide a blood transfusion. For most Protestants the bread and wine are regarded as sacred *symbols* of Jesus Christ's body and blood.[2]

After praying together at the monthly prayer breakfasts, uniting in worship services on numerous occasions throughout the year and finally experiencing a united celebration of the Eucharist on Worldwide Communion Sunday, there emerged a genuine spirit of ecumenism within the Christian community at Charlestown. That spirit was often manifested in expressions of Christian love, of *agape*, and it was not uncommon for my wife Barbara and me to be the recipients of lots of hugs from parishioners who were old enough to be our parents, but what was special about it was that we received almost as many hugs and kind words from our Roman Catholic friends as we did from our Protestant parishioners. The Sulpician priests showed a truly magnanimous degree of collegiality and Christian brotherhood toward me and invited me to have lunch with them in their refractory at least once a month.

*   *   *

When I led a pilgrimage to the Passion Play in Obergammgergau, Germany in the spring of 1990, among the sixteen Charlestown residents who accompanied us were five members of the Charlestown Roman Catholic congregation including our beloved Nun, Sr. Mary Pierre Newman, MM, who was the sister of Bishop Newman of the Archdiocese of Baltimore. When we were in Venice, Italy, I accompanied our Catholic friends to Sunday morning Mass at St. Paul's Cathedral. The Holy Scriptures were read in five different languages to accommodate the multi-national congregation and foreign visitors in attendance, but most of the liturgy was spoken in Latin and was recited by Sr. Pierre from memory while I followed along in the Missile drawing upon the Latin I had learned as a high school student in Columbia, Pennsylvania. We quickly came to love Sr. Pierre and to regard her as one of the living saints of our time who like Mother Teresa of Calcutta set for all of us examples of righteous living and Christian charity.

At Charlestown Fr. Frank Sweeney's office was next to mine and directly across the hall were the offices of Sr. Pierre and Fr. Stockmeyer's and the office of Rev. Trent Owings, the Disciples of Christ minister who served as my Assistant Pastor. We shared a receptionist/secretary whose desk was located at the entrance to our Pastoral Care & Counseling suite of offices.

During the school year we might have as many as six seminarians from St. Mary's Roman Catholic Seminary serving internships under the mentoring of our clergy staff.

One of the highlights of our day was when Rudy Wilson would pay a visit to our offices. He would stop to chat for a few minutes with whomever he might happen to find in their office at the time, and eventually he would knock on my door. In my office there was a little alcove area where I had placed four chairs by a small table upon which were a lamp and reading materials. I used this as an area for informal counseling and for small committee meetings. The coffee pot was always on and usually I had cookies which I obtained from the community's Food Services department. When Rudy would come in I always welcomed his good company and would take a break from whatever I was doing to visit with him. I knew that whatever news he carried would be of interest and sometimes he would provide me with important information about things within our parish and the larger community of which I was unaware and about which I was grateful to learn through the filter of Rudy's careful scrutiny. No football running back ever had a better team to run interference for him as he carried the football down the field toward the goal line. Rudy was my lead blocker and also a great receiver when I'd pass the ball to him.

Rudy Wilson was my own personal *Colombo*. Just like Peter Falk's comical TV detective Lieutenant Colombo, Rudy would start to leave, and then thinking of something that just happened to pop into his mind as he reached the door, he would pause and say, "Oh, Pastor, one more thing . . ." Rudy was unintentionally really comical but I never let Rudy catch me chuckling at his Colombo mannerisms. Sometimes after he had closed the door behind him and gone down the hall to visit with someone else, something would come to his mind and he would come back, rap on the door, stick his head in and say, "Pastor, one more thing . . ." But there was never anything unkind or not genuine about Rudy. And he seemed to find a special place in his big heart for my wife Barbara who was about thirty-five years younger than Rudy. Barbara who is younger than I am is also like Rudy, a gregarious and vivacious person. The two of them seemed to hit it off well from the very beginning and it was soon apparent that Rudy had become very fond of Barbara and regarded her almost as if she were a daughter. Rudy was a widower and spent many hours each day alone in his apartment listening to music aired on the Christian radio stations and on the good music stations that he could tune into on his stereo recorder. Knowing that Barbara loves good music, Rudy began making sixty and ninety minute cassette tape recordings especially for Barbara and he seemed to find a special pleasure presenting his tapes to Barbara as unspoken expressions of his fondness for her.

Rudy Wilson was more than just another parishioner to us; he was more even than one of the key lay officers in our CUP congregation. Rudy Wilson became a trusted confidant and a beloved friend and elder brother in Christ. Any pastor who is fortunate to find among his parishioners such a loyal, trustworthy, knowledgeable and dedicated friend is a lucky and blessed minister. May Rudy's tribe increase.

NOTES:

[1]   To view the Charlestown Community and its magnificent inter-faith basilica visit the Charlestown website at: ***http://www.retirementcommunitiesonline.com/Listing.php?lid=124.***

[2]   It was my privilege in 1976 to be an invited guest of the Roman Catholic Diocese of Harrisburg, PA and to participate with a selected group of other Protestant clergyman in the World Congress of the Holy Eucharist that was held in Philadelphia that summer. At that historic occasion the Reverend Bishop Fulton J. Sheen in his major address acknowledged that Protestants are correct in their recognition that the wafer/Host is not magically transformed into *literal* human flesh nor is the wine magically transformed into *literal* human blood. Bishop Sheen then went on to explain that for Christians the bread and wine nonetheless become in a *mystical* and metaphysical sense the body and blood of Jesus Christ." His explication of the Roman Catholic understanding of *the mystical presence* of Jesus in the celebration of the Holy Eucharist conforms to the Scriptural assurance that wherever and whenever two or three gather together in His name he is present with them. In that Scriptural mystical and spiritual sense Bishop Sheen's explication can be affirmed by Protestant Christians. Knowing the affinity of my Protestant theological convictions to the Roman Catholic theological understanding of the Eucharist I was invited to be a co-celebrant with my Catholic fellow clergy at the holy altar, and I was able to do so without violating my own theological understanding of the Holy Sacrament of Communion.

John Marvin Brown, PhD

CHAPTER 16

JOHN MARVIN BROWN

JOHN MARVIN BROWN, PhD, is blessed with a deep baritone voice and a love of music. I thoroughly enjoyed listing to him sing in our church choir and to hear him sing the familiar old Gospel hymns and the Negro spirituals which are an integral part of the Black American heritage in which he grew up. In 1992 Marvin and his wife Lydia and their children began attending **St. Luke's United Methodist Church in the Woodlawn district of Baltimore, Maryland**.

At its zenith in the 1960s the St. Luke's UMC in Woodlawn had a membership of over one thousand communicant members and an additional constituency who participated in the Church's Boy Scout, Cub Scout, Girl Scout and Brownie Scout units and in the Senior Citizens Association and Congregate Meals programs, etc., St. Luke's United Methodist Church was then one of the strongest Methodist congregations in the Baltimore Central District of the United Methodist Church.

The St. Luke's UM Congregation traces its historic origins back to a group of godly and dedicated Christians who lived in the area back in colonial times when the surrounding region was known as Powhatan (named after one of the tribes of American Indians whose tribal hunting and fishing grounds reached to the headwaters of the Patuxent River near what is today the Woodlawn community). In 1856 a group of these Christians began holding old-fashioned Methodist Class Meetings in a second floor weaving room of a cotton mill building which stood within what are the present precincts of the Woodlawn Cemetery.

These class meetings continued until 1873 when a church building was erected close by and given the name "Powhatan Methodist Episcopal Church." That building was moved by oxen across the frozen pond waters of Gwynn's Falls in the winter of 1904 to the present church site. When a new and larger sanctuary nave was erected in 1930, the old Powhatan Church was moved once again, this time to the back of the church property where it remains part of the church building complex today.

From those early humble beginnings, nearly a century and a half later the Powhatan congregation was merged into the nearby St. Luke's Methodist Episcopal Church (founded in 1859) and the present sanctuary was completed in 1931. In 1953 a large building was purchased from a WW II Army Base that was surplused; the building was dismantled and moved over 30 miles and reassembled on the church property where it has since served as an excellent Parish Hall. In 1992 air-conditioning was installed in the sanctuary, annex and parish hall, and each of the buildings was redecorated, giving the church a much needed refurbishing.

Following WW II the U.S. Social Security Department offices were located in the Woodlawn area which began to undergo a rapidly accelerating demographic transition from an all-White residential area to what has become a predominantly Black neighborhood. Marvin and his wife Lydia were among the first *Christians of color* who began to worship with the St. Luke's United Methodist Church and because of their professional training and winsome personalities they were welcomed and quickly integrated into the life and leadership positions within the congregation.

At the age of thirteen Marvin formed a local rock group, the *Softones*, in his neighborhood of Baltimore. He was the lead singer in the *Softones* musical group, which became well-known on the East Coast. The *Softones* recorded five albums and traveled to England and Europe where they landed singing engagements on the stages and in the night clubs of the cities to which they traveled.[1] But there was a downside to the fast-track life of a group of Black musicians on the move from singing gigs in one city after the other. As with so many musicians traveling in the subcultures, locales, and the night life of the entertainment world, it was not long before Marvin became an alcoholic and a drug addict, and his life began the downward slide to which that path often leads.

Marvin realized that drugs and alcohol were slowly and agonizingly but surely killing him and that unless he could somehow manage to climb out of the cesspool into which he was sinking, he would die young. Wanting to live, he entered a program to treat his addictions. It was through contacts made during his alcohol and drug therapy that he met Lydia, a pretty Hispanic girl who was also seeking recovery from drug addiction. Marvin and Lydia fell in love and were married and soon had a daughter and two little boys in their family.

Because both Marvin and Lydia have bright minds and winsome personalities and had successfully managed through rehabilitation therapy and abstinence to regain sobriety, they were recruited to enter training to become professional drug and alcohol therapists and counselors. Eventually Marvin was named the Assistant Director of the Drug and Alcohol Rehabilitation Treatment (DART) Clinic founded and sponsored by the St. Luke's United Methodist Church of Woodlawn, Baltimore, Maryland.

Because of the growing illicit drug traffic that surfaced in the transitional Woodlawn neighborhood, we began to explore the possibility of establishing a *Drug and Alcohol Rehabilitation and Treatment* clinic, which came to be known as our DART program. With the assistance of Marvin and Lydia and several of their associates in the addiction treatment field, I undertook the task of writing and filing the DART protocol and licensure application for the clinic. The protocol and application encompassed over five hundred pages of documentation that had to meet the very same requirements as the addiction clinic at the world famous John's Hopkins Hospital in Baltimore. The St. Luke's DART Clinic pioneered in the development of a full-fledged *holistic* counseling program that included a *pneuma-psycho-somatic* understanding and discipline in the treatment of addictive diseases and emotional-psychological disorders and pathologies. St. Luke's DART Clinic was the first addiction treatment clinic to be licensed by the Maryland State Board of Health for holistic counseling treatment, and it became a model for future clinics in the State of Maryland. Today there are numerous holistic addiction treatment clinics throughout Maryland and the United States that are now practicing the kind of holistic treatment programs pioneered by the St. Luke's DART Clinic.

Following the example of St. Luke the Physician and Evangelist of the New Testament, the DART clinic provided a needed "healing ministry" of professional counseling and therapy to persons suffering from addiction disorders. I served as the Administrative Director of the clinic. A physician and a registered nurse offered the required medical supervision and treatment. Marvin Brown and several part-time counselors provided group and one-on-one training and guidance to patients/clients and the parish secretary served as an adjunct secretary to the clinic. As an outgrowth of the DART program, a Narcotics Anonymous program was developed at St. Luke's UMC in Woodlawn. NA groups meet five nights weekly at the St. Luke's Church, and this year the NA programs celebrated their eighteenth year of continued ministry to persons in recovery from addiction.

*　　*　　*

Marvin Brown was elected the Lay Leader of the St. Luke's Congregation and it was in that role that Marvin distinguished himself by manifesting a noble spirit of personal integrity in a particularly difficult situation in which I became the target of a mean-spirited racial attack upon my person. In that confrontation Marvin demonstrated an exceptionally high level of Christian integrity and commitment, devotion to Christ and a much appreciated loyalty to his pastor. Severe pressure was placed upon Marvin by his testimony and in his loyalty and prayers for me. In that crucible of inter-racial tension Marvin demonstrated his personal integrity, his commitment to Christ, and the backbone to stand up for what he believed was right and true.

*　　*　　*

I came to respect and regard Marvin as a true fellow-servant of Jesus Christ and will always be grateful to him for his high moral ethics and Christian character. In the course of my ministry it has been my good fortune to know and love as brothers and sisters in Christ many good and godly Black Christians, and I am glad that *"in Christ there is no east or west, in Him no south or north; but one great fellowship of love throughout the whole wide earth."* It is not the color of our skin but the attitude of our heart and our faith in Jesus Christ that knits us together as brothers and sisters and members of the family of God. For this we give thanks and praise to our Heavenly Father.

*　　*　　*

Marvin earned an undergraduate degree in ministry and counseling, and in 2001 he earned the Master of Science in Human Services degree from Lincoln University. In 2009 he received his PhD in Psychology degree from Capella University, Minneapolis, Minnesota. Dr. Brown is the program director for intermediate care and detoxification at Gaudenzia, Inc. in Baltimore, Maryland. He is an adjunct professor at Lincoln University, Pennsylvania where he teaches counseling systems, psychology, and ethics. He continues to serve the Lord as a Christian layman and a leader in his church and community.

NOTES:

1　　Their new CD, *The Very Best of the Softones*, is available through Amherst Records, Buffalo, New York. See their website:
http://www.amherstrecords.com/store/store_browse_detail.php?PID=52&CID=73

L. B. Holcombe, MSEd

CHAPTER 17

L. B. HOLCOMBE

L. B. HOLCOMBE, MSEd, is truly a Southern gentleman and one of the finest Christians it has been my privilege to know. He is an outstanding leader and member of the **Johns Creek United Methodist Church, Duluth, Georgia.**

His initials stand for Leonard Bob, but to his family and friends he is affectionately known as "L.B.," and in good Southern tradition that seems to fit him just fine. He was born on Oct. 4, 1931 in Whitfield County, Georgia[1] He attended public schools in the North Georgia mountain town of Dalton, which is known as the "Carpet Capital of the World," nestled in the foothills of the Blue Ridge Mountains.

During the Korean War L.B. served in the U.S. Navy assigned to an LST 846 landing craft engaged in amphibious assaults upon Korean beachheads and river landings of troops. Following his discharge from the Navy, he earned an MSEd degree from West Georgia College, and taught 8th grade mathematics in a middle school. In 1963 he married Kathryn Tangle who was also from Whitfield County, and became employed as an agent for the Cotton States Insurance Company where he worked for the next 33 years. He became the Senior Vice President of Marketing for the Property and Casualty Department of that company, retiring in 1996.

After moving to the North Atlanta area, the Holcombes joined the Johns Creek United Methodist Church and L.B. very quickly became one of the leaders of that growing congregation. In North Fulton County, there were two small rural churches, each having about a dozen active members. Warsaw

Methodist Church was established in the early 1800s on property known as the Warsaw campground, which served as a planning site for soldiers during the Civil War. The Ocee Methodist Church was founded much later, around 1915. It was under the pastoral leadership of the Rev. Wayne Johnson that these two small congregations merged on September 7, 1987 forming the new Johns Creek United Methodist Church. The church received the current property as a gift from Johns Creek Technology Park and began constructing a new church building in Duluth, Georgia. Today the congregation has grown to a membership of over two thousand and carries on an active outreach ministry through its extensive sports program, its child day care center and a host of various congregational activities.[2]

* * *

Rev. Wayne Johnson was a large man standing well over six feet tall and weighing over three hundred lbs. In college he had been a varsity lineman for the University of Mississippi's football team. When the Vietnam War broke out, Wayne Johnson was recruited and trained as a Green Beret special ops field officer and served valiantly in Vietnam. His military mission had been to train and deploy Vietnamese soldiers and to deploy with them into front-line combat operations. His orders were to "search and destroy and take no prisoners." Wayne was engaged in numerous hand-to-hand fire fights and was one of the few survivors when his jungle outposts were over-run by throngs of Vietcong. It was in a devastating combat engagement that Wayne Johnson witnessed the slaughter of the entire platoon under his command. It was only by a miracle of God's grace that he survived.

Unfortunately, Wayne Johnson became a victim of the post-traumatic stress syndrome experienced by many military personnel who were engaged in the life and death struggles for survival in the midst of repeated severe combat engagements.[3] Although he had an outstanding ministry as the "organizing pastor" of the Johns Creek UM Church, the haunting demons and nightmares of Vietnam tormented him, affecting his ministry and ultimately leading to his early demise. He was a man who truly loved the Lord but who was a victim of the madness and insanity of war. We choose to remember him for his love of Jesus Christ and his deep desire to make a difference as a builder of His kingdom on earth.

Upon returning home after the war, Wayne Johnson became an officer in a bank in his hometown in Mississippi; but feeling the call from God to the Christian ministry, he attended Candler School of Theology at Emory University in Atlanta and became a United Methodist minister. Rev. Johnson had a deep love of Christ as his Savior, and more than anything else he wanted to "make disciples" who would on a daily basis live lives of true commitment to God. With the assistance of a group of dedicated laymen, Pastor Johnson developed a criterion for serious Christian commitment, and out of that mode of discipleship he developed the Love One Another Fellowship (LOAF) program. The LOAF clusters were small groups who engaged in Bible study and personal accountability, following the pattern of John Wesley's class meetings and the personal accountability reporting that distinguished early Methodism. Through his leadership and that of the group of lay leaders who worked with him, the Johns Creek Church experienced a phenomenally rapid growth from a handful of people to a large membership that today continues to grow and to expand its outreach ministries.[4]

* * *

After I retired from pastoral ministry in July of 1994, we moved to Georgia from Annapolis, Maryland and built a new home in the Olde Atlanta Club in Forsyth County north of Atlanta. We transferred our membership to the First United Methodist Church of Duluth, Georgia, and Barbara sang in the choir. Occasionally I was invited by the pastor to preach and assist in the worship and other services.

It was out of curiosity and interest that I visited the Johns Creek UM Church on a Sunday just before Christmas in 1995. I learned that Rev. Johnson who was also a pilot had suffered an accident while working on his twin engine Beechcraft airplane and had undergone surgery to remove a metal shaving that had spun off a drill and embedded itself in his eye. That morning there was no clergy present but a layman had led the service and given a short talk. After the service I offered my services to the congregation as a temporary supply minister until Pastor Johnson could return to the pulpit. That led to an invitation from Pastor Johnson for me to serve as the Minister of Pastoral Care & Counseling for the Johns Creek Congregation, and later that position was expanded to include responsibilities as the congregation's Minister of Christian Education. It was in those capacities that I came to know L.B. Holcombe.

* * *

The Johns Creek Church has a large and vibrant senior adult "Good News" Sunday School Class with an average attendance of around fifty persons and a larger constituency. This same group of people also formed the core of a mid-week "Basics" Bible study group that met regularly on Tuesday evenings with an average attendance of around thirty persons. L.B. Holcombe was the *de facto* leader and "President" of both of these groups. In addition, L.B. was also the leader of a "LOAF" (Love One Another Fellowship) small orientation/study-group for new members that regularly met for fellowship and Christian nurture in the parishioners' homes. He was also a Facilitator for the *Disciple I* through *the Disciple V* series of Bible Study groups, and a participant in the Stephen's Ministries, a visitation and counseling outreach ministry of the church. L.B. was involved in the church up to his elbows and gave unstintingly of his time and energies in those leadership capacities.

It was not a surprise to me when L.B. approached me asking for my help by filling in for him as a substitute teacher for the Sunday morning "Good News" class. I was retired and not really interested in engaging in any additional pastoral responsibility, so I declined his invitation. Then a week or two later once again L.B. pleaded with me to spell him off for a Sunday or two or to take a couple of the midweek Basics Bible Study sessions. Again, I declined. But when he begged me for the third time to give him a break by substituting for him, I didn't have the heart to turn him down again. I finally consented to fill in for him on the following three Tuesday evening sessions. I asked L.B. what he wanted me to speak about, and he said, "You can talk about any subject you choose."

That was a pretty wide-open *carte blanche* invitation. I didn't have the slightest idea about what kind of subject I should choose, so I asked my wife Barbara and she suggested, "Why don't you use the material from your sermons about the Apostles?" Over the years I had developed sermons about first one and then another of the Apostles, until I finally had accumulated a whole series of sermons devoted to each one of the Twelve Apostles. "Just take your pick," Barbara had prompted, so for the first lesson I selected a sermon discourse on St. Matthew who was quite a colorful character.

To my surprise, the group responded enthusiastically and asked me to choose another one of the Apostles from that series of sermons. Next I selected St. Andrew, the first of the Galilean fishermen to become a disciple of Jesus Christ (St. Andrew is my favorite of the Apostles.) Again the Basics Bible Study group was enthusiastic and the crowd had grown a little. The third week I chose Jude Lebbaeus Thaddaeus, the son of St. James the Great and the nephew of his father's brother, St. John. I have come to regard St. Jude as the most likely New Testament character to be identified as the boy with "the loaves and fishes" with which Jesus fed the multitude (see St. John 6:1-13). After the third evening, the Basics study group was intrigued by the lives of the Apostles about whom I had spoken, and the whole group joined L.B. in imploring me to continue with the series until I had completed the entire list of Apostles including Matthias who took the place vacated by Judas Iscariot.

When we returned home that evening, Barbara surprised me by stating: "David, you really ought to write a book about the Apostles and have it published." I had not previously given any thought to writing another book. In 1980, Skipworth Press had published my first book, *The Pastoral Mentor*, which was a distillation of my doctoral dissertation, but I was so busy with pastoral responsibilities that I had enough on my hands just keeping up with the weekly preparation of sermons, college courses that I taught at Drew University, and occasional other lectures and public addresses. Now that I was retired I had the time to devote to the writing of a book manuscript about the Apostles. There is, however, a marked difference between writing a sermon manuscript for delivery as a pulpit discourse and the research and writing of a book, especially one which is designed to be a reliable and fully documented work suitable for use in academia as well as in a local church for reading by a lay audience. When I mentioned to the Basics Bible Study Group that Barbara had suggested that I write a book about the Apostles, they gave their enthusiastic support and agreed to be my "pilot" critique group; so over the next four months an average of thirty-five persons met each week as we worked our way through the biographical sketches of the Apostles.

Shortly thereafter we moved to Fort Wayne, Indiana where I completed the writing and editing of the book entitled **The MINYIAN,** which was published by *Xlibris*, one of the affiliates of the Random House publishing conglomerate, and in the fall of 2004 the book was released.[5]

Not long after the book's release, I received an E-mail from a well known movie producer offering me a role in two major documentary films about the Apostles. My interest was piqued and when I responded requesting more information, the producers sent me a contract with two scripts to learn for my appearances as one of the New Testament scholars in each of the two films, **Twelve Ordinary Men** and **Miraculous Mission,** produced by Grizzly Adams Film Productions and Shadow Play Films.[6]

The book and the movies resulted from L.B. Holcombe's persistence and persuasion and from the encouragement of my wife, Barbara Ann, and the good people in the Good News Class and the Basics Bible Study group at Johns Creek United Methodist Church. We continue to correspond with these grand Christian people and they graciously keep us on their class mailing list and permit us to be prayer partners with them. Their loyal friendship and prayers are greatly appreciated, and we consider ourselves fortunate to be part of their fellowship.

NOTES:

[1] Whitfield County, GA is named after the famous preacher Rev. George Whitfield who was a colleague of John and Charles Wesley at Oxford University, England and was associated with the Wesley brothers in bringing the religious "Great Awakening" to America in the 18th Century.

[2] To learn more about the congregation visits its website: *http://www.johnscreekumc.org/index.php*

3   Post Traumatic Stress Disorder (PTSD) is a condition distinct from *traumatic stress*, which has less intensity and duration, and combat stress reaction, which is transitory. PTSD has also been recognized in the past as **stress syndrome, shell shock, battle fatigue, traumatic war neurosis, or post-traumatic stress syndrome (PTSS)**. Diagnostic symptoms include reexperience such as flashbacks and nightmares, avoidance of stimuli associated with the trauma, increased arousal such as difficulty falling or staying asleep, anger and hyper-vigilance. Per definition, the symptoms last more than six months and cause significant impairment in social, occupational, or other important areas of functioning (e.g. problems with work and relationships.)—*http://en.wikipedia.org/wiki/Post-traumatic_stress_disorder*

4   To learn more about the Johns Creek United Methodist Church you may visit the church's website at: *http://www.johnscreekumc.org/*

5   You can visit it *The MINYAN* websites at: *http://www.chapelquartet.org/theminyan.htm* and *https://www2.xlibris.com/bookstore/bookdisplay.asp?bookid=19564.*

6   To learn more about these films, you can visit the following website: *http://www.grizzlyadams.com/Public/ChristianReleases/index.cfm?productID=40*

David Tibbitts

CHAPTER 18

DAVID TIBBITTS

DAVID TIBBITTS is a successful building contractor specializing in the design and construction of residential and commercial entrance porches, decks, patios and fences. He is the owner and President of the Atlanta Decking & Fence Company, Shiloh Road, Cumming, Georgia. David was Chairman of the Administrative Council of the **Shiloh United Methodist Church, Cumming, Georgia** during the brief time I served that congregation as its interim pastor in 1998. David and several other men of the congregation used their talents as skilled craftsmen to keep the Shiloh UM Church and its parsonage in good repair and made improvements on these structures from time to time as funds permitted. They were an active group of Christians who shared a strong bond of fellowship and a deep commitment to the church and to their Lord. I am especially grateful to David for the important leadership role that he contributed throughout my tenure as pastor of the Shiloh Church and my extended tenure as a trustee of that congregation later on. The following account will provide the reader with some idea of the prevailing circumstances and the importance of David's role during that critical time in the life and history of the Shiloh UM Church.

* * *

The Shiloh United Methodist Church traces its beginning back to the antebellum pre-Civil War days of the 19th century. Like many rural churches of that era, the church was first begun in 1842 as a Sunday School that met in the county schoolhouse on what is now Shiloh Road in Forsyth County southwest of Cumming, Georgia. The congregation was founded by the Methodist Episcopal families who lived in the surrounding rural area and farmed the land, raising livestock, chickens, cattle and dairy cows, cotton, and whatever crops would grow, in addition to the vegetables and other produce they raised to feed their own families and to sell in the local farmers' market.

When General Sherman and his Union Army cut a seventy-five mile wide swath through the South, past Atlanta and eastward to Savannah, the little country church located about fifty miles north of Atlanta was bypassed by the marauding troops, and the surrounding farms were spared. But Forsyth County, which lay at the southern end of the foothills to the Blue Ridge Mountain Range, shared the Southerners' hatred for the Yankees and what their armies had done to their beloved South. To the east, the Chattahoochee River is the county line and to the north and west lay the North Georgia Mountains. Cumming is the Forsyth County seat and until the 1990's had remained a typical small town, but the burgeoning growth of the Greater Atlanta area has in the last two decades pushed northward toward the small rural town. The opening of State Highway 400, a major arterial corridor running north from Atlanta through Cumming, has helped bring about in that county one of the fastest growth rates in the nation.

Following the emergence on the national scene of Martin Luther King and the rapid racial and demographic changes that the federal government implemented under the Kennedy administration, Atlanta had become a center for the Black community and its civil rights activism. Forsyth County was one of the very last strongholds of the Ku Klux Klan and at the Chattahoochee River bridge and all of the points of entry into the county signs were posted that read "Nigger, be gone before sundown." Although a few Negroes mustered the courage to cross the county line to work for some of the wealthy townspeople and farmers, it was not a good place for Black folks to be after sunset. Furthermore, Yankees, of whatever color, were no more welcome than were the Black laborers. That mind-set was made clear to me soon after we moved to Georgia in 1994. The first time I had my hair cut at a local barber shop in downtown Cumming I was made keenly aware of the still lingering and seething bitterness of the KKK rednecks living in the area. I guess those Southerners had no trouble recognizing my Yankee accent and I was rudely baited by the barber and several of the other Rednecks in the shop. I was not certain that I would get out of the barber's chair without accidentally being nicked by the straight razor he used to trim around my ears and the back of my neck. I never went back to that particular barber shop and from that time on I was more careful where I went and with whom I tried to strike up a conversation. Additionally, I was disappointed but not surprised when I was given a polite but very cold shoulder by some of the United Methodist pastors who regarded me as an "outsider" and an interloper and intruder into the precincts of their

Southern clergy circles and churches. Some of the ministers who were graduates of Candler School of Theology at Emory University showed their provincialism and Southern Dixie prejudices toward me. I was a graduate of Drew University, Madison, New Jersey, which was sufficient evidence in their minds that I was definitely from above the Mason-Dixon Line, even though my home Conference is the Baltimore-Washington Conference, which is below the line charted by the surveyors, Charles Mason and Jeremiah Dixon, to separate the Southern Confederacy from the Northern Union states.

The phenomenal and rapid influx of people not only from the Northern states but from around the world has made Atlanta the largest metropolitan area in the Southeastern United States. Many of the people who have moved to the Atlanta area were relocated there from other cities as the American and international regional corporate headquarters of hundreds of industrial and commercial corporations have opened offices, warehouses, and commercial business centers in and around the greater Atlanta area. This tremendous influx of people has had a pronounced leveling influence to alter and counter the old animosities that had existed in past generations; but unfortunately racial tensions are still painfully evident particularly in the inner-city areas and Black neighborhoods in the central and south sides of Atlanta.

Whatever the demographic and racial attitudes may be elsewhere, when I was requested by the Roswell District Superintendent to serve as the interim pastor of the Shiloh United Methodist Church, that congregation received Barbara and me with a warm Christian spirit and the gracious hospitality for which Southern ladies and gentlemen are known. Perhaps part of that welcome was an expression of the relief they felt that someone whom they could trust and respect had come to the rescue of their church following the havoc that had been wrought upon their congregation by the previous pastor. They hoped that I would be able to help them salvage and rectify the wrongs that my predecessor had perpetrated against them.

*　　*　　*

As is typical of small churches within driving distance of the seminaries, a young seminarian had been appointed as the part-time pastor of the Shiloh UM Church and part of his stipend had been the privilege afforded him of living in the church's parsonage located behind the church. The student pastor, Joseph Kennedy, had received deacon's orders and subsequently was granted elder's orders during the two years of his tenure at Shiloh. Mr. Kennedy's father was a Caucasian, a United Methodist minister who married a Chinese woman, and Joseph Kennedy was born with pronounced oriental features. He also had a driving ambition and had learned from his father how to "con" people and take advantage of innocent and unsuspecting persons. Kennedy was determined to make a big impression on his district superintendent and upon the new neophyte bishop who had only recently been appointed to serve the North Georgia Conference of the United Methodist Church.

Some of the liberal professors and young Turks at Emory University had persuaded Kennedy that the magic key to growing a large congregation was to adopt a "modern" genre of worship made fashionable by Bill Hybels and his staff at the Willow Creek Church enterprises in the Chicago area. Hybels and his associates developed an iconoclastic kind of "modern" approach to Christianity, rejecting the historic models of church architecture, religious symbols, music, sermon discourse, and anything that traditionally had been associated with the mainline Christian churches of Europe and America. In the place of the traditional church settings and forms of worship Hybels and his staff solicited followers who gathered in non-traditional halls, theatres, and small groups. Instead of a traditional pulpit, robed clergy and choir, pipe organ and hymnals, a setting was created that was closer to a theatre or night club where some comedian sat on a bar stool and told stories and cracked humorous jokes. The music they presented was generated by guitars, jazz instruments and drums, and sermon discourses were displaced with conversational teaching and stage shows produced by amateur actors portraying some Biblical "truth" through drama and theatrics. Casual dress, jeans and anything except a business suit or robe became the accepted order of the day. It was a conglomeration of "come as you are" religiously illiterate curiosity seekers who were first attracted by Hybels and his company. Just recently, however, Willow Creek Church parishioners are demanding a recovery of the traditional heritage of Christendom and a return to more liturgical forms of worship and celebration; and attempts are being made by the Willow Creek Church leadership to cater to the resurfacing desires of their patrons for a more traditional worship.

In an attempt to mimic Hybels' *modus operandi* the young seminarian Joseph Kennedy took it upon himself to give away the Shiloh Church's pulpit, communion table, chancel chairs, organ, piano and pews! Without discussing it with the officers of the congregation and getting written approval from the Board of Trustees to do so, Kennedy unilaterally exceeded his pastoral prerogatives and gave the church's furnishings to a Black congregation on the south side of Atlanta. And without any authorization to do so, Kennedy ordered folding chairs, costing approximately $2,500 dollars, which he placed in a semi-circle around a barstool upon which he sat. From his bar stool he attempted to accompany the congregation's singing with a guitar and whatever jazz musicians he could recruit as his back-up band.

Kennedy also removed from the wall of the chapel a bronze memorial plaque that had inscribed upon it the names of the benefactors who had donated the pews, pulpit, organ, piano, etc. and the names of the persons in whose honor or memory the various church furnishings had been given. Moreover, it was discovered that Kennedy had salted the church's record books by removing from the membership roster anyone who disagreed with him and adding to the roster the names of his acquaintances and total strangers to pad the rolls in an attempt to inflate the membership as if he had single-handedly brought into the church a large number of new parishioners to "grow" the church. Kennedy's tampering with the membership books of the church, as part of his deliberate and cunning attempt to "con" and fool the district superintendent and the bishop, succeeded in pulling the wool over their eyes.

Kennedy hosted a Roswell District meeting at the Shiloh Church and padded the church with his friends and people who were total strangers and "ringers" unknown to the members of the congregation, and led the gullible superintendent and bishop into believing that Kennedy had been instrumental in bringing all these new people into the Shiloh membership. For that ruse and fraud, Superintendent Smith awarded to Kennedy a dubious certificate of recognition as the Roswell District's "most successful minister" in the area of church growth and new member accessions. What a joke! To hide his fraud, Kennedy also stole and disposed of the Church's membership book, and that historic document has never been recovered.

When the parishioners arrived on a Sunday morning and discovered that their church had been vandalized by the theft of its pews, organ, and other chapel furnishings, they immediately called the District Superintendent to report the missing items and ask for his help in recovering the items which Kennedy had stolen in an act described by the county sheriff as a crime of "theft by conversion (illegal transfer)" of the church's properties.

The District Superintendent, a Reverend Harold Smith, met with the Board of Trustees and other church officials and instead of disciplining Mr. Kennedy, Smith mounted what became an outrageous attempt at a "cover-up" of Kennedy's deceit and theft. Instead of disciplining Kennedy, Smith "promoted" him and appointed Kennedy to serve as an Assistant Pastor at a nearby church, Johns Creek United Methodist Church in Duluth, Georgia, where I had served previously as the Minister of Pastoral Counseling and also as the Minister of Christian Education. Kennedy vacated the Shiloh parsonage and began his new duties at Johns Creek UMC immediately.

In an effort to find an interim pastor for the Shiloh Church, Superintendent Smith phoned me and requested that I serve in that capacity until a permanent pastor could be found to fill the vacancy Smith had created by the transfer of Kennedy to the Johns Creek Church.

On my first Sunday as their interim pastor a small group of nineteen parishioners gathered in their "trashed" sanctuary, and we worshipped in a makeshift manner with the folding chairs and a borrowed piano; but I refused to sit on a bar stool and instead found a small podium which we used as a combination lectern/pulpit, and we used a folding table from the parish hall as a communion table. After the service the distraught, frustrated and angry parishioners explained to me the theft of their church's pews and other furnishings and asked me to help them recover the stolen items if we could.

The Superintendent authorized me to contact the Black church and arrange for the recovery of the stolen items. When I asked the trustees if the theft had been reported to the Forsyth County Sheriff's Department, I learned from them that the District Superintendent did not want the crime reported to the civil authorities but hoped he could somehow cover up Kennedy's theft and retrieve the missing furniture without having the incident reported in the local Cumming and Atlanta newspapers. It was transparently obvious that Smith was not as concerned about the missing church properties as much as he was about protecting himself since the crime had occurred on his watch and was his administrative responsibility.

The church's leaders had met previously with the Superintendent and expressed their dissatisfaction with Kennedy, but Smith had tried to stonewall and had completely ignored their complaints until Kennedy's theft compelled Smith to take action. When I inquired of the church's insurance agent about the filing of a claim for the lost property (and of several thousand dollars of money that Kennedy had also illegally misappropriated) the agent stated that it would be useless to file an insurance claim until a report of the crime had first been filed with the police.

The congregation's treasurer, Mrs. Nina Anderson, accompanied me on a trip to consult with the Georgia State Insurance Commissioner at his office in the Georgia State Office building in downtown Atlanta. When we explained the circumstances of the theft and the loss of the Shiloh Church's properties and asked for his counsel as to how the Church might obtain from its insurance provider a full compensation for the financial loss associated with that theft, the Commissioner courteously read the Shiloh Church's insurance document and with a sincere sense of regret over what he found he informed us that the insurance policy did not cover this particular incident of theft! It seems that neither the insurance agent nor the Board of Trustees had ever considered the possibility that any member or employee of the church would be guilty of theft or embezzlement, so in order to reduce the insurance premium, church members and employees were excluded as persons covered under the policy! It was the responsibility of the District Superintendent to ensure that the each church was properly covered by adequate insurance coverage, so here again the ultimate responsibility for this tragic set of circumstances lay upon the District Superintendent. That "penny wise and pound foolish" choice to exclude church personnel in order to gain a reduced insurance premium proved to be a myopic short-sightedness that would now cost the congregation the forfeiture of any compensation for the damages and loss of its property via its useless insurance policy. The only remedy left to the congregation was to seek redress through criminal and civil actions against Kennedy in the public courts.

When I was made aware that the District Superintendent had consulted with the neophyte bishop, Lindsey Davis, and that they had colluded with the Conference Chancellor (who was an "old boy network" acquaintance of the Forsyth County Prosecuting Attorney) in an effort to avoid the public prosecution of the Rev. Mr. Kennedy, it became evident that the Shiloh Congregation needed to hire its own attorney to represent the interests of the church. The Conference Chancellor was unabashedly representing only the interests of Superintendent Smith, Bishop Davis and the North Georgia Conference UMC.

A local attorney (who later became a court judge) was retained and a criminal complaint of *theft by conversion* of the properties and funds that Kennedy had misappropriated was filed by the congregation's attorney with the Forsyth County Sheriff's Department and with the Forsyth County Prosecuting Attorney, but the conference attorney managed through the exchange of political "courtesies" to head off a criminal investigation and the prosecution of Kennedy.

Following the Superintendent's instructions, I contacted the pastor of the Black church who had received the stolen properties of the Shiloh Church and explained to him what had happened and that a criminal complaint had been filed with the local police. When I asked that he assist us in arranging for the return of the stolen properties, he immediately became defensive and threatened me with a lawsuit for falsely implicating him in the receipt of stolen property. When I requested that he phone the Forsyth County Sheriff's office to verify the information that I had reported to him, he became very excited, angry and abusive in his language and further threatened me, finally hanging up on me.

When Superintendent Smith learned that the Shiloh Church had hired an attorney and was seeking redress and the recovery of its church properties through the courts, he hit the panic button because he realized his own complicity with Kennedy in the whole affair would be exposed. Smith phoned me and in a panicked voice and with a single sentence he declared that I was "no longer the interim pastor of the Shiloh UM Church." Without asking me for a report on what we were doing or without giving me any explanation, in a very cowardly and unprofessional manner he rudely and abruptly hung up the phone on me! Bang . . . the line went dead and that was the last time I ever spoke with Smith. Nor did Lindsey Davis ever extend to me the professional courtesy of phoning me to inquire regarding the Shiloh Church or to ascertain for himself the details regarding what had occurred.

* * *

The Shiloh Congregation was once again stunned by the unethical and unprofessional behavior of Smith and the new bishop. The Board of Trustees and other officers of the church were in a real quandary and left without a pastor. They decided to elect me as a trustee, since it is permissible under the canon law of the UM *Discipline* for non-members to be elected as church trustees as may be deemed desirable or necessary by a local congregation. When Smith and Davis learned that I had been elected as a trustee and in that capacity I could continue to represent the Shiloh congregation in consulting with the congregation's attorney and the civil authorities and courts in seeking redress under the law, Lindsey Davis wrote to the bishop of the Baltimore-Washington Conference complaining that I had mishandled the matter and requesting that Bishop May (who is a Black minister) intervene by using his episcopal office in an effort to pressure me to cease and desist from any further efforts on my part to assist the Shiloh Church. When I received a letter from Bishop May inquiring about my involvement with the Shiloh Church, I sent Rev. May a complete 50+ page legal brief delineating the details of the case, and suggested that he advise his neophyte Episcopal colleague that he should be very careful lest he become guilty of tampering with a witness of the court by trying to pressure and manipulate me with threats while I was acting in my capacity as a legal trustee of the Shiloh Church! Apparently that caught Mr. Lindsey Davis' attention because I never heard another word from Bishop May or a single peep out of Smith or Davis.

Eventually the Black pastor and his congregation were persuaded that it was in their best interest to return the stolen properties of the Shiloh Church without further delay, and a truck was sent by Smith to retrieve the Shiloh properties. The badly damaged pews and other items that were retrieved required restoration by a furniture repair company and the expense had to be borne by the Shiloh Church. However, the church's organ was never recovered. It was learned later that when the men from the Black church had tried to remove the organ, they had handled the instrument roughly and had broken off the foot pedals. Having badly damaged the organ, they decided that they didn't want to bother with the broken instrument, so Kennedy gave it to a neighboring UM church where it was sold for $250 in a rummage sale. The North Georgia Conference of the UMC never reimbursed or compensated the Shiloh Church for the damage to its pews or the loss of its organ, and the bronze memorial plaque was never recovered nor were the membership book and other church records ever recovered.

*   *   *

During this time, it came to my attention that Joseph Kennedy's father, who claimed to be an ordained United Methodist minister and a licensed professional counselor, was hired as a pastoral Counselor by the large First United Methodist Church of Norcross, Georgia (a suburb on the northeast side of Atlanta). The senior Kennedy had misrepresented himself and when he was repeatedly requested to furnish the Norcross UM Church with copies of his official college transcripts and his ordination and counseling licenses and credentials, he failed to do so. Without proof of the authenticity of his credentials he was uninsurable under the church's malpractice insurance policy and posed a serious risk from possible litigation against his employers, so he was dismissed. Almost immediately upon his dismissal the senior Kennedy applied for and was granted a staff position as the Director of Pastoral Counseling at the Johns Creek UM Church and that congregation was unwittingly stuck with both of these renegade ministers.

When Harold Smith had appointed Joseph Kennedy to the position of an assistant pastor at the Johns Creek UM Church, neither he nor Bishop Davis were completely honest with the congregation or with its Senior Minister, Dr. Dee Shelnutt, who was a former district superintendent and colleague of Smith's on the Bishop's Cabinet. I had guessed that rather than to honor the code of professional ministerial ethics and advising the Johns Creek congregation about the younger Kennedy's unacceptable criminal behavior at the Shiloh Church, Smith and Davis had decided to cover up Kennedy's despicable activity in the hope that word would not be spread throughout the Conference or the public press which would have caused an embarrassment to Smith and Davis for their complicity in the matter.

As a ministerial courtesy, I invited Dr. Shelnutt to our home and presented him with a complete copy of the legal brief that our attorney had presented to the Forsyth County Prosecuting Attorney concerning Joseph Kennedy's "theft by conversion." I also informed Dr. Shelnutt about the problem that the Norcross UM Church had encountered with the senior Kennedy and their decision to terminate his services as a pastoral counselor. Dr. Shelnutt must have confronted both of the Kennedys with the documented information I had given him and may have informed them that a complaint of criminal charges had been filed with the Forsyth County Sheriff's Department against the younger Kennedy. Both or these renegade ministers were summarily dismissed and the younger Kennedy fled to California, perhaps out of fear of being apprehended and prosecuted. It was later learned by David Tibbitt's wife, Virginia, from a private investigator, who had been hired by the Johns Creek Church to investigate Joseph Kennedy, that Kennedy had no less that five different social security numbers! What a fraudulent charlatan he is.

*   *   *

In his position of leadership as the Chairman of the Shiloh Congregation's Administrative Council, David Tibbitts took an active and aggressive stand, challenging Superintendent Smith about certain inappropriate correspondence and actions that Smith had taken and over his failure to properly supervise and discipline Kennedy once his unacceptable behavior was discovered and reported to the District Office.

When the Shiloh trustees were met with inconsiderate rebuffs and with no decisive remedial action by Superintendent Smith, David's disappointment and anger grew over what appeared to be the betrayal of the congregation: both the superintendent and the bishop seemed to show an indifference toward the congregation and only a self-interest in protecting their own images and the public image of the Conference above the rights of the local church. The trustees held several meetings to consult together and to decide upon a course of action in an effort to recover the church's missing furnishings and funds. When Smith unceremoniously and callously dismissed me from my position as their pastor, David's sense of fairness and justice and righteous indignation reached a boiling point. He felt he had to do something that would get the superintendent's attention and prompt Smith to take seriously the damage that Kennedy's behavior and Smith's efforts and collusion to absolve Kennedy of any wrong doing had inflicted upon the Shiloh Church. He cast about in his mind and soul for a way to demonstrate in some tangible way the disappointment and disgust that he and the members of the congregation felt over Smith's mishandling of the situation. A course of action began to take shape in his mind and he knew what he had to do.

David Tibbitts is a master builder and craftsman. He decided quietly and stealthily to do something that would provide Mr. Smith with a little bit of the sense of utter frustration that the trustees and members of the Shiloh Church were feeling. After the sun had gone down, David drove to the District Office where he took his power screwdriver and drove three inch long screws through the front and rear doors into the door jambs of the office. David drove the screws in deeply so it would not be easy for Smith or anyone else to extricate them. David effectively sealed the District office to prevent Smith from carrying on "business as usual" as if nothing were amiss at Shiloh or in any of the other churches of the District where Smith's bungling and malfeasance had cause irreparable damage to the congregations that had suffered under Smith's bureaucratic ineptness. When Smith arrived at his office the next morning he literally would be "screwed" out of his office!

Wanting to see with his own eyes the frustration that Smith would experience when he found that he could not gain access to his office, David arrived early and parked his car in an inconspicuous spot where he could observe Smith's arrival. When Smith approached the front door of his office he inserted his key and the door opened easily. It was only after Smith had gained access to his office that David realized that in the darkness of the previous night he had screwed shut the door to the wrong suite of offices! Without saying anything to anyone, David took his power screwdriver and reversed the power drive removing the screws he had so carefully placed at strategic points to seal the doors against entrance. No serious damage had been done and nobody would be the wiser, though they might wonder what had caused the strangely placed holes in the doors and their door jams.

Having vented his anger by his prank, David had to laugh at himself and his own futile quest for revenge for the wrongs done by Kennedy and Smith and Bishop Davis against his beloved Shiloh Church. Though Smith never knew how close he came to feeling the sting of frustration that he had helped to inflict upon the Shiloh congregation, Smith's despicable behavior would eventually catch up with him. Harold Smith had inflicted inexcusable pain and anguish upon several other pastors and churches in the Roswell District, but instead of Lindsey Davis removing Smith from the superintendency, Davis became an example of *the Peter Principle* working overtime.[1] Rather than imposing some sort of remedial discipline against Smith, Davis rewarded Smith's incompetence by promoting him and appointing him as the Superintendent of the Athens District! Not long afterward, the Athens and Atlanta papers carried articles reporting that the Athens police had arrested Harold Smith for sexual misconduct—for publicly exposing himself, and for the sexual solicitation of male students on the University of Georgia campus. Though Smith was disclosed for what he is, neither Lindsey Davis nor Dee Shelnutt ever contacted me to apologize for their misjudgment of my professional integrity or ever thanked me for the pastoral leadership that I gave to the Shiloh congregation. That's the way it goes with church bureaucrats who are more interested in their own image and agenda than they are with fulfilling the high calling of their office to provide spiritual assistance and righteous examples to those for whom they are responsible. But there is a righteous judge before whom each of us will some day stand to give account of the deeds we have done while living in our mortal bodies here on earth.

God must have a sense of humor, and I can imagine Him watching over David as he drove those screws into the doors of what he thought was Harold Smith's office. God knows David's heart, and certainly He must feel the kind of indignation that Jesus expressed as he cleansed the temple and condemned the religious rulers of his day who by their actions perverted the message of God's love for mankind. God must surely have a very special place in His kingdom for those persons like David Tibbitts who seek with all their hearts to do what is right in His sight.

I am grateful to David Tibbitts for his loyalty, for his support and his prayers for me and for his fellow Christians in the Shiloh United Methodist Church.

And I rejoice at David's success in his vocation and for his sense of personal joy over the family that God has given him.[2] May God bless David and all of those other good and godly laymen who have been to their pastors as David's Mighty Men were to him.

NOTES:

[1]   The Peter Principle is the principle that "In a Hierarchy Every Employee Tends to Rise to His Level of Incompetence." While formulated by Dr. Laurence J. Peter and Raymond Hull in their 1968 book The Peter Principle, a humorous treatise which also introduced the "salutary science of Hierarchiology", "inadvertently founded" by Peter, the principle has real validity. It holds that in a hierarchy, members are promoted so long as they work competently. Sooner or later they are promoted to a position at which they are no longer competent (their "level of incompetence"), and there they remain. Peter's Corollary states that "in time, every post tends to be occupied by an employee who is incompetent to carry out his duties" and adds that "work is accomplished by those employees who have not yet reached their level of incompetence".—http://en.wikipedia.org/wiki/Peter_Principle

[2]   You can visit David Tibbitt's website at: ***http://www.atlantadecking.com/*** When you visit the website of David's company, Atlanta Decking and Fence Co., be sure to take time to click on the video where you can see and hear David speak about his own work ethics and his commitment to providing a superior quality of craftsmanship. David's Christian faith is reflected in his business practices.

Rev. Glenn David Jones

EPILOGUE

THE ALMIGHTY in His divine providence selects for His own purposes persons in whom He sees certain possibilities and whom He chooses to carry out His will in and through their lives. King David in his psalms and hymns recognizes the profound influence and direction upon his life by the wisdom, foreknowledge and providence of God.[1]

The formation of the character and soul of David began in his home. The Lord sent the prophet Samuel to the house of Jesse in the village of Bethlehem of Judea. Jesse had eight sons, all of whom were strong and handsome young men. It was not the eldest, however, but the youngest boy whom God chose to become the king of Israel.[2] "David was ruddy, with a fine appearance and handsome features . . . and the Spirit of the Lord came upon David in power."[3]

Without his father or his brothers realizing it, God had been preparing David for a life of heroic service to which he would be called as the king. During the lonely hours passed in the fields of Ephratha below the village of Bethlehem, David had learned how to play the harp and to compose shepherds' songs that he sang to his sheep, and he sharpened his skill in the effective use of the sling as a weapon against marauding wild animals and if necessary against thieves. He had defended his sheep against attacks by a lion and a bear and other beasts that roamed the hill country of Judea. And he cultivated a spirit of faith and trust in his god, Yahweh. When the safety and freedom of Israel was threatened by the Philistine's and their champion, the giant warrior Goliath, David was ready, with a faith that had been honed in the solitude of a shepherd's watch over his flocks, to meet the challenge of this pagan savage giant. David's father Jesse, his brothers, the old prophet Samuel, the prince Jonathan and King Saul all had a part in shaping and molding David into the man who would lead the tribes of Israel into the formation of the greatest nation of that era in human history.[4]

*   *   *

LIKE DAVID, our lives and destinies are influenced by divine providence and by our own personal response to both the opportunities and the difficulties that are presented to us over the course of our days. We are shaped not only by the genetic imprint of our DNA, but perhaps even more profoundly by the day-to-day experiences through which we pass on our earthly pilgrimage. Our character formation begins in the home, under the tutelage of our parents. Then our small world expands beyond our home when we enter the world of academia which for some children begins with day-care at the early age of two or three, and advances to kindergarten and elementary through intermediate school, high school and college. All along the way we are being groomed for entry into the adult life of the work-a-day world of vocational or professional careers, for the institutions of courtship, marriage and for the building of our own families and social relationships.

*   *   *

The list of this author's—David Jones'—"Mighty Men" would be incomplete if it did not include those men (and women) whose influence, guidance, support and assistance helped prepare me for the time when I would begin my professional careers as a Christian minister, a university professor and an author. Of all the individuals who helped form and shape my life, none were more important nor contributed a more profound influence than my own father and mother.

THE REVEREND GLENN DAVID JONES, SR. was born in a log cabin located up on South Mountain, between Frederick and Boonsborough, Maryland. An older sister, Ruth, and a brother, John Grayson, had already been born into the family of John David Jones and Loretta Fox Jones, when on November 8, 1904, a third baby—a boy, Glenn David Jones, was born. The father, John David Jones, worked as a skilled stone mason during the months when construction jobs were available in the neighboring cities of Hagerstown, Frederick and Washington, DC. During the winter months, he worked at home crafting woven baskets from willows and oak wood which he shaped with a draw-knife and skilled hands, and he would weave cane and lath seats for chairs to be sold in the markets and shops of the nearby towns. His wife, Loretta, was the daughter of a country doctor who was well respected in the surrounding countryside. During the summer months she would work in the garden, and like mothers of farm families in those days, she would prepare dried apples and nuts and canned fruit and vegetables for the winter months to feed the growing family. Soon a second little girl, Orpha

Victoria, and then another son, Alonzo, and finally a baby girl, Helen, were born to the family. Fate was not kind, however, to this family of Welsh/German and Scott/Irish descent. The father became ill, and due to the bungling of a quack doctor, he died of complications resulting from a bursted appendix. Times were hard for the young widow with her brood of six small children.

The courageous mother was determined to keep her family together though others offered to adopt the children and some thought they should be placed in orphanages or foster homes. With all the grit and determination of her fiery and undaunted spirit, "Reddy" (a nickname that came from her name Loretta and her red hair) Jones went to work in the fields, and the children joined her when they were old enough to work for neighboring farm families. During the summer months the children went barefooted to save their shoes for school days. The family seldom missed church services on Sundays. The mother sat on the women's side of the old country church house, and the boys sat at the back on the men's side. When they talked or scuffled in the back of the church, they could never understand how their mother, sitting in front of them would know of their misbehavior, since she never turned around lest someone might think that the widow Jones was making eyes at someone else's husband. It was not until years later that they learned their mother had asked the other ladies of the church, whose husbands were sitting on the men's side, to keep an eye on her mischievous boys so they were never able to get away with misbehaving in God's House without receiving a severe punishment when they returned to their humble log cabin home.

The older children attended the country school across from the graveyard where their father was buried. A marker placed there by the local lodge of the *Improved Order of the Redmen* marked the site of their father's grave, and often the children would look out of the one-room school house windows and brush back the tears as they remembered their father. The schoolmaster was a mean-hearted man and stern, and would whip the children with a hickory stick if they disobeyed or failed in their studies. Glenn and his brother John knew the brutality of that cruel hickory stick, because as boys-would-be-boys they engaged in their share of rough-and-tumble childhood fights and mountain children's scraps. In that old country school the children learned from the *McGuffy Readers* and from literature books, and they learned to appreciate poetry and music.

Until the day he died, Glenn Jones could recite from memory poetry learned in that old school house—poems like *The Village Blacksmith*, and other classics beloved by the people of that era. One of his favorite poems *All things Bright and Beautiful* describes God's creation. In my memory I can hear his resonant voice reciting the lyrical words of those poems. I can see him standing in the pulpit and articulating with deep conviction and faith the exposition of the Holy Scriptures, and leading us in prayers of contrition, thanksgiving and supplication to the God in whom he placed an unwavering faith and trust.

The widow Jones moved with her brood of little children down off the mountain to Frederick, Maryland, and the older boys, John and Glenn went to work in a brickyard hauling wheelbarrow loads of bricks from the hot kilns up steep ramps to be loaded into railroad cars for shipping to distant construction sites in Baltimore and Washington, DC. One hot summer day, Glenn was overcome by the heat and fatigue and dropped from sheer exhaustion. Unable to keep the pace with full-grown men, he went home, and prayed that God would provide him with a job so he could support his mother and brothers and sisters. In the providence of our merciful Heavenly Father, "Glenny boy," as his mother affectionately called him, was given a job as a "printer's devil" or apprentice on the Frederick newspaper. That was the beginning of a skilled trade which was to serve him well from time to time over the coming years. Later he went to work for a book-binding and printing company in Hagerstown, Maryland.

While living in Frederick, he would hire a little mare from the local livery stable and drive the horse and buggy up to the farm of his Aunt Lil and her family. He and his brother John became debonair young men about town and were eligible bachelors who courted young maidens whom they met in the churches around the town. Glenn began to attend the Men's Bible class at Calvary Methodist Episcopal Church in Frederick, and sometimes the family would attend the Church of God or the Lutheran Church in whose cemetery their grandparents and some of their other relatives were buried.

When the celebrity evangelist from California, Amie Semple McPherson, held a revival campaign in the Evangelical United Brethren Church in Baltimore, the family traveled on the train to the big city to attend the meetings, and there Ruth, John and Glenn were introduced to the emerging "Pentecostal" revival movement that was sweeping the country during the second decade of the last century. Glenn had been given a deep spiritual sensitivity by the Lord, whose Holy Spirit had visited him in some mystical way and placed His divine hand upon the lad on an occasion when at nine years of age he was alone in their humble log cabin, singing familiar hymns as he went about his daily chores of sweeping and cleaning their small living quarters. When asked about that particular experience, with a lingering sense of awe he would describe how the room lighted up and he was aware of the presence of *a heavenly being* standing with him. Years later, when he was in his eighties, he was taken to the hospital for an emergency operation, and alone lying in his hospital bed near the point of death, once again he experienced a similar visitation from the Lord. In words of reverent amazement he described how once again a strange and marvelous and indescribable light filled the room and a figure whom he believed to be *the risen Christ* stood at the foot of his bed and ministered to him. From that moment he began an amazing recovery and lived several more happy years afterward.

As a young man Glenn turned to the Lord and consecrated himself to serve God as a minister of the Gospel. Under the encouragement and mentoring of the

Reverend Ralph Jefferies of Hagerstown, and the Reverend Bowie, Potomac District Superintendent, and others, the young man was directed to his first pastorate in the college town of Beaver Falls, Pennsylvania (the town from which football's famous quarterback, Joe Namath, would come). Recognizing a gift and a calling to evangelistic ministry, the young minister held campaigns for neighboring pastors and often traveled in his automobile to Cleveland, Ohio to visit his mother and sisters and his younger brother, Alonzo. Then, in the providence of God, Glenn Jones was called to supply the pulpit of the Calvary Pentecostal Church in Jamestown, New York. It was there that his life would be indelibly influenced by a young blond Swedish-American girl whose beauty and charm would capture the heart of this young southern minister from below the Mason-Dixon Line.

Evelyn Marianna Hallin, wearing a pretty pinafore dress and a neatly embroidered little apron, hurried from the family kitchen to answer the knock at the front door. When she opened the door, there standing in front of her was the debonair young interim pastor, Rev. Glenn D. Jones, who had just recently been appointed to fill the pulpit of her church until the congregation could select a senior minister to pastor their congregation. As their eyes met it was truly "love at first sight."

Sometime during the last part of the eighteenth century there was born in Sweden a soldier, Johannes Paff, who had seven sons, five of whom would also become soldiers like their father. One of those sons, Soldaten (soldier) Anders Snugg, born in 1821, married Stinat Hellena Cathrina Nicolaidotten. Anders and Hellena Cathrina had three sons and four daughters. Among these children was Carl Johan, who was born in 1841 and who took as his wife Hallina Christina Ecklund (born in 1838.) Carl Johan Anderson (Ander's son) and his wife Hallina had a son, Johan August Carlson (Carl's son) born March 8, 1874. Fate was not kind to Johan, whose mother died when Johan was a small boy. His father remarried, and his second wife was jealous of Johan and his sisters, Ida and Albertina. Johan's step-mother was cruel to him, but not to her children Gustav, Oscar, Anna, and Elmer. Johan decided to leave home and to seek his destiny in the new world of America, so he left Hakarps-Sosken, near HuskVarna, Smoland, Sweden, and at the age of twenty, he made the trans-Atlantic voyage to America aboard a sailing vessel, spending seven weeks in passage at sea.

Like thousands of other immigrants, the young *Svenske poika*, Johan August Carl's Son, landed in America almost penniless, not able to speak the language of this new and strange land, but yearning for the freedom from want and suffering which America promised to the teeming masses which thronged to its shores. At Ellis Island, Johan was asked to register with the Immigration Office. Disappointed and sad over the cruel treatment given to him by his stepmother, Johan decided not to take his father's name: he would not be Johan Carlson (Carl's son); instead, he would adopt his mother's name, "Hallina" but he would omit the feminine ending of her name and he would take the name John August Hallin. When his younger brothers and sister came to America, and even when his half-brothers came to the United States later on, they all adopted John's new surname and they would become known as Gustav Hallin, Oscar Hallin, and Elmer Hallin.

John (Johan) Hallin made his way from Ellis Island to the Swedish settlement of Jamestown, New York, on the shores of Cahatquah Lake in the western part of that state. There John found employment as a woodworking craftsman in one of the numerous furniture factories in the Jamestown area. Developing and refining his woodworking and finishing skills, John energetically became an entrepreneur and President of the Elk Furniture Company in Falconer, New York. He and his partner developed a noble manufacturing business with a fine reputation for creating excellently crafted furniture worthy of the credit given to old-world master craftsmen.

When he first moved to Jamestown, the young Swedish craftsman found room and board in the home of the Swedish immigrant family of Carl Johan Peterson and his wife Anna Louise Hagg Peterson. The Peterson's ancestors, like those of John Hallin and most Swedes, had been baptized and raised in the Lutheran state church of their homeland. But somewhere they had come under the influence of the Anglican Englishman John Wesley, and had become devout and staunch Swedish Methodists. Carl and Anna Peterson had five sons and a daughter, Anna Marie (born April 4, 1876). Carl, who was a Steward in the Epworth Swedish Methodist Church in Jamestown, was determined that no man would court his daughter unless he was a Swede and a Methodist!

John August Hallin attended the Epworth Swedish Methodist Episcopal church with the Peterson family, and it was not unpredictable that he would fall in love with their beautiful and demure daughter Anna Marie. The couple was married in the Epworth Church on October 8, 1896, and to their union were born a son and four daughters, the third or whom, Evelyn Marianna, was born April 30, 1909.

Glenn David Jones and Evelyn Marianna Hallin were married on February 17, 1931 and to their union were born two sons, Dr. C. (Calvin) David—aka Glenn David, II, Rev. Everett Warren, and two daughters, Eileen Elizabeth and Lois Marie.

Glenn D. Jones, Sr. was granted a certificate as a "licensed preacher" by the Assemblies of God denomination in 1928, and began his ministry as an itinerant evangelist. Following his first pastorate in Beaver Falls, Pennsylvania, which began in the latter part of 1928, and the brief interim pastorate in Jamestown, New York, where he met Evelyn, he was appointed to become the pastor of the Assemblies of God Church in Erie, Pennsylvania in 1930. He was ordained as an elder/minister in 1931, and continued to serve the fledgling church in Erie, where their two sons were born. Over the four decades of his pastoral ministry (1928-1968) he served fourteen different congregations from four separate denominations in Pennsylvania, New York, and Michigan. In 1958 he transferred into the

Evangelical United Brethren Church and when in 1968 the EUB denomination was absorbed into the United Methodist Church, he became an ordained itinerant elder in that denomination, from which he was granted honorable retirement the following year and in which he remained until his death in October, 1991.

The saga of his four decades of pastoral ministry is too long to recount here. In the early days of his ministry he was an enthusiastic and fiery evangelist in the mold of his idol, Billy Sunday. In his middle years he was an energetic and faithful pastor whose sermons were marked by sound doctrine and fascinating illustrations from the Holy Scriptures and life experiences that were applicable to the lives and pilgrimage of current day Christian disciples. In his latter years, his pulpit discourses, pastoral counsel and administrative expertise were distinguished by scholarly wisdom, a humble spirit of reverence toward God, and the dignity and bearing of a veteran soldier of the Cross that became richer with each passing year. The legacy of his godly example and life of devoted Christian ministry continues on in the lives of his children, grandchildren and great-grandchildren and in the lives of his many parishioners and their Christian progeny.[5]

In particular, the influence of the life of the Reverend Glenn D. Jones, Sr. is most profoundly acknowledged and evidenced by the author of this book, whose own life and ministry was impacted and blessed by the righteous example and mentoring of his father. It was my father, Glenn David Jones who was the first and most beloved by me of all of those who were among this author, David Jones' *Mighty Men of God*.

*   *   *

The author acknowledges with gratitude those who helped in the publication of this book. My sincere thanks and appreciation go to:

Barbara Ann Hillman Jones, my devoted and loyal wife, who is also my best critic, editor and proof-reader, and without whose encouragement and assistance many of the successes accounted in this book would not have been possible. Barbara's next book, ***Recollections of a Jamestown Swede***, will be released in the fall of 2009. You can visit her website at: https://www2.xlibris.com/bookstore/bookdisplay.asp?bookid=43656 ;

To my children, Daniel Stephen, Deborah Marilynne, and Mark Bradley, who loved and encouraged me in those endeavors which they shared with us, both in the churches I served and in the secular pursuits and private family times we enjoyed together;

To the many friends and parishioners whose partnership in the Gospel as *workers together with God* was invaluable to the success of our congregations; and also to the various business associates who invested their energies and resources in the several secular enterprises in which we engaged;

To those colleagues in academia and professional organizations, especially those in the Academy of Parish Clergy, Inc. and the American Association of Christian Counselors; and also those in the civic and fraternal organizations, Rotary International and others with whom we shared common ideals and goals and community life;

To Nina Anderson for her editorial skill and her expertise as a proof reader for carefully scrutinizing every sentence and paragraph of the manuscript for this book (and for the key role she played in the life of the Shiloh UMC where she was the church treasurer during the saga reported in Chapter 18). Nina is an author in her own right and has recently published **The Bumble Bee Miracle**—*A Story of Survival from Inflammatory Breast Cancer.* You can visit her website at: https://www2.xlibris.com/bookstore/bookdisplay.asp?bookid=43205;

And to my publishers *Xlibris*, an affiliate of *Random House Ventures* whose technical skills contributed immeasurably to the development and printing of this book . . .

To all of you, my dear family, colleagues and friends . . . a great big "Thank you!"

C. David Jones
Fort Wayne, Indiana
2009

NOTES:

[1]   See Psalm 139 for a description of God's providential direction of the lives of righteous and faithful people.

[2]   I Samue16:34-13.

[3]   Ibid., v. 13.

[4]   The deeds and exploits of King David are an inspiring saga and worth taking the time to read (See the Old Testament books of I Samuel, beginning with chapter 16 through II Samuel, and I Kings beginning with Chapter 11.) The poetry and hymns of David found

in the Psalms are also inspiring literature that offers insight into the heart and soul of this great warrior king who, in spite of his flaws and failures, remained "a man after God's own heart." *Vide.* I Samuel 13:14; Cf. Acts 13:22.

5 For a more detailed account of the life and legacy of the Reverend Glenn David Jones, Sr. see his biography, *A Man After God's Own Heart—An Account of [the life and ministry of the] Reverend Glenn David Jones, Sr.* by Lois Marie (Jones) Oster. Penn Laird, VA: © the author, 2001, 200 pages.

Made in the USA
Middletown, DE
12 February 2022

61048945R00137